SECRETS
of
MOUNT SINAI

The Story of the World's Oldest Bible —
Codex Sinaiticus

James Bentley

Foreword by
James H. Charlesworth

DOUBLEDAY & COMPANY, INC.
GARDEN CITY, NEW YORK
1986

To my daughters

Photographs were supplied by Archivio IGDA, Helmut Behrend, Werner, Braun, by courtesy of the Trustees of the British Museum, Garo Nalbandian and Pictorial Archive (Near Eastern History) Est., Jerusalem. Special photography by Dr Philip Mavroskoufis.

ISBN: 0–385–23297–7

Library of Congress Catalog Card Number: 85–10385

Library of Congress Cataloging in Publication Data

Bentley, James, 1937–
   Secrets of Mount Sinai.

   Bibliography: p.
   Includes index.
   1. Bible. Greek. Codex Sinaiticus. 2. Tischendorf, Constantin von, 1815–1874. 3. Saint Catherine (Monastery: Mount Sinai) I. Title.
BS64.S5B46   1986   220.4'8   85–10385
ISBN 0–385–23297–7

© James Bentley 1985
Foreword by James H. Charlesworth copyright © by Doubleday and Company, Inc. First published in Great Britain by Orbis Publishing Limited, London 1985 First published in United States of America by Doubleday and Company, Inc., 1986

Printed in Great Britain.

Contents

Foreword

Reflections on the Mysteries of
St Catherine's Monastery

James H. Charlesworth

George L. Collord Professor of New Testament Language and Literature, Princeton Theological Seminary

For thousands of years southern Sinai has been a center of sacred traditions: It contains the mountain on which Moses received the Ten Commandments, the nearby hill where the Israelites worshipped the golden calf, the caves where Elijah found refuge and the majestic walls of the monastery of St Catherine's. It was those walls I approached on my first trip there in 1979. The final leg of our journey had been covered in an open-windowed, dilapidated bus which made me empathetic with Constantin Tischendorf, who suffered considerably from the sun, desert and uneven gait of the camel during his visits to St Catherine's.

I recall that at the time, the monastery was within Israeli-occupied territory. Too often did we see the Israeli soldiers with their mini machine guns counterpoised by the noisy, disrespectful tourists. The state of siege even extended into the monastery and I was able to speak with Archbishop Damianos only over the telephone.

How different was my most recent trip to St Catherine's several years later. We had an uneventful flight to Cairo where we rented a Peugeot to make the eight-hour drive. Our only stop was for refueling from a 'filling station' which was simply a pipe protruding from the desert sand. After one final turn around a bend beneath a mountain the gigantic sixth-century walls of St Catherine's were revealed. The awesome weight and height of the monastery's Justinian walls, the colossal feeling of antiquity, the unearthly silence, the eerie cold of the night, the piercingly bright planets and stars and the holy bulk of Mount Sinai combine to create an overwhelming experience of other-worldliness.

4

In this charged atmosphere my mind turned to the discovery in 1975 of a sealed room in the northern wall. Among its contents were art treasures and ancient manuscripts. After publishing three articles and a monograph on these sensational discoveries I still had no answer to the question from many scholars as to the content and location of these artifacts. Several specialists offered the opinion that they were re-hidden outside the monastery in places known only to the monks.

This second visit offered a glimmer of an answer and provided me with the most memorable moment of my visit. As Archbishop Damianos grew to know me better, he felt confident enough to extend the opportunity to see the ancient manuscripts. I leapt at the chance and he took me to the south section of the monastery. We passed one of the most advanced microfilm readers I have ever seen and stepped into a back room that was lined with bookshelves. A winding staircase led to a second level where more manuscripts were stored.

After examining some Greek manuscript fragments, I was asked if I would like to examine the recovered leaves of Codex Sinaiticus. I answered 'Yes!' My mind and heart raced ahead as a rare experience was about to become personal. My privilege carried its price, though, as at the end of this feast, Archbishop Damianos asked me not to reveal what I had seen and learned. I have kept this promise. The announcement and first publications belong to the Archbishop and his fellow monks.

As *Secrets of Mount Sinai* discloses, these monks have been abused by western imperialism; they deserve our long overdue support and deep respect.

Today Biblical scholars know that we are far from possessing the original manuscripts written by the New Testament authors. Even with the manuscripts we do have it is well to remember that all the gospel manuscripts contain errors: some mistakes were caused by a scribe's faulty hearing or eyesight; others occurred because of poor spelling or inattentiveness; others were deliberate alterations due to changes in doctrinal or theological beliefs.

We are fortunate that indefatigable scholars, including Constantin Tischendorf, discovered early manuscripts such as the fourth-century Codex Sinaiticus, which was found in St Catherine's Monastery.

Tischendorf was obsessed with finding a manuscript of the

Bible which was pure and authoritative and so I can imagine the intense excitement he experienced when he beheld the revered treasure and began reading it alone at night. Spread before him the pages lay, illuminated by the flickering light of a candle. He bent over the pages and copied the Greek text onto a separate sheet.

We may well find texts more authoritative than Codex Sinaiticus and some of the papyri found in this century do contain material more important than this codex; but we are no longer looking for a text free from corruption for we are no longer convinced that we can reconstruct the text as it existed in the first century.

Centuries ago, Codex Sinaiticus began to lose some of its leaves. Tischendorf knew of this because he had recovered 43 leaves in St Catherine's in the 1840s. These leaves are now preserved in Leipzig. At some point in the 1850s he discovered 346 leaves and a fragment which are in the British Museum. Tischendorf never knew that more than a dozen leaves of Codex Sinaiticus remained in the monastery. No one knew this until ten years ago. It seems that these leaves had been stored in a room in the northern wall of the monastery almost 100 years before Tischendorf's visit. The room itself and its thousands of manuscripts were forgotten until the fire uncovered it in 1975.

Codex Sinaiticus, Codex Syriacus, Codex Vaticanus and Codex Bobiensis do not contain the last twelve verses of the Gospel of Mark. This is a notable omission: it is these verses only which contain the description of Jesus' resurrection appearance. Since Mark's account seems to be not only the earliest but also that on which Matthew and Luke based their accounts, a question arises: What is the basis for the accounts of Jesus' bodily resurrection according to Matthew, Luke and John?

During this century there has been a distinct shift by scholars regarding the ending of Mark. Early in this century, many influential scholars doubted that Mark originally ended without some description of Jesus' appearance to his disciples in Galilee. Today, most New Testament scholars doubt that the twelve final verses in Mark are original.

Any attempt to assess the significance that Mark may have originally ended at 16:8, 'and they (the women) said nothing to anyone, for they were afraid,' must discuss the meaning of two other verses. The first of these is Mark 16:7, which contains the promise of the young man in the tomb: 'But go, tell his disciples and Peter that he is going before you into Galilee; there you will see him, as he told you.' The second is Mark 14:28 in which we find Jesus' words referred to: 'But after I am raised up, I shall go before you into Galilee.' These verses have led some excellent scholars to contend that while Mark may not have recorded the physical resurrection of Jesus, he undoubtedly knew about the Hebrew traditions of bodily resurrection (cf. 2 Maccabees 14:37-46). Also predating Mark are all of Paul's authentic letters. In Romans, a creedal formula is quoted that may be decades older than Romans. In it we find emphasis clearly placed on Jesus' resurrection (cf. Romans 1:3-4).

It is clear that the essence of Christianity is bound to a canon of cherished texts which are shaped and better comprehended by an intense examination of the Greek text as preserved in authoritative witnesses, especially Codex Sinaiticus. We can thank the previous generation of scholars for raising the questions we are grappling with today and which we may bequeath yet unanswered to future generations.

Looking back on the above comments reminds me of a particularly unforgettable afternoon.

The summer sun had begun to take its toll on me one afternoon and so I took my camera and left the monastery through the small opening in the western wall. I climbed the red granite slope of the mountain to the north and after about 30 minutes of climbing I sat down to gaze back upon St Catherine's Monastery, now diminutive beneath the massive rock of Gebel Musa or Mount Sinai. Before me on this barren and beautiful stage, thousands of years of history, tradition, service and piety had been played out. Then my gaze was attracted to a small image moving from the pass below. I watched it continue through the valley, past the stone walls of the monastery. It was a lone camel with its driver, heading toward the west.

JHC
Princeton
30 May 1985

Acknowledgements

One of the greatest pleasures about writing books lies in finding new sources of evidence. The chief character in this book is Constantin von Tischendorf. F.H.A. Scrivener once wrote of Tischendorf that because he left no papers behind him, writing about his life 'might seem to resemble . . . making bricks without straw'. Since that time a few letters had appeared — three in the British Museum; another, along with a draft Tischendorf penned on rough paper, in the university library in Leipzig; and five more important letters discovered by Professor Ihor Sevcenko in the monastery of St Catherine on Mount Sinai. A few other letters by Tischendorf were quoted in the German account of his travels written by his granddaughter, Hildegaard Behrend.

In researching this book I learned that Tischendorf had become extremely friendly with a Scotsman, the Revd Dr Samuel Davidson, trusting him enough to commission Davidson with the translation of his monumental last edition of the New Testament in Greek. Thirteen remarkably frank and informative letters from Tischendorf to Davidson eventually found their way (along with Tischendorf's collection of some 3000 early printed books)

8

into the library of the University of Glasgow. So far as I know, these have not been used by researchers before now. I am deeply grateful to the University Librarian for making these letters available to me and allowing me to use extracts from them.

In addition I should particularly like to thank Dr Michael Clanchy, Mr Gary L. Fisketjon, Miss Caty Mallender, Dr Philip Mavroskoufis, Mr Charles Merullo, and Professor Jürgen Moltmann for their help.

Finally I record my thanks to the archbishop and confraternity of St Catherine's monastery on Mount Sinai, to Egyptair, and to Air Sinai.

JAMES BENTLEY

Prologue

The Air Sinai plane leaves the stretch of apparently endless sand-dunes and tarmac that is Cairo International Airport and cruises 1500 ft above the wrinkled yellow ridges of the desert. Looking down on that inhospitable sand with its occasional metalled road and rare stunted tree, I thought of the ancient story of Moses, leading the children of Israel on their dangerous journey from Egypt to the promised land, through the same wilderness.

According to the book of Exodus, the children of Israel pitched camp at a place called Rephidim, where there was no water for the people to drink. There they found fault with Moses. Tormented by thirst, they complained, 'Why did you bring us out of Egypt to kill us and our children and our cattle of thirst?' The biblical stories of Moses bringing water out of a rock, and of God feeding the people with manna in the desert, take on a new meaning and potency in the presence of this fearful barrenness.

But a twentieth-century scholar thinks of other miracles too — miracles of discovery and modern scholarship — for this intensely dry desert has preserved the secrets of centuries. Slowly over the past 100 years many of these secrets have been revealed. Their effect on believers and unbelievers alike has been and will be profound.

Soon the Air Sinai plane leaves the miles of desert behind and begins to climb over mountains, sometimes slightly threatening, sometimes looking little more than knolls from our height. The mountains are bluish in the shade, sand-coloured where the sun strikes them, some-times rippled and sometimes scooped out into whorls, with the passes clearly visible. Then another stretch of sand leads to the Red Sea, which is in fact very blue and sometimes even ultramarine. There are sandy beaches, a few solitary vessels and an oil derrick until at the other side rocks appear again, in places rising sheer from the sand. These mountains are greener than the earlier ones, with russet streaks and hues dating from volcanic times. At the foot of some of them grow a few green trees. Over new peaks and ridges and a few towering blue crags appears the narrow black airstrip built by the Israelis a couple of miles from Mount Sinai, during the period when this was Israeli-occupied territory as a result of the Arab-Israeli War of 1967.

The plane goes on to Eilat, if any passenger asks to go there, but that rarely happens. From the airport a coach takes you up a tarmac road, avoiding the many potholes, past donkeys and mules and camels. The land is inhospit-able, with tiny patches of scrub and silent burnt peaks, which grow bigger until the coach reaches the top of the pass. Occasionally we drive past a man standing with his wife, child and a loaded mule by the roadside, or simply sitting down. Today this is Moslem country and we pass a small, white, square mosque. The road winds through a few Bedouin encampments. Occasionally we pass little stone villages of three or four huts, alongside parched trees and sometimes a tiny walled garden. The coach passes a little chapel marking the spot where the Christian father and solitary St Jerome is said to have died.

By now we are 8000 feet (2500m) above sea level, and suddenly we glimpse a massive 160-foot long wall and gateway: the defences of the ancient monastery of St Catherine on Mount Sinai. The coach creeps up a narrow boulder-strewn road, and we have arrived.

Once monks of many religious persuasions lived inside St Catherine's — for the Orthodox faith of the Christian east embraced Syrians, Georgian, Ethiopians, etc. as well as Greeks. Today all the monks belong to the Greek Orthodox Church. The monastery guest-room testifies to their respect for the now-deposed Greek monarchy: its walls are covered with photographs of the entire Greek dynasty from 1863, along with all the royal consorts (including the German-loving wife of Constantine I, who was the sister of Kaiser Wilhelm II).

These pictures have a deeper historical significance. The monks of Mount Sinai still consider themselves to be an imperial foundation, guardians of a shrine built for them over fourteen centuries ago by the Emperor Justinian.

In the monastery guest-room hang also many pictures of the late President Sadat of Egypt — a Moslem whose protection was much valued by these Christian monks — as well as a photograph of Archbishop Makarios, signed in his characteristic red ink on a visit to mark the 1300th anniversary of the monastery's foundation. And because this is the land where Moses spoke and acted for Jehovah, other spaces on the walls are covered with British coloured engravings of attempts by Victorian artists to depict his exploits: crossing the Red Sea with the children of Israel as the pursuing Pharaoh and his army drown; bringing the tablets of the law down from Mount Sinai, and so on.

Justinian presented to the monastery 200 Egyptians and 200 Wallachians to serve the monks of St Catherine's as serfs. Descendants of these servants still work for the monastery. Known as *Dschebelijah*, they are not quite

13

Bedouin, though they have often intermarried with members of genuine Bedouin tribes. These men and their ancestors have served every visitor to the monastery since its foundation, as well as looking after the monks. On my arrival one of them brought me thick sweet coffee in a tiny cup along with a glass of water. And this Dschebelijah, whose name was Selim, cooked for me delightful food during my stay in St Catherine's. I rewarded him with two cigarettes a day.

Once the monastery was rich, drawing money from branches in Lebanon, Crete, Greece, and Cairo, from a sister nunnery devoted to the prophet Moses, and from lands in Russia and Romania. Today, its revenues depleted, the monks rely on tourism for much of their income. Money from UNESCO has paid for some tourist accommodation outside the monastery wall, next to its beautiful garden. Each day they welcome forty or fifty visitors, who spend an hour looking at the treasures of this remarkable place.

One of these is the exquisite church built inside the walls on the orders of the Emperor Justinian. This sixth-century building is one of the finest and certainly one of the most important of all early Christian basilicas.

The twentieth-century visitor, like a postulant or *catechumen* of early Christianity, enters the church by means of a kind of ante-nave, the *narthex*, separated from the main church by a great wall and doors. To reach the huge wooden doors of the narthex, the worshipper must descend steeply, because the church, built alongside the traditional site of the burning bush, is lower than almost any other part of the interior of the monastery walls. To compensate for this, its architect, Stephanos, made sure that the two great walls at the west and east ends projected far higher above the roof than was structurally necessary. As a result, the building, seen from the outside, con-

14

structed out of the red, worked stones of the area, still imposes, without appearing on the one hand too huge, or on the other, abnormally sunk into the ground.

Two huge doors guard the entrance to the narthex. But these are not contemporary with the building itself. They were built out of cypress wood in the twelfth-century (or perhaps a little earlier) and are still in virtually perfect condition, intricately carved with angels and the Christ, with flowers, trees and leaves. They lead the visitor into the narthex itself, which now houses some of the monastery's greatest treasures. Behind glass are displayed the earliest icons in the world, as well as a beautiful and famous twelfth-century icon of St John Klimakos climbing up a ladder to heaven. On a stand is the monastery's latest icon, painted in Greece by a monk named Jerbacis in 1977.

Displayed in the narthex too are some of the monastery's literary treasures. Supreme place belongs today to Codex Syriacus, recognised in 1892 as a fifth-century translation of the gospels, partly erased three or four centuries later so that the parchment could be used again. It is older than the monastery itself, evidence that the monks of St Catherine's either were given or collected manuscripts dating from before their own foundation. And here too is a copy of an even greater ancient Biblical manuscript — Codex Sinaiticus, which takes its name from the convent on Mount Sinai but, as we shall see, was lost to it over 100 years ago.

Inside the sixth-century church itself icons hang on the massy pillars holding up the roof. And over the apse of this church you see an astonishing mosaic, depicting the transfiguration of Jesus. On either side of the transfigured Saviour stand Moses and Elijah, and at his feet are three apostles, Peter, James and John. Above, on the left and the right, are two scenes from the life of Moses. On the left he takes off his sandals before the burning bush. On the right, he receives the ten commandments on Mount Sinai. (Oddly enough, in this mosaic the commandments are written not on tablets of stone, as in the Biblical accounts, but on a scroll.) This great mosaic incorporates medallions portraying John the Baptist and the Virgin Mary, as well as portraits of the Old Testament prophets and the twelve apostles. But since Peter, James, and John already appear in the central scene of the transfiguration, the artist who created the mosaic was able to fit into it the portraits of the apostles St Mark, St Luke, and St Paul, instead of Peter, James, and John.

He also included portraits of two other persons who were almost certainly living on Mount Sinai when the mosaic was made. These were an abbot of the monastery, called Longinus, and a monk identified in the mosaic simply as 'John the Deacon'. It is probable that this man was the famous John who in the late sixth century wrote a celebrated treatise on how to get to heaven. He called it 'The Ladder of Perfection' (and as a result he is generally known as John of the Ladder, or John 'Klimakos'). John's treatise has thirty chapters and his ladder has thirty steps, representing the thirty virtues a man or woman must attain before reaching heaven.

The only comparable mosaics to this masterpiece are in Italy, in the churches of San Vitale and Sant' Apollinare in Classe, Ravenna, which were created in the same century. It represents one of the most remarkable treasures of the monastery. Then, in the opinion of Professor Kurt Weitzmann, 'With the exception of the apse mosaic, the greatest artistic treasure of Sinai is the collection of icons'.

To me also these icons — unparalleled anywhere else in the world — appeared overwhelmingly beautiful. Later in this book I shall explain how such a unique treasure comes to be found in such a remote spot.

But both to the Christian scholar and the student of

man's religious quest, in spite of the wealth and beauty of the icons of St Catherine's monastery, a greater treasure is to be found in its 3000 ancient documents and manuscripts. Because Syrian, Georgian, and Ethiopian monks once lived here alongside Greeks, these precious documents include Syrian, Georgian, and Ethiopian as well as Greek manuscripts. Many of them remained unknown to the outside world for centuries, often unread by the monks themselves. But increasingly, and especially over the past two centuries, the quest for spiritual truth has brought men and women to Mount Sinai, to try to unlock the secrets of these ancient documents. What they found has proved both startling and even frightening.

Introduction

The Emperor Justinian built his monastery on Sinai, at the foot of Gebel Musa, as if he intended it to last for ever. So thick and powerful were its defensive walls that they stand today substantially as Justinian's architect left them, dressed with red local granite and in places towering more than 80 feet (30m) high.

This monastery, now dedicated to St Catherine of Alexandria, is the oldest continuously inhabited convent in the Christian world. Its beauty, and the fact that it has survived intact for so long, are both astounding.

St Catherine's monastery was built to defend monks from the attacks of marauding Saracens at a time when most of the Sinai was under the sway of Christianity. Within a century the followers of Mohammed were conquering Egypt, and soon St Catherine's monastery was a lonely bastion of Christian monasticism in an Islamic world. As tradition has it, in AD 625 the monks sent a delegation to Mohammed himself, begging his protection. Later Mohammed allegedly visited the monastery, and travellers were and are shown the divinely enlarged imprint of his camel's hoof on a rock. In any event the monks did obtain a document, purportedly from Mohammed, that guaranteed their safety. A later Sultan is said to have carried this away, leaving an authenticated copy still displayed in St Catherine's.

Whatever the truth in these traditions, the monks of Mount Sinai undoubtedly managed to gain recognition and protection from the Sultans, and took great care not to jeopardize their precarious security. Yearly they persuaded the Sultans in Constantinople to renew their charter of protection. And these Christian monks developed a uniquely tolerant relationship with Islam.

Remarkable evidence of this is provided today by an Islamic mosque standing within the walls of the Christian monastery itself, to serve the religious needs of its Moslem servants. An immediately arresting sight in this singularly Christian context, it was built in the eleventh century, at a time of great danger to the monks — either when Kalif Hakim was ravaging and pillaging Christian foundations or slightly later in the 1090s when Archbishop John the Athenian was murdered by hostile Moslems. One account has the monks building the mosque overnight, as a means of protection against marauders who might have burned St Catherine's to the ground; the sight of the minaret rising above the monastery walls would turn away militant Islam.

For the next three centuries Christian crusaders brought pilgrims to the convent on Mount Sinai. The crusaders even offered themselves as special protectors of the monastery. But in accepting this protection the monks were careful not to offend their Islamic neighbours. In AD 1115 they even dissuaded Baldwin, the crusader king of Jerusalem, from paying a visit to the mountain, so as not to anger the Sultan.

Throughout the Middle Ages these Christians sought, gained and retained independence and peace in a potentially hostile land. When Selim I of Turkey became Sultan of Egypt in 1517, Turkish rule brought two-and-a-half

19

centuries of greater tranquillity to the monks on Mount Sinai. The monastery acquired land and possessions as far away as Crete, Romania, and Moldavia. So long as they offered no hostility to the rulers of the Sinai, the monks found protection from the Turks. In 1551 the Sultan granted the monastery a charter ordering his officials not to prevent the monks from selling their traditional wares — 'animal foods, silks, wine, soap, olive oil, carpets, lentils, peas, beans, cheese, honey, coarsely-woven cloth, furs,' and so on. The charter also forbade the monks from selling anything useful to the Sultan's enemies, such as horses or weapons, an order the monks were entirely willing to obey.

But the threat of instability in Sinai was always present. In 1769 the Mameluke ('military knight') Ali-Bey revolted against Turkish rule and was not defeated until 1773. Meanwhile, the monks remained studiously neutral. The next threat came from Napoleon Bonaparte's brief Egyptian adventure in 1798. The monks of St Catherine's obtained a *firman* or decree of protection from the French, because, Napoleon explained, 'he was filled with respect for Moses, the Jews and also the monks, who were learned men living in the barbarity of the desert'.

Napoleon was expelled from Egypt by the British and the Sinai was restored to the Sultan in 1802. But for several dangerous years the struggle between the Mameluke leaders of Egypt and Mehemet Ali made access to St Catherine's risky and difficult. A Swiss explorer named Johann Burckhardt managed to reach it in 1816 and again in 1822 only by disguising himself as a Bedouin.

Mehemet Ali and his son looked favourably on the convent during the nineteenth century. It survived the British protectorate and occupation of Egypt without harm. For over 1300 years the monks had learned to survive and live in peace. They had developed the skill of not provoking neighbours whose faiths differed from their own, of withdrawing in times of stress and of keeping monasticism alive — almost, as it were, unnoticed by the warring nations around them.

Such skill has proved as necessary in our own time as in the past. After World War II the inhospitable Sinai became the focus of Israel's struggle to survive amidst her Arab neighbours. In 1965 the Israeli general Moshe Dayan wrote that 'military victory in Sinai brought Israel not only direct gains — freedom of navigation, cessation of terrorism — but, more important, a heightened prestige among friends and enemies alike'. These gains, crucially important for Israel, were nevertheless bought at the cost of great anxiety for the monks of Mount Sinai, who survived three Arab-Israeli wars, and between 1967 and 1982, when their monastery lay in Israeli-occupied territory, were at times scarcely accessible to western visitors. The monks' *raison d'être* — to live and worship in peace — meant stringent avoidance of any action that might provoke either their former protectors or their present ones.

Inside St Catherine's monastery were never more than thirty monks at any one time, and even in the seventh century AD, when upwards of 300 hermits and monks lived and prayed in solitude on Mount Sinai, these Christians would seek refuge in the monastery in times of danger. Today St Catherine's houses fewer than a dozen monks.

But over the course of 1400 years the monastery has become the home of invaluable treasures, preserved largely by its very isolation. When Christians elsewhere decided to destroy exquisite icons painted with images of God, Jesus, and the saints, believing that these pictures were idolatrous and contravened the second commandment, the monks of Mount Sinai by contrast preserved their icons, building up what is today the greatest collection in the world.

21

At the same time the monks so enriched their library that today its collection of ancient books contains over 3000 manuscripts. Only the Vatican library possesses more. Some of the manuscripts now in St Catherine's are older than the monastery itself. Among its treasures are revelations that make St Catherine's of great significance thousands of miles beyond the desert where it stands, and these few monks the guardians of secrets of utmost importance to millions of men and women throughout the rest of the world.

On 26 May 1975 these monks made a new, remarkable discovery. A few days earlier a fire had gutted the small chapel of St George, built into the north side of the monastery's great wall. Underneath this chapel the monks were in the habit of storing wood, drying it slowly to use as fuel; for safety's sake they decided to clear this wood away. As they did so, they uncovered a long-disused cell whose ceiling had caved in — almost certainly during one of the earthquakes that shook the monastery in the eighteenth century. When the monks began to clear away the rubble in this cell, they discovered an enormous mass of ancient manuscripts.

Altogether this find numbered well over 1000 previously unknown documents, written in Greek, Arabic, Syrian, Armenian, Ethiopian, Georgian, and Latin. This astonishing collection, buried for nearly 200 years and unknown to the outside world for nearly 2000, must be included in the sequence of major twentieth-century discoveries that includes the Dead Sea Scrolls and the Gnostic gospels.

But the one absolute masterpiece preserved for centuries by the monks of St Catherine's is no longer there. The great Codex Sinaiticus — the oldest virtually complete Bible in the world — is today in the British Museum. As the Museum proudly and rightly proclaims, the manuscript 'is a jewel beyond price'. Yet it remained unknown to the outside world until it was discovered in the middle of the nineteenth century in the ancient monastery on Mount Sinai.

This book is in part the story of how Codex Sinaiticus went from the Middle East to London and in part the story of the remarkable man for whom this Codex was the Holy Grail — an obsession which brought him three times to St Catherine's and which was his life's work. But, more importantly, it is about how this great Codex profoundly alters our understanding of the Christian faith.

Codex Sinaiticus is supreme among Biblical manuscripts: the oldest surviving Bible in the world containing the complete New Testament, and an unparalleled witness to the text of the Old Testament. The differences between the text of Codex Sinaiticus and the New Testament as perceived by Christians even today are nearly shocking, and it is fair to say that although scholars have worked on the manuscript, few Christians even know of these differences and that fewer still have come to terms with them.

Finally and above all, the discoveries at St Catherine's dramatically force us to reconsider one crucial element in Christianity: the resurrection of Jesus Christ himself.

BOOK I

CHAPTER I

The Scholar

On 18 January 1815 the wife of Dr Tischendorf, medical practitioner of Lengenfeld, a small town south of Leipzig in what is today East Germany, bore her husband a son. The pious Lutheran parents baptised the boy Lobegott Friedrich Constantin. He was destined to become the most famous as well as the most controversial Biblical scholar of all time.

Lengenfeld was an obscure manufacturing town in the Kingdom of Saxony, situated in a region of forests and breathtakingly beautiful valleys, where the local inhabitants still wore a curious and distinctive peasant costume. The boy's ancestors on his mother's side had lived there for centuries. One of these, a charcoal-burner in the fifteenth century, had achieved local renown when the lord of nearby Schloss Altenburg, Kurz von Kauffungen, kidnapped two royal princes. Attempting to spirit one of the princes into Bohemia, von Kauffungen came across Tischendorf's ancestor in the forest, burning charcoal. While the charcoal-burner set about the kidnapper with his stirring-pole, his wife summoned other charcoal-burners and together they overpowered von Kauffungen. The royal hostage was saved and his kidnapper later beheaded.

Constantin Tischendorf grew up to revere his charcoal-burning ancestor and to share his veneration of the Saxon royal family. When Tischendorf himself was knighted, he included in his coat of arms the figure of a sturdy charcoal-burner, stirring-pole on his shoulder.

None of his other Saxon ancestors achieved such fame, though they graduated from charcoal-burning to running a paper-mill in nearby Greiz. Tischendorf adored his mother, and her death when he was still in his twenties deeply affected him. He felt her to have been his greatest friend, and ten years after her death still was often aware of her presence. 'How little death is able to divide our hearts', he wrote. 'It binds together even tighter such true friends as my mother and myself.'

But if the boy derived his sensitivity from his mother, his brains came from his father. Dr Tischendorf was not a local man. Born in Thüringia, he had qualified at the University of Jena. He sent Constantin to learn Latin and Greek at the Gymnasium (grammar school) in Plauen, the chief and largest town in the district, picturesquely situated over 1000 feet above sea level and washed by the Weisse Elster. The boy was well-taught and a prize-winner. At the beginning of the Michaelmas term, 1834, he entered the theology school of the University of Leipzig.

Founded in 1409, Leipzig was one of the most ancient and important universities in Germany. Constantin Tischendorf became one of its students at an auspicious moment. The patronage of the Saxon royal family was bringing about a powerful expansion in the university. In Tischendorf's lifetime the number of students rose from 800 to over 3000. Magnificent new lecture halls were on the verge of completion. The young student responded to his teachers with alacrity — especially the New Testament professor J.G.B. Winer. He published two prize-winning essays and in 1838 became a doctor of philosophy. He also wrote a volume of romantic poems called *The Buds of May*, some of which were set to music. Tischendorf was developing literary skills as well as a formidable intellect.

The untimely death of his father forced Constantin to leave university and earn a living by teaching in a school near Leipzig run by a Lutheran pastor. There he fell in love with a fellow teacher, Angelike Zehme, the pastor's daughter. He also further developed his literary skills by publishing (under the pen-name of Dr Fritz) a novel called *The Young Mystic*.

But Tischendorf aimed at more than schoolmastering and writing novels. He passionately desired to do a great work for God and Jesus Christ. And though he was destined to become one of the outstanding Biblical scholars of the age, he had no intention of becoming a dry-as-dust academic. He longed to communicate his discoveries and his learning to ordinary men and women.

At the age of twenty-five he returned to the University of Leipzig, this time as university lecturer and a member of the faculty of theology. To a man already committed to defending the truths of Christianity, Tischendorf's return to the academic life came not a moment too soon. The Christian scriptures, both the Old and the New Testament, were under attack as never before.

One school of German theologians had come to doubt the reliability of virtually all the New Testament. Whereas Christians had formerly believed that nearly every book in the New Testament had been written either by one of Jesus' own followers or by a close associate of those followers, some theologians now asserted that scarcely any part of the New Testament contained the authentic record of Jesus' disciples.

In the Bible thirteen letters are attributed to the Apostle Paul. Now German theologians were claiming that only four of these (I and II Corinthians, Galatians, and Romans) were actually written by him. As for the four Gospels, some sceptical theologians were maintaining that they were composed long after the events which they purported to describe. Instead of trustworthy and accurate accounts of the sayings and doings of Jesus Christ, they contained, it was asserted, little but unreliable myths. Scarcely anything recorded in them — and certainly next-to-nothing in the fourth Gospel of John — could be regarded as eyewitness testimony of the life, death, and resurrection of Jesus.

All this horrified Constantin Tischendorf. In his view the four Gospels as written down by Matthew, Mark, Luke, and John were entirely trustworthy. Two of the evangelists, John and Matthew, he believed to have been 'direct eyewitnesses' of the events of the Saviour's life. He accepted that the two others, Mark and Luke, were 'men intimately connected with these eyewitnesses'. Because John, in his belief, was the disciple specially loved by Jesus, the last Gospel was in Tischendorf's view 'the most important of the four'. All that Christians needed was an accurate text of the New Testament, from which they might learn sacred truths. With such a text Christians could confute what Tischendorf described as 'the dazzling wit and ingenious sophistry' of those who 'torture and twist the facts which occurred 1800 years ago'.

Accordingly in 1840 Tischendorf published his first attempt at producing an authentic New Testament in Greek. It did not satisfy him (though his friend Bishop Dräseke called it 'the foundation stone of your literary immortality' and presented a copy to the King of Prussia).

Tischendorf's whole professional career would be spent in defending a Bible under attack. For this reason he laboured and lectured, suffered and searched the Orient, looking for proof that Holy Scripture could be trusted.

His work came not a moment too soon. Although many men and women had previously doubted some of the words of the Bible, in public such doubts were generally suppressed until, in the eighteenth century, two Englishmen brought them out into the open. One of these men was the famous historian Edward Gibbon.

Gibbon's *Decline and Fall of the Roman Empire* shocked the devout by asserting that the early Church fathers defeated heretics by using forged testimonies. He went further by insisting that the 'rash and sacrilegious hands' of these Church fathers had even contaminated Holy Scripture itself. He concentrated his attack on one text in particular. The first Epistle of John, chapter 5, verse 7, had long been used to prove the truth of the difficult doctrine of the Trinity — that Jesus, his heavenly Father and the Holy Spirit are in fact three persons united in one God. The text reads, 'there are three that bear record in heaven, the Father, the Word and the Holy Ghost, and these three are one'. Gibbon declared it to be spurious.

Others had done so before him, but only in academic and learned circles. Gibbon did so before the general public, in language designed to offend. 'This memorable text,' he wrote, 'which asserts the unity of the THREE who bear witness in Heaven, is condemned by the universal silence of the orthodox fathers, ancient versions, and authentic manuscripts.' In short, it had been inserted into the genuine text at some later time.

So why had scholars continued to accept it? Erasmus, said Gibbon, suspected it to be false but kept it out of 'prudence'. Erasmus' rivals — both Roman Catholic and Protestant — stuck to the spurious text out of 'honest bigotry'. Since that time, Gibbon concluded, 'the pious fraud, which was embraced with equal zeal at Rome and at Geneva, has been infinitely multiplied in every country and every language of modern Europe'. In effect Gibbon implied that Christians were defending the doctrine of the Holy Trinity (and thus that Jesus was God as well as man) by fraudulent means.

Many of the faithful were scandalized. In Britain the clergy instantly attacked Gibbon. They were led by the Revd George Travis, Archdeacon of Durham. Unfortunately Gibbon happened to be right; and Archdeacon Travis was an incompetent scholar. And to Gibbon's defence leapt one of the most bizarre geniuses of the century, Richard Porson.

A.E. Housman, the Cambridge classicist and poet, held that Porson was Britain's second greatest classical scholar. Yet Porson's career ended in failure. Although he had been born into a poor Norfolk family, the young Porson's precocious brilliance led him to an education at Eton and Trinity College, Cambridge. But two things prevented greater success. One was drink. The other was Porson's refusal to take Holy Orders, which effectively barred him from university preferment.

After leaving Cambridge, Porson was once found drunk in a turnip field, and forced to give up his job as tutor to the son of a rich family in the Isle of Wight. Byron described him as the most bestial of all the disgusting brutes that he knew. Porson, he wrote, was sulky, abusive, and intolerable, adding, 'In private parties he was always drunk or brutal, and generally both'. He became librarian to the London Institution, but scarcely attended to any of his duties, frequently coming home dead-drunk long after midnight. But for his early death (asserted his successor as librarian) the directors of the Institution would certainly have dismissed him. A.E. Housman once made a brilliant after-dinner speech in the great hall of Trinity College, Cambridge, alluding to Porson's tragic affliction. 'This great College, of this ancient University,' said Housman, 'has seen some strange sights. It has seen

Wordsworth drunk and Porson sober. And here am I, a better poet than Porson, and a better scholar than Wordsworth.' For all his drunkenness, Porson's brain was formidable. Along with Edward Gibbon, this depraved Englishman brought into the open the dubious authenticity of parts of the Christian Bible.

Porson greatly admired Gibbon. He considered the *Decline and Fall* incomparably the greatest literary work of the eighteenth century. He loved to quote long passages from it. To admire a sceptic like Gibbon and also to enter the eighteenth-century church was scarcely possible. At any rate, when faced with the decision whether or not to seek ordination, Porson said, 'I found that I should require about fifty years' reading to make myself thoroughly acquainted with divinity — to satisfy my mind on all points'. In any case, his doubts about orthodoxy — and especially about the doctrine of the Trinity — were all too obvious. Once, discussing the matter with a Trinitarian friend, he saw a buggy pass by containing three men. 'There', said Porson's friend, 'is an illustration of the Trinity.' Porson replied, 'No, you must show me one man in *three* buggies, if you can'.

Faced with such doubts and aware of the great intellectual problems confronting the Christian faith, Porson was appalled at the cocksure incompetence of Archdeacon Travis's defence of the three heavenly witnesses of I John chapter 5, verse 7. He published a brilliant and devastating reply.

Porson's technique reveals a breakthrough — for which he was in large part responsible — in the textual criticism of the Bible. It was the technique later used by Tischendorf and every other competent textual scholar. Porson faced the question of how to decide, out of many different manuscripts of the Bible, which gave the correct text. His answer was to group them in 'families'. All the texts that

31

shared common errors, misreadings, misspellings, alterations and so on, belonged to the same family, he decided.
This enabled him to eliminate later manuscripts which
were obvious copies of earlier ones.

He found it possible to build up a family tree of any
text, discovering the various stages at which the text had
undergone change or alteration. His aim was to get back
to the ancestor from which all the different, later texts
were descended. This text, the ancestor of all the rest, and
no other, was the closest to the original that anyone can
expect to find.

Porson proceeded to use this technique to destroy the
claim to authenticity of the proof of the three heavenly
witnesses in the first Epistle of John. He showed that none
of the extant oldest Greek manuscripts of the Bible
contained it. The spurious text first appeared in Latin
manuscripts around the year AD 400. Not one of the early
fathers ever quoted or cited the text. Through its inclusion
in the Latin text, it reached a few, very late Greek
manuscripts, and in 1522 Erasmus included it in the third
edition of his Greek Bible.

Gibbon was overjoyed that his attack on the text had
been so powerfully vindicated. 'I consider Mr Porson's
answer to Archdeacon Travis as the most acute and
accurate piece of criticism', he wrote. 'His strictures are
founded in argument, enriched with learning, and en-
livened with wit, and his adversary neither deserves nor
finds any quarter at his hands. The evidence of the three
heavenly witnesses would now be rejected in any court of
Justice; but prejudice is blind, authority is deaf, and our
vulgar Bibles will ever be polluted by this spurious text.'
In fact, they are not. No modern Bible now contains the
interpolation. Porson's attack proved decisive.

Some still vainly tried to defend the spurious text. The
German scholar Johann Albrecht Bengel had argued that

the words *must* have been part of the original Bible because of their great importance for Christian doctrine — an argument patently absurd.

Other scholars set about trying to find old Greek manuscripts that did contain the disputed words. None could be found. In 1827 the Rector of Lincoln College, Oxford, and the Bishop of Peterborough claimed that they had seen the text in an old Greek manuscript that had since disappeared! Porson had already dealt with such desperate claims. Mythical manuscripts like this, he mocked, were apparently too good for this world. They were, perhaps, deposited in a snug corner of the moon, along with Archdeacon Travis's supposed learning.

By Tischendorf's time scholars were forced to admit that the generally accepted text of the New Testament was inaccurate, based on manuscripts written far later than Gospel times. They were forced to the reluctant conclusion that the first published edition of the New Testament in Greek — that made by Erasmus in 1516 — was faulty. Not only was Erasmus slapdash in his work. He had also used poor manuscripts.

Unfortunately, Erasmus's faulty text — partly because it was blessed by Pope Leo X — soon became the accepted basis of all new translations of the New Testament, Catholic and Protestant alike. When Martin Luther translated the whole Bible into German in 1520, he translated the New Testament directly from the second edition of Erasmus' Greek version. Soon Protestants everywhere came to regard this faulty Greek text by a Roman Catholic humanist as the inspired word of God, from which Christians, scholars and laymen alike, deviated at their peril.

Even Roman Catholic scholars were ill-advised to question Erasmus' received text of the New Testament. In the late seventeenth century, a learned French priest called

Richard Simon perceived that he could make fun of
Protestants by pointing out that the Bible they revered as
the sole source of revelation was inaccurate. Since, he
wrote, 'the original manuscripts have been lost,' Protestants can consult 'the Bible only in the form we have it
today'. Richard Simon hoped to demonstrate that the only
sure way to Christian truth was to accept the inspired
teaching of the Church and not the Bible alone. But so
great was the alarm caused by his attacks on the received
text of Holy Scripture that his own ecclesiastical superiors
had much of his work destroyed.

What they could not destroy was the truth in his
assertions. The text of the Christian Bible was inadequate.
Richard Simon's work came to the attention of an Angli-
can clergyman, John Mill, who early in the next century
produced a remarkable edition of the Greek New Testament. Mill himself did not dare depart from the received
text; but his voluminous notes to it — derived from many
earlier manuscripts than those used by Erasmus — demonstrated absolutely clearly that this received text was in
many places wrong.

Mill's caution in presenting his conclusions seemed
amply justified, for in the same century a Swiss clergyman, Johann Jakob Wettstein, began to publish a new
edition of the Greek New Testament which did depart
from Erasmus' text, and found himself deprived of his
holy orders.

But the demands of scholarship could not be ignored for
ever. By the time of Constantin Tischendorf the problem
of the text of the New Testament was generally recognized as one desperate for a proper solution. The problem
could no longer be swept under a scholarly carpet. Gibbon
and Porson had deliberately opened the eyes of the general
public to the mess the scholarly world had got itself into.
Tischendorf found himself in the middle of the great

nineteenth-century debate about whether the Bible could be believed at all.

Tischendorf was no longer concerned merely with problems of the textual accuracy of the New Testament or the attack on the spurious reference to the Holy Trinity in the first Epistle of John. By now scholars had begun to cast doubt on the Gospel records of the life of Jesus himself. 'It is well known,' Tischendorf said, 'that several learned men have, quite recently, written works on the life of Jesus, purporting to prove that He whom Christendom claims as her Lord did not really live the life that the Gospels record of him.' These learned men, Tischendorf believed, struck at the very foundations of Christian belief. 'If we are in error in believing in the person of Christ as taught us in the Gospels, then the Church herself is in error, and must be given up as a deception,' he said. The whole Christian faith seemed at stake.

The supreme problem, not surprisingly, concerned the many miraculous aspects of the traditional account of Jesus's life. As early as 1800 a theologian from Heidelberg, Heinrich Eberhard Gottlob Paulus, set about writing a life of Jesus which suggested that the miraculous stories in the Gospels were in fact inadequate explanations of what had really happened. Paulus did not believe that the Gospel writers were liars. On the contrary, in his view they did set down reliably what Jesus had done; but they also misinterpreted it. Once, Paulus asserted, Jesus had walked on a sandbank towards his disciples who were in a fishing boat. The Gospel account erroneously suggested that he had walked on the water.

Paulus's greatest wish was, he wrote, that his views on the miracle stories 'should not by any means be regarded as the most important matter'. It was a vain hope. By the time of his death in 1851 views such as his were causing enormous unease in the churches, so much so that one

Oxford divine publicly expressed the wish that all the German critics were at the bottom of the German ocean.

Scholars with even more radical views were reaching a wide public and, inevitably, distressing many of them. The most radical was David Friedrich Strauss, whose views so shocked conservative Christians that the University of Zurich offered him the chair of theology there in 1839 and then pensioned him off before he took office.

Strauss's *Life of Jesus* assumed that every single part of the Gospel accounts had been subject to mythical re-interpretation. Even though he accepted a historical basis behind the Gospel stories, Strauss argued that the boundary line between the historical and the unhistorical would 'for ever remain fluctuating and unsusceptible of precise attainment'.

Strauss did not regard the 'mythical' as necessarily 'untrue'. Spiritual truths, he argued, were independent of whether or not an episode in the life of Jesus actually happened. He was, he wrote, 'aware that the essence of the Christian faith is perfectly independent of his criticism. The supernatural birth of Christ, his miracles, his resurrection and ascension, remain eternal truths, whatever doubts may be cast on their reality as historical facts'. To Tischendorf and many other Christians, such arguments were valueless. Their belief in, say, the resurrection, depended on trust in the absolute trustworthiness of the Gospel witness. That Strauss was undermining.

In so doing Strauss undoubtedly undermined the faith of some intelligent Christians. His *Life of Jesus* was translated into English by the young George Eliot. During the work she was, she said, 'Strauss-sick'. She said it made her ill, dissecting the beautiful story of the crucifixion. To endure this pain, she would gaze on an engraving of the face of Christ which she kept on her study wall, and on a twenty-inch-high cast of Thorvaldsen's statue of the risen

Jesus. But in the end she lost her faith. Later, when the identity between the author of *Adam Bede* and the translator of Strauss became known, many critics were shocked. To cease to believe in the truth of the Gospels and the risen Jesus seemed to destroy the very basis of Christian morality. The eighty-four year old critic Crabbe Robinson declared that George Eliot's work had destroyed 'all comfortable notions of right and wrong, true and false'.

'I falter where I firmly trod', wrote Alfred Tennyson in his poem *In Memoriam*. One acute observer noted in 1877 that even at 'Sunday luncheon-tables' men and women could be heard professing disbelief in what were once held to be central tenets of the Christian faith. Above all many religious leaders feared for beliefs of the common man. Writers such as Strauss were 'robbing the poor man of his Saviour', asserted the angry novelist Charles Kingsley.

Only in this context can Tischendorf's life's work be fully appreciated. He was passionately determined to refute those who were destroying the faith of the Christian world. Many Christians desperately longed for such a refutation. In a pamphlet published in March 1864 Tischendorf wrote, 'May my writing serve this end: to make you mistrust those novel theories upon the Gospels — or rather, *against* them — which would persuade you that the wonderful details which the Gospels give of our gracious Saviour are founded upon ignorance or deceit'. Tischendorf's pamphlet sold out the entire edition of 2000 copies within three weeks.

But the works he was attacking were also runaway best-sellers. The latest attack on the historicity of the Christian Gospels had been published by a Frenchman in the previous year. Ernest Renan's *Life of Jesus* scandalized the German scholar. Renan, as his critics complained, treated the life of Jesus as a kind of romantic piece of theatre. Renan, said one of them, 'is at once the author of the play, the stage-manager, and the director of the theatre'. At a sign from him the open-air stage is lit up, 'the footlights are turned higher, and while the flutes and shawms of the orchestra strike up the overture, the people enter and take their places among the bushes and by the shore of the Lake'. Then Jesus begins to preach what Renan described as 'the delicious theology of love'.

Tischendorf was in part simply scornful of Renan's ignorance of the geography of the Bible. 'M. Renan', he pronounced, 'has taken strange liberties with the Holy Land.' But what he found appalling was Renan's suggestion that the Lord's miracles were based on deceit, deceit aided by Jesus's astute friends. Far from being dead, Jesus's friend Lazarus arranged to be wrapped in the winding sheets of a corpse and laid in a tomb. 'Lazarus, yet pale with sickness, had himself been wrapped up in grave clothes and laid in the family sepulchre.' Jesus raises him, apparently from the dead, and later discovers the family deception.

This for Tischendorf was the final scandal in a book he dubbed 'nothing else than a caricature of history from beginning to end'. Renan's attitude to the resurrection of Jesus himself seemed at first sight less obviously heretical than his account of the raising of Lazarus. It did not therefore strike quite so much horror in Tischendorf's heart. But other Christian scholars found it far from acceptable.

After recounting the death of Jesus, Renan begins to eulogize the Saviour:

> Rest now, amid thy glory, noble pioneer. Thou conqueror of death, take the sceptre of thy kingdom, into which so many centuries of thy worshippers shall follow thee, by the highway which thou hast opened up.

Incredibly, Renan never analyses the discrepancy between his assumption of some sort of resurrection for Jesus and the alleged duplicity of the Gospels about the other miracles, and in particular about the raising of Lazarus. In truth, Renan hurriedly brushes over the whole question of the bodily resurrection of Jesus Christ. As Albert Schweitzer later commented, 'The bell rings; the curtain begins to fall; the swing-seats tilt. The epilogue is scarcely heard: "Jesus will never have a rival. His religion will again and again renew itself; His story will call forth endless tears; His sufferings will soften the hearts of the best; every successive century will proclaim that among the sons of men there hath not arisen a greater than Jesus" .' In that lay Jesus's immortality.

Ernest Renan's *Life of Jesus* was furiously attacked by the orthodox. Partly because of this, it went through eight editions in three months. But for Tischendorf it was not Renan's sentimental son of man who would survive the centuries. Renan, along with the other critics of the authentic Gospels, were destined, Tischendorf said, to oblivion. Tischendorf firmly believed that as a result of his own discoveries the Gospel record was established more firmly than ever. As a result, he asserted, 'The Gospels, like the Only-begotten of the Father, will endure as long as human nature itself, while the discoveries of this pretended wisdom must sooner or later disappear like bubbles'.

Tischendorf's confidence came partly from awareness of his own immense abilities. But it also derived from his recognition that some scholars were fighting back against those who doubted the Bible. One of these was a man Tischendorf greatly admired, the Berlin professor Karl Lachmann.

Lachmann was not a theologian but a student of classical and Old German texts. When he turned to the study of the text of the Bible, he did so reverently, but with the same scholarly independence as he had applied to pagan works.

In preparing his texts, he declared he had no interest either in their meaning or their interpretation. Indeed, he once said he didn't care if he produced a text that was ungrammatical. The meaning, theology, and even the grammar of the Bible would come later. What Lachmann set out to do was produce a text based entirely on the oldest manuscripts he could find.

Lachmann's edition of the New Testament appeared in 1831. It was phenomenally learned but as Tischendorf realized, it was still inadequate. He identified the principal problem: Lachmann had failed to discover and make use of enough early manuscript material to produce an impregnably authentic text of Holy Scripture.

Tischendorf made it his life's work to solve that problem. To do so he built up a personal library of over 3000 rare volumes which is now to be found in the University of Glasgow. Consulting it even now the visitor cannot fail to be impressed by the care and industry with which Tischendorf trained himself for his life's task. The library contains his copy of Erasmus's first edition of the Greek New Testament, published in Basel in 1516, as well as a small copy of the second edition of this work published in 1521. He owned a first edition of Luther's translation of the New Testament into German. Tischendorf had bought and studied editions of the Bible by early Christian fathers of the church, such as St Jerome. And he had got hold of a copy of John Mill's revolutionary work on the Greek New Testament, published in Leipzig in 1710.

Equally impressive is the evidence of Tischendorf's study of handwriting of ancient manuscripts. He bought the famous seventeenth-century book by the French Benedictine monk Jean Mabillon which established how Latin script had developed over seventeen centuries. In the field of Greek manuscripts, Tischendorf obtained a work by another famous Benedictine monk, Bernard de

Montfaucon, which in 1708 virtually created the study of Greek and Byzantine palaeography.

Tischendorf's own achievement was, if anything, to be even greater than that of these two men. 'I am confronted by a sacred task,' he wrote to his fiancée Angelika, 'the struggle to regain the original form of the New Testament.'

At his disposal were four great ancient manuscripts — or nearly so, for two of them were virtually inaccessible. The first was the famous manuscript known as the Codex Alexandrinus. This, it was thought, was 1300 years old and had come to rest in the British Museum. The second ancient manuscript, the so-called Codex Claramontanus, was in the National Library of Paris. Both these manuscripts contained early copies of part, though not all, of the Bible.

One of the inaccessible manuscripts was the Codex Vaticanus in Rome. Dating perhaps from the middle of the fourth century AD, it ought to have been of inestimable value in establishing the true text of the Bible. But the Vatican authorities simply refused to let anyone see it.

The fourth great manuscript, the Codex Ephraemi in Paris, was inaccessible simply because no-one could read it. It preserved a text of the Bible written probably as early as the fifth century AD. But several centuries later this text had been more or less erased, so that the parchment could be used again to record the writings of a Syrian teacher called Ephraem. No-one had been able to decipher the original Biblical text underneath.

Nothing daunted by these difficulties, Tischendorf decided that within a year he could produce a new, definitive edition of the Greek New Testament. The task did indeed prove difficult. 'This gigantic undertaking has weighed heavily on me,' he told Angelika, 'and later on it will seem unbelievable, even to me, that I could write a book in less

41

than a year which will bring me both cursings and blessings.' The cursings he expected from jealous colleagues, who were already accusing him of arrogance. But Tischendorf was convinced of God's call in this work. 'I lay its future in God's hands', he wrote. 'Though jealousy and narrow-mindedness cast suspicion upon me, I know I am struggling in an earnest and holy endeavour, though all my strength is weakness.' He urged Angelika to ignore the criticisms of his rivals. 'If others suspect me of following any other than a heaven-sent goal,' he told her, 'you must not believe it.'

Tischendorf decided he must visit Paris, London, and elsewhere, to examine the ancient manuscripts of the Bible in person. He therefore applied to the Saxon Ministry of Public Worship and Education for a grant to enable him to do this. His academic rivals tried to stop it. 'I am not going to despair', Tischendorf wrote to Angelika. 'I believe with Christian joy that the Father in Heaven loves me, for he chastises me. What after all is the crime for which I am suffering? That I leave the comfortable path of study, where I might achieve something excellent, and turn my face to the unusual.' Repressing the ambitious hopes involved in his remarkable project, he wrote, 'before God I feel it in the depths of my soul that it is not a conceited, arrogant desire on my part, but an inspired, high-minded endeavour which I myself cannot resist'.

Yet Tischendorf could also at times be candid about his magnificent ambitions. 'I have other aspirations and aims', he told his fiancée. 'One lies as far away as Rome! I am prepared for anything and throw myself, a daring though cautious swimmer, into the whirlpool.' Tischendorf was determined to work even on the forbidden Codex Vaticanus. He failed in the end to achieve this ambition; but he came within an inch of success.

And in 1840 he was entirely successful. In spite of the

efforts of Tischendorf's enemies, the Minister of Public Worship and Education, Dr von Falkenstein, made him a small grant of 200 Thalers. Tischendorf's brother generously matched the sum with another gift. And in October the scholar set out. 'My destiny calls me onwards,' he wrote to Angelika, 'and I must follow.' He arrived in Paris, and for the first time his genius was confronted with and triumphed over a worthy task. Not only did he examine the Codex Claramontanus. Tischendorf also managed to transcribe the 64 faded Old Testament leaves and 145 New Testament leaves of the Codex Ephraemi.

A later story of the Tischendorf family tells how his mother, pregnant with the future scholar, saw in the streets of Lengenfeld a blind man. 'Oh God,' she exclaimed, 'do not let my child be born blind!' Instead, her son was born with prodigious eyesight. For two years he toiled over the pale, washed-out Greek letters of the Codex Ephraemi, overlaid by the Syrian text. Then, early in 1843, he published his edition of the deciphered Codex. It was an outstanding achievement.

Though Tischendorf's extraordinary impact on the general public was yet to come, his scholarly reputation was made. Now he visited London, Holland, Switzerland, and Italy, poring over fresh manuscripts of Holy Scripture. Only in Rome did he meet opposition. It is difficult to know who put obstacles in Tischendorf's way. According to his own account, Pope Gregory XVI would have let him see the Codex Vaticanus; but Cardinal Mai — who wished to publish his own edition of that text — blocked Tischendorf's plans. The German scholar was allowed to examine Codex Vaticanus for no more than six hours. His experience soured his later relationships with Roman Catholic scholars of the day.

And the cost to Tischendorf had been great. He had suffered financially. The Ministry of Public Worship and

Education had given him 200 Thalers. His journey to Paris alone had cost him 750 Thalers. Tischendorf had been obliged to carry out menial tasks — transcribing manuscripts for others, and so on — in order to survive.

Worse, he had failed to achieve the ambition he had set for himself in 1839: 'to reconstruct if possible the exact text of the Bible as it came from the pen of the sacred writers'. Tischendorf knew in his own heart that his first critical edition of the New Testament was unsatisfactory. The manuscripts at his disposal were still inadequate. It was clear to Tischendorf that he must find new sources for establishing the authentic text of the Bible.

Tischendorf's son-in-law analysed the changing ambition of his famous father-in-law. Initially, he wrote, Tischendorf was convinced 'that nothing in theology was as important as the careful study of the oldest manuscripts of the New Testament to prove their genuineness'. After years of brilliant, costly scholarship he came to see that this was not enough. Now, 'to prove the early existence and authenticity of the Gospels his main aim was to go in search of manuscripts that would afford this proof'.

This was the quest that brought him to the convent of St Catherine on Mount Sinai.

CHAPTER II

The Monastery

Where might a scholar in the nineteenth century find new sources of the authentic Gospels? The obvious answer was in the Middle East. The age of the great collectors — some would say plunderers — had already dawned, and much of their treasure came from oriental monasteries. Robert Curzon, the unscrupulous fourteenth Baron Zouche, seeking ancient manuscripts on behalf of the British Museum, boasted of getting a blind, grey-bearded abbot drunk in order to take away his old books. In the mid–eighteenth century an English bishop named Richard Pococke had found his way into the library of the monks of St Catherine's on Mount Sinai where he saw a large number of manuscripts. He reported that none of them were valuable ones.

He was wrong, but his error misled others. William Turner who visited the monastery in 1815, reported, 'To my enquiries after manuscripts and a library the priests answered, that they had only three Bibles, and I took their word more readily, as Pococke states they had no rare manuscripts'. So he came away empty-handed.

Others found and took away remarkable treasures. William John Banckes, who also visited Mount Sinai in

1815, recorded that 'by persevering and rummaging' he found 'a library of two hundred volumes, of which three quarters were manuscripts, and of them nine-tenths were Greek'. Banckes, a son of the Enlightenment, had little respect for religious books. 'The greater part were theological,' he observed, 'but some were interesting.' He managed to bring away with him five manuscripts, containing:

1. Hephestio on Greek metres, an oration of Isocrates, and the letters of Phalaris;
2. the first three books of the *Iliad*, along with part of the fourth book, the tragedies of Aeschylus, and much Greek poetry;
3. Euripides' *Medea*, and the beginning of his *Hippolytus*;
4. a work by the Byzantine historian Cedrenus;
5. all of Aristotle's *Physics*.

William Banckes managed to see only a small part of the monks' literary treasures. Johann Burckhardt on his visit to St Catherine's in 1822 reported that 'They have a good library, but it is always shut up; it contains about fifteen hundred Greek volumes and seven hundred Arabic manuscripts'. The monks' habit of keeping visitors out of their library annoyed westerners who had made the arduous journey to Mount Sinai. Some of them angrily assumed that the monks themselves never used their valuable books. An American visitor, Dr Edward Robinson, reported in 1838 that 'The Library is utterly neglected, private reading forming no part of the duties or pleasures of these worthies'.

In fact the monks were well aware that they possessed priceless treasures and that their visitors would have liked to take them away. A year after Robinson's visit, Archdeacon Henry Tattam and his travelling companion Miss Platt arrived at St Catherine's monastery. Tattam desperately wished to buy the monastery's oldest Biblical codex. The archbishop of Sinai scarcely allowed him to see it. Ten years earlier, he explained, another Englishman had tried to buy it for £300, but the Greek patriarch in Cairo had instructed the monastery not to part with the manuscript on any account.

Tattam was indignant at not being able to take away the precious codex. Miss Platt was equally indignant that anyone should have offered so much money to these despised monks! £300, she observed, was an 'imprudently high price for things of this kind, and gives to the Oriental an impression that they must be of immense value'.

To such Orientals Constantin Tischendorf now looked to complete his life's work. As he told his brother Julius, he was convinced that 'many a monastery still contains unexamined recesses'. More than ever Tischendorf now believed in his own genius and his superiority over his rivals in the field of Biblical textual learning. 'No-one', he told Julius, 'has explored recently with so definite a purpose as myself. I have learnt to distrust the labours of my predecessors.' He was certain that he must search for new manuscripts himself.

Again he approached the Ministry of Public Worship and Education for funds. At the end of 1843 he set off 'to attempt', as he put it, 'to win a blessing for the church, for knowledge and for the Fatherland, together with immortal laurels for myself'. In March 1844 he sailed from Leghorn, Italy, in a French war steamer, for Alexandria by way of Malta. From Alexandria he took a small ship up the Nile to Cairo.

There the monks of St Catherine's on Mount Sinai welcomed him to their daughter house. In the fashion of many western Protestant visitors, Tischendorf took an instant dislike to his hosts. He judged their protracted worship 'ridiculously out-of-tune'. Their attitude to scholarship he completely despised. They seemed not to care for his own urgent concerns. A library with these monks, he wrote, occupied 'the place that ladies' what-nots occupy with us'. When he asked the monks whether they possessed any ancient manuscripts in Cairo, they told him that all their manuscripts were in the monastery on Mount Sinai. Nevertheless, Tischendorf persuaded them to open the cupboard that served as their library in Cairo. It took them, he said, half-an-hour to find the key. When they opened the cupboard they discovered it to be stuffed with ancient manuscripts.

This find made him all the more eager to cross the desert to the mother house on Mount Sinai. The modern travel industry was about to begin. Paddle-steamers already plied between the Lebanese and Palestinian ports. Murray and Baedeker would soon publish their guides to the Orient. Before long Thomas Cook's tours would be in operation. Yet travel in those regions remained hazardous. In 1862 the eminent Victorian Henry Thomas Buckle set out to tour Egypt and the Holy Places with two school-boys, twenty camels, and two donkeys. He and his companions wore heavy flannel underclothing. Even so Buckle contacted typhoid and died at Damascus, lamenting: 'Oh my book, my book! I shall never finish my book'.

Tischendorf's aim in 1844 of crossing from Cairo to Mount Sinai was a difficult and even dangerous one. The great French novelist Alexandre Dumas the Elder had made the same voyage in 1836. Crossing the desert, short of water, he recalled, 'I asked myself what madness had sent me to the place whither I was going'. Past skeletons of dead dromedaries, whose flesh had been eaten by jackals and hyenas, he described how 'We proceeded at a sound trot, with our heads down, compelled from time to time to close our eyes, which were scorched by the reflection of the sand'. During the day he suffered sun-stroke and his skin blistered. 'I may venture to assert, that while we were travelling in the desert, I had regularly a new nose every evening', he remembered.

Dumas's account revealed to westerners the romance of the desert — and its hazards. Few westerners are skilled at riding camels. For Dumas, 'Every sharp trot of the dromedary was like the blow of an invisible sword, inflicting acute torture'. As a result of the pains he endured by day, he also spent detestable nights, with 'dull pains in every part of the body'. Moreover, he was well aware that he would face the same torments on his way back to Cairo. (In fact, the return journey was worse. Dumas confessed to temporary insanity and delirium during a sandstorm which prevented the party from eating for thirty hours until it blew itself out.)

The supply of water in the desert was totally unpredictable. Professor Flinders Petrie, examining Egyptian remains in Sinai in 1906, recorded that once 'it rained without ceasing for two days and a night, creating rivulets and a waterfall down the mountain slope. A week later the valley floor was carpeted with verdure and flowers, and the thorny bushes were masses of bloom'. This erratic pattern of rainfall presented dangers. In December 1867 the Revd F. W. Holland, travelling in the Sinai desert, saw thirty persons and scores of sheep and donkeys swept to their death in a sudden raging torrent down the Wadi Feiran. Equally dangerous was lack of water. The Revd C. Pickering Clarke, describing the Sinai monastery and its approaches in 1881, recalled another traveller's complaint of insufficient halts for rest or sleep, 'at most two or three hours, soon to be interrupted by the oft repeated monition, "If we linger here, we all die of thirst", sounding in our ears'.

Yet travellers to Mount Sinai were rarely disappointed. Of the four days spent sketching, exploring, and conversing there, Dumas wrote, 'I verily believe that these four days were the most perfectly happy and completely busy of my life'. The desire for solitude, for an escape from 'civilization' drove men and women — especially intrepid Englishwomen — to the holy wilderness. Dumas climbed to the top of Mount Sinai and sat down on a stone to eat the food the monks had brought for him. He stood up again and noticed that on that very stone an English lady had carved in deep letters, 'Miss Bennet'. In the visitor's book back in the monastery he counted the names (he says) of one American, twenty-two Frenchmen, three or four thousand Englishmen and Miss Bennet.

Other visitors found the same peace as Dumas on Mount Sinai. At the end of the century Professor Bensley of Cambridge took his wife there. He died suddenly three days after their return to England. Mrs Bensley recalled their time together in Sinai as a kind of paradise. 'I think of the boundless freedom of the desert, of its golden light and eternal sunshine', she wrote. 'I listen to the sound of falling waters and to the waving of the palm trees, where I wander hand in hand with my beloved, and I hardly know: is it a dream of the past? is it a vision of the future?'

Then as now the monastery of St Catherine was a romantic spot. In 1600 a Frenchman, Henri Castale visited Mount Sinai and, for the first time, mentioned that the only access to the monastery was by rope and pulley. No-one could gain access unless the inhabitants agreed to pull them up. Castale visited St Catherine's when its fortunes were at a low ebb. He found there only one monk and recorded that he was starving. Another twenty-five monks lived elsewhere on the mountain side. By the time Dumas made his visit the monks' fortunes had revived. Dumas found sixty monks and perhaps 300 servants. They fed him on eggs, almonds, pastry, camel cheese, dates, and brandy. The monks' oasis was flourishing. Innumerable vines more than supplied their needs. When he left, they gave him oranges, raisins, and date brandy, in exchange for sugar. Yet the romantic rope and pulley was still the only way into the monastery. 'We skirted the interminable walls of the convent,' Dumas wrote, 'meeting at every step wretched Bedouins, ragged and naked, attracted by the neighbouring monastery and living on the charity of the monks as the poor at the gates of churches in Catholic countries live on the alms of the congregations.' Dumas had only a paltry letter of introduction, and feared that the monks might be unwilling to let him in. But they let down by rope and pulley first a basket. In this they pulled up the letter and the traveller's baggage. Then they let down the rope, this time with a cross-bar, and pulled up Dumas and his party.

In some respects Alexandre Dumas's account of his visit to St Catherine's monastery offered his readers the same satisfactions as did his novels. Dumas was helping them to escape from their own jaded lives into a far-off, unreal world. No longer was St Catherine's seen as a spiritual power-house, in spite of the remarkable impact it still made on westerners who arrived there. The monastery was depicted as a remote paradise, untouched by the troubles of the real world. It was in this spirit that the novelist Pierre Loti, tired and dissatisfied with his life in Paris, set out in 1894 for Mount Sinai, hoping to recover a faith which feverish civilization had all but destroyed. On 22 February he sat under the palm trees of the oasis of Moses, half-an-hour's journey from the Red Sea, and was overcome by contradictory feelings. 'All about us was the empty infinitude,' he wrote afterwards, 'the twilight desert swept by a great cold wind, the desert that rolled, in dull, dead colours, under a still more sombre sky which, on the circular horizon, seemed to fall on it and crush it.'

So sinister seemed the desert that a strange melancholy mingled with Loti's desire for solitude. Yet he felt also a kind of ecstasy. 'It is terrifying in its magnificence', he wrote. 'The limpidity of the air gives an extraordinary depth to the perspectives, and in the clear and far-receding distances the chains of mountains are interlaced and over-laid in regular forms which, from the beginning of the world, have been untouched by the hand of man, with hard dry contours which no vegetation has ever softened or changed.'

On 1 March, after climbing for two days in snow, thunder, and tempests, Loti's party saw at last the tall ramparts and cypress trees of the convent of St Catherine on Mount Sinai. The holy mountain seemed to him to be silent, sinister, and chill, 'as empty now as the soul of modern man'. Trembling with cold, the party reached the gigantic walls of the convent, their summit lost in the swirling snow, and a little iron-clad door opened. 'Two more doors of a similar kind led through a vaulted tunnel into the rampart. They closed behind us with the clang of armour, and we crept up some flights of rough, broken stairs, hewed out of the rock, to a hostel for pilgrims at the top of the great fortress.'

Some hospitable monks in black robes, with long hair like women, hurried to cheer the party with a little hot coffee, warmed in copper vases on charcoal. 'Everthing has an air of nonchalant wretchedness and Oriental di-lapidation in this convent built by the Emperor Justinian fourteen centuries ago', recorded Loti. 'Our bare, whitewashed bedrooms are like the humblest of Turkish dwellings, save for the modest icon above the divan, with a night-light burning before it.' But he noticed that in spite of the wretchedness of the surroundings and the apparent desolation of the place, the walls of the little room were covered with the names of pilgrims gathered from the ends of the earth, with Russian, Arabic, and Greek inscriptions predominating.

In the morning Loti awoke and was amazed at what he found inside the monastery walls. 'A Byzantine church, a mosque, cots, cloisters, an entanglement of stairways, galleries and arches, falling to the precipices below; all this in miniature, built up in a tiny space; all this encompassed with formidable ramparts and hooked onto the flanks of gigantic Sinai!' Mount Sinai itself astounded him, 'all of a blood-red granite without stain or shadow, the peaks so vertical and so high that they dizzy and appal. Only a fragment of sky is visible, but its blueness is of a profound transparency, and the sun is magnificent.'

Inspired by the same Romanticism, European artists had begun to sketch and paint the monasteries and holy sites of the east. One of the most enterprising, the Englishman Frederick Catherwood, took with him a 'camera lucida' (a drawing device in which the image is made to appear on the paper by reflection) on his first visit to Egypt in 1823 and 1824. Eight years later Catherwood was back again, taking part in Robert Hay's excavations of ancient sites and carefully drawing them. French artists too (in particular, Count Léon de Laborde) sketched and painted St Catherine's monastery as they explored the exotic east. Usually they seemed always to be sketching just as some quaintly dressed traveller was being hoisted into the monastery by means of the rope and pulley. Oddly enough, this romantic feature is absent from the work of the greatest of these topographical artists, the Scotsman David Roberts. None the less, his journey to the Orient, a dream since boyhood, proved a sound commerical venture. To facilitate his travels, Roberts secured an introduction to Mehemet Ali. He then sketched with enormous facility, building up a collection of drawings which could be speedily transformed on his return to

Europe into prints and pictures. Between 1845 and 1852 he produced a twenty-part publication, *Egypt, Syria and the Holy Land*, which was a tremendous success. The work included his justly celebrated lithographs of St Catherine's monastery and Mount Sinai. Westerners were again opening up the Orient.

But how in the first place had this celebrated monastery come to be built in such a remote and inhospitable spot? The answer involves the God of the Jews and his servants Moses and Elijah; it involves the brutal murders of hermits and holy men; it derives from the devotion of the most exotic of all Byzantine empresses, Theodora, the wife of Justinian.

The wilderness of Sinai was the spot where the Jews believed God had supremely revealed Himself. Three months after they came out of Egypt, according to the book of Exodus, the Children of Israel reached this wilderness. There, facing the mountain, they pitched camp. On the morning of the third day there was thunder and lightning on the volcanic mountain-top, and a thick cloud, and a blast like a great trumpet, so that all the people in the camp trembled with fear. Then, on top of Sinai, God gave Moses the ten great commandments.

Here too, according to another Exodus tradition, Moses had seen God for the first time, when he was looking after the sheep of his father-in-law Jethro. The angel of God appeared to him, it is said, in the shape of a flame of fire coming from the middle of a bush. Moses was amazed to see a bush burning but not consumed. Then God called to him from the bush, 'Do not come near. Take off your shoes from your feet, for the place on which you are standing is holy ground'. Moses hid his face, for he was afraid to look on God.

According to the Exodus tradition, Moses did in fact see God. When he brought down from Sinai the tablets of stone, carved with the ten commandments, the skin of his face shone and the people were afraid to come near him. Moses veiled his face whenever he spoke with them, and he took off the veil whenever he spoke with God. After his death, the Bible says, 'there has never been such a prophet in Israel as Moses, the man who knew God face to face'.

Now scholars have argued for many years about the precise location of all the events recorded in the Bible concerning the wanderings of the children of Israel in the wilderness. No-one can be certain that these revelations to Moses really did occur on what we now call Mount Sinai.

The Bible witness itself certainly causes problems. In the first place, the traditions of Moses were handed on by word of mouth through many centuries. The story of the Exodus itself occurs in more than one version in our Old Testament. From the narratives as we now have them it is impossible to be certain exactly where the Children of Israel crossed the Red Sea. In their present form the stories do not even tell us who was the Pharaoh who tried to prevent the Children of Israel leaving for the Promised Land.

Secondly, the 'mountain of God' itself in the stories is sometimes called Horeb and sometimes Sinai. As they stand in the Bible the names now appear to be inter-changeable. But did they once refer to two different mountains? Are we to assume, with some scholars, that Horeb is the range of the mountains and Sinai the peak; or vice-versa? Or is it possible, as other scholars have sug-gested, that — because many different tribes inhabited the region — Horeb is the name used by one tribe and Sinai the name used by another for the same mountain? So far no-one has been able to answer these questions with any certainty.

Next, scholars have pointed out that the mountain as described in Exodus chapter 19 and chapter 20 seems to be a volcano. Mount Sinai (says chapter 19, verse 18) 'was altogether on smoke, because the Lord descended upon it in fire: and the smoke thereof ascended as the smoke of a furnace, and the whole mount quaked greatly'. Chapter 20, verse 18, records that 'all the people saw the thunderings and the lightnings, and the voice of the trumpet, and the mountain smoking; and when the people saw it, they trembled, and stood afar off'.

But other scholars have discounted this argument. They claim that the descriptions of Sinai in Exodus chapters 19 and 20 by no means necessarily imply a volcanic mountain. Since there is nowhere any mention of ashes, the phenomena described (which are, of course, attributed to the presence of God) are far more those of a tremendous and dangerous storm than of a volcano. In this way, even though there are no volcanoes on the Sinai peninsula, the traditional site of the appearance of God to Moses is defensible.

A fourth difficulty proposed by scholars is a tactical and, so to speak, military one. It has been argued that the Sinai peninsula lay within the control and jurisdiction of the Pharaohs. In seeking to escape them, the Children of Israel and their leaders would surely have fled elsewhere. However, we now know that Egyptian troops manned the peninsula only during those months when valuable mining took place there. And Moses led his people out of Egypt at the time of the year when no mining took place.

Whatever conclusion the reader reaches, it is necessary to bear in mind the warning of the twentieth-century German Old Testament scholar, Gerhard von Rad, that the traditions about Moses 'were not laid up in archives all through the centuries; they were passed on as living traditions from mouth to mouth and from soul to soul'. Von Rad pointed out that a picture handed on like this from generation to generation cannot remain unaltered in the process. His conclusion is that 'in consequence Moses, as he is presented to us, rises to gigantic stature; he surpasses the limits of ordinary human capacity; he stands as a colossus high above all the sons of men. And yet, for all that, here is the true and genuine figure of a man, a figure that has power to move us by its very humanity'.

In the end I personally warm to the words of the Dominican scholar, Fr Louis Grollenberg, whose monumental *Atlas of the Bible* was first published in 1954. Notwithstanding the cogency of some of the arguments offered by other scholars against the acceptance of Sinai as the site of God's revelation to Moses, Grollenberg robustly described such critics as 'armchair scholars'. He concluded that, 'A visit to the traditional Mount Sinai suffices to dispel all these doubts. The huge granite formations are an awe-inspiring spectacle. The atmosphere, the light and the colours, the incredible stillness, all conspire to make the scene an unforgettable setting for the meeting of God with man'.

By the time of the Christian era the tradition was firmly fixed, along with the belief that the prophet Elijah too had met with God on this same sacred spot. According to the first book of Kings, Queen Jezebel had decided to kill the prophet, who fled from her and took refuge in a cave on the mountain side. The word of God came to him, saying, 'What are you doing here, Elijah?' He stood on the mountain and God himself went by.

> There came a mighty wind, which tore the mountain and shattered the rocks before God. But God was not in the wind. After the wind came an earthquake. But God was not in the earthquake. After the earthquake came a fire. But God was not in the fire. After the fire came the sound of a gentle breeze.

The story indicated that God was a spiritual being who spoke intimately with his prophets. The monks of Mount

57

Sinai were later to build a chapel over a cave where, their tradition held, Elijah was granted this revelation.

These appearances of God to men were commemorated in the original name of the monastery on Mount Sinai. Today it is dedicated to St Catherine of Alexandria, but it was first dedicated to the transfiguration of Jesus Christ. In the first three Gospels we are told that Jesus went up a mountain, where his face shone and Moses and Elijah appeared talking with him. To be transfigured as Christ was, to see God as Moses and Elijah did, these goals constitute the apogee of the monastic life. It was natural to wish to build a monastery on the spot where these events traditionally took place.

But long before the building of the monastery groups of Christian hermits and anchorites — both men and women — were living on this sacred mountain, reverencing the holy sites. St Catherine's monastery was built here partly because the monastic tradition of the whole Christian church developed in this wilderness. After the year AD 313 (when the Emperor Constantine recognized Christianity as one of the permitted religions of the empire) these hermits petitioned the Empress Helena, Constantine's mother, for her protection. In 330 she built a small church on Mount Sinai, dedicated to the Virgin Mary, and a tower to protect the site of the burning bush. The place was becoming one of the most favoured Christian sites.

In the next century a Spanish noblewoman called Etheria made a pilgrimage to Mount Sinai. Hers is the first record of such a voyage ever made. She observed that 'There were many cells of holy men there, and a church in the place where the bush is'. In front of the church was a pleasant garden with abundant water. Etheria was shown the spot where God told Moses to take off his shoes. And, she recorded, the burning bush itself 'is alive to this day and throws out shoots'.

And it was in this remote region that the Christian spiritual tradition developed — a third reason for the eventual construction of a great monastery. St Antony was the first Christian ascetic to withdraw into the Egyptian desert. A rich young man, whose parents had died when he was aged twenty, he sold his 300 acres of land, put his sister in the care of a community of virgins, and with the help of other ascetics, devoted himself to prayer and the godly life, having given his money to the poor. In need of solitude, he lived for fifteen years among tombs, before withdrawing to the mountains for the last twenty years of his life. Even there he could not remain alone, for many visited him, to learn how to overcome their own temptations. Occasionally he would leave the mountain to combat heresy, or to comfort Christian prisoners of the Emperor Maximian. When the end of his life was drawing near, he returned to the mountains, with two companions.

St Antony died in 356, aged 105. In the year 357 St Athanasius wrote an account of his life. Athanasius saw Antony as the ideal monk, a man who could work miracles and discern good and evil spirits. His *Life of St Antony* became immensely influential throughout the Christian world. St Jerome and St Augustine read and revered it. Before the end of the century the Bishop of Antioch had translated it into Latin.

Antony's example inspired many others. Their lives to modern ears sound strange, almost barbaric. One such was a hermit named Onophrius, whose life was written by an Egyptian monk called Paphnutus. When they met, Onophrius said that he had been living in the desert for seventy years or so. At first he had lived with a community of monks, but the example of Elijah and John the Baptist drove him into the desert. His clothing fell away. Hungry and thirsty, he had lived on dates. He had suffered extreme heat and extreme cold. He was spiritually at peace.

Paphnutus described how Onophrius had invited him into his hut. Suddenly, the hermit grew pale. He asked Paphnutus to bury him, and died there and then. Paphnutus wrapped a piece of his own cloak around the dead hermit, and put him in a crack in the rock. Pilgrims were still visiting the grotto, where Onophrius had lived, many centuries later.

Many such hermits must have died alone. A monk called Raithou later in the fourth century described how he came to a cell in the desert and found inside it a dead monk, whose body dropped to dust as soon as Raithou touched it. Other hermits ceased to live by the ordinary rules of the world. Another visitor to Mount Sinai in the fourth century, an Italian named Postumianus, came across a hermit who had lived on top of the mountain for fifty years. 'He wore no clothes,' reported Postumianus, 'but was covered in bristles growing on his body, and of divine gift knew not his nakedness.'

From these unwashed men and women of the desert came an odour of sanctity much prized by the Christians of the early Middle Ages, as is well illustrated by the beautiful story of St Mary the Harlot. Niece of the monk Abraham, who had brought her up after the death of her parents, she had turned to vice as a prostitute. The old monk shed the garmets of a hermit and dressed in worldly clothing to visit her, in the guise of a customer but really to beg her to return to the godly life. Posing as a soldier, keeping his hat over his face, he even forsook his lifelong abstinence and drank wine, in order to keep up his disguise. 'The girl came and put her arms around his neck, beguiling him with kisses. And as she was kissing him, she smelt the fragrance of austerity that his lean body breathed, and remembered the days when she too had lived austere: and as if a spear had pierced her soul, she gave a great moan and began to weep.'

These men were the spiritual predecessors of the monks of St Catherine's. As time passed, their cells were grouped around chapels on Sinai, where they met for worship on Sundays. Some shared cells with younger monks. One called Silvanus made baskets, and filled them with dates. These he sold to keep him and his young friend Zacharias, though since he believed Zacharias was better employed reading godly books rather than eating, he frequently failed to call the younger hermit when it was time for food! Another devout Christian, named Galaction, set off with his wife Episteme for Mount Sinai. They took only ten days to cross the desert. Then he lived with ten male hermits, and she lived with four virgins, some way off from her husband.

These ascetics were revered by their fellow Christians. An Egyptian monk who visited some of them in the late fourth century, noted the extreme rigour of their lives. 'Their aspect was that of angels,' he said, 'for they were so pallid and, so to say, incorporeal, owing to their abstaining from wine, oil, bread and other food that tends to luxury, living only on dates, just enough to keep themselves alive.' Many became famous for their bizarre practices. A hermit called Stephen trained a leopard to guard his vegetables from marauding animals. Another was said to have transformed himself into a palm tree, to escape from marauding Saracens. Several of the most renowned spent their lives entirely on top of pillars.

They lived, not only bizarrely by our standards, but also in charity with one another. Rufinus of Aquilea observed in 374, 'I have seen among them many fathers that lived the life of heaven in the world.' He added, 'I have seen some of them so purged of all thoughts of suspicion or malice that they no longer remembered that evil was still found upon the earth. They dwell dispersed throughout the desert and separate in their cells, but bound together by love. They are quiet and gentle. They have, it is true, one great rivalry amongst themselves: it is who shall be more merciful, kinder, humbler and more patient than his brother'.

Not surprisingly, the sayings of these men became famous. Until Helen Waddell collected them in her book *The Desert Fathers*, much of this wisdom had been forgotten, if not despised in western Christendom. Helen Waddell quoted an astonishing remark by the great German church historian Adolf von Harnack: 'If I may be permitted to use strong language, I should not hesitate to say that no book has had a more stultifying effect on Egypt, Western Asia and Europe than the *Life of St Antony*.'

But in the Middle Ages the holy places inhabited by St Antony were deeply reverenced by the Christian world. His wisdom inspired countless followers. It exalted *solitude* — so that the holy men advised a young would-be saint: 'Go and sit in your cell, and your cell will teach you everything.' At the same time these desert fathers knew that solitude alone was insufficient for *holiness*. One famous abbess called Matrona used to observe that it was better to live in a crowd — leading the solitary life inwardly, in the will — than to be locked up in a cell longing all the time to be a part of that crowd.

Similarly the desert fathers urged would-be saints to curb their bodies by *fasting*, while again insisting that this alone could not lead to holiness. An abbot named Hyperichus went so far as to say that to eat flesh and drink wine was better than to eat the flesh of one's brothers by backbiting them.

War against the flesh nonetheless ought to be ceaseless, in the opinion of the desert saints. And even harder than this war was, they believed, the battle against the evil spirit in the heart. Abbot Anthony used to say: 'The one who sits in solitude and quiet has escaped from three wars: hearing evil, speaking evil and seeing evil.' Yet, he added, 'against one thing we still, we must constantly battle — against our own hearts'.

The ultimate aim of all these hermits, anchorites, abbots and abbesses and would-be saints was the same: super-human humility and the total denial of the self. According to one celebrated tale illustrating this achievement, 'The devil appeared to a certain brother, disguised as an angel of light, and said to him, "I am Gabriel and I am sent unto thee." But he said, "Look to it that thou wast not sent to some other: for I am not worthy that an angel be sent to me." And the devil was no more seen'.

The spiritual tradition of St Catherine's monastery was built on the wisdom of these desert fathers. But the desert monks were not universally revered, and the attacks on them by marauding Saracens was one final reason for the building of the monastery on Mount Sinai. Even the protection of the Empress was insufficient to shelter men and women who lived in caves on the mountainside. On a visit to Mount Sinai in the fourth century, an Egyptian monk named Ammonius hid in a tower and watched Saracens attacking godly hermits. When he emerged he counted thirty-eight dead. Another died of his wounds four days later. Not long afterwards came news that forty hermits, as well as some women and children, had been killed by marauders near Raithou.

These attacks continued. In the early fifth century St Nilus, one of the emperor's highly-placed officials in Constantinople, visited the holy mountain, along with his sons. They decided to live as hermits. Nilus saw fellow-hermits killed by marauders, and he helped to bury the dead.

The monastery of St Catherine's exists partly because of

this habit of people of different beliefs persecuting and even killing each other.

In the ninth century AD a Patriarch of Alexandria named Eutychios wrote an account of the building of the present monastery. This account is still preserved in the monastery library. Although written nearly 300 years after the events it describes, Eutychios's account is certainly not without historical value. He tells how, weary of persecution, the monks of Mount Sinai approached the Emperor Justinian for protection. They begged him to build for them 'a monastery where we shall be safe'. Justinian agreed, adding that the monastery 'should be fortified so that no better could be found'.

The Emperor Justinian had married a remarkable woman. According to the *Secret History* written by the court historian Procopius, in her early life the Empress Theodora had been an actress and dancer notorious throughout Constantinople. Born around the year 500 in Cyprus or Syria, she came to Byzantium with her parents. Her father, whose job was to guard the bears in the amphitheatre, died leaving a widow and two daughters, the second of whom was Theodora. She followed her elder sister onto the stage. Not yet twenty years old, she was, according to Procopius, small and pretty, with beautiful black eyes and heavy eyebrows. Her performance on stage was of such vulgarity that the historian Gibbon preferred to leave a description of it to a footnote in the decent obscurity of Greek. Yet Gibbon's famous description of the youthful courtesan bears repeating:

> The beauty of Theodora was the subject of more flattering praise, and the source of more exquisite delight [than her skill as an actress]. Her features were delicate and regular; her complexion, though somewhat pale, was tinged with a natural colour; every sensation was instantly expressed by the veracity of her eyes; her easy motions displayed the

graces of a small but elegant figure; and either love or adulation might proclaim, that painting or poetry were incapable of delineating the matchless excellence of her form. But this form was degraded by the facility with which it was exposed to the public eye, and prostituted to licentious desire. Her venal charms were abandoned to a promiscuous crowd of citizens and strangers, of every rank, and of every profession; the fortunate lover who had been promised a night of enjoyment, was often driven from her bed by a stronger or more wealthy favourite; and when she passed through the streets, her presence was avoided by all who wished to escape either the scandal or the temptation.

Theodora left the stage to go to live with her lover who became governor of Pentapolis in Africa.

Soon she fell from his favour and he cast her out. Wandering penniless, she was helped by holy men. Now aged almost forty, she was more respectable and managed to captivate the emperor-to-be. Procopius says that she entrapped him with magic and love potions. His aunt, the empress, was certainly opposed to their marriage, but she died in the year 523. The emperor, Justinian's uncle, made Theodora a patrician. He abrogated the law forbidding senators (such as was Justinian) marrying actresses or courtesans. In April 527, after his uncle's death, Justinian became emperor. Theodora was crowned empress on Easter Day in St Sophia.

She remained a patroness of the arts and (perhaps because of the charity shown to her by holy men in the days of her penury) a protectress of the church, even against her husband's wishes. When, for example, Justinian excommunicated and exiled Anthemius, Patriarch of Constantinople, he took refuge in Theodora's apartments. He was thought to be dead, and discovered only twelve years later after the death of the empress.

She was also a woman of great courage. When in

65

January 532, rebels attacked the imperial palace, Justinian was ready to flee. She said, 'Flee if you will, emperor. You are rich. Your ships are ready. The sea is clear. But I shall stay, for I adore the proverb, "The purple is the best winding-sheet" .' The emperor recovered his nerve and the rebels were defeated.

Theodora reigned for twenty-one years. She could be cruel to her enemies (as to Pope Silverius, who was brutally deposed). But she was also devout. She received many Syrian and Egyptian monks in her palace. She died on 29 June 548, of cancer. Her image can be seen in the mosaic of S. Vitale in Ravenna, where she wears a long purple robe with a golden border, braided with gold and jewels, with pearls in her hair. But her greatest monument is the church and fortress of St Catherine on Mount Sinai.

According to Eutychios, Justinian wished the monastery to be built on top of the mountain, but since there was no water there, the site of the burning bush was chosen instead. (Eutychios asserts that for this change of plan the emperor had the architect of the monastery put to death, but this is almost certainly untrue. An inscription in St Catherine's prays for the architect, his wife and family: 'Lord God, who appeared on this spot, save and bless your servant Stephanos of Aila, the builder of this monastery, and Nonna, and give rest to the souls of their children George, Sergius and Theodora'.) The account of the monastery by Procopius does, however, indicate that a site on top of the mountain might have been considered. He wrote:

> Since these monks have no desires but are superior to all human passions, and as they possess nothing and spend no care upon their persons, nor seek pleasure from anything else whatever, the Emperor Justinian built a church for them, which he dedicated to the Virgin, that they might therein spend their life in continual prayer and the service of God.

Procopius adds:

> He did not build this church on the summit of the
> mountain, but a long way below it, for it is not possible
> for a man to pass the night upon the peak because at night
> continuous thunderings and other yet more terrible divine
> manifestations take place.

Procopius had never visited Mount Sinai. 'I count it a
toilsome and perilous task,' he once wrote, 'to cross a
great ocean in a crazy vessel.' He seems not to have
realized that Justinian's fortress walls actually surround the
church built by Stephanos as well as the site of the burning
bush. He was, nonetheless, clear that such a fortress had
been built. 'At the foot of the mountain,' he wrote, 'our
emperor also built a very strong fort, and placed inside it a
considerable garrison of soldiers, in order that the bar-
barian Saracens might not from that point secretly invade
Palestine.'

If Procopius is here to be believed, Justinian had other
reasons — more secular ones — for building the fortress
on Mount Sinai, besides his laudable aim of protecting the
monks. Nonetheless, his piety and that of his empress are
what today allow us to determine almost exactly when the
church on the mountain was constructed. Two parallel
inscriptions on the roof beams read: 'To the salvation of
our pious emperor, Justinian', and 'To the memory and
the rest of the soul of our empress'. The church must have
been built sometime between the death of Theodora in AD
548 and the death of Justinian seventeen years later.

Now this monastery was the home of the spiritual
wealth of the desert fathers. It also housed the site of the
burning bush — and possibly that bush itself. (In 1216 a
visitor named Magister Thietmar was told that Christians
seeking relics had divided it up and taken it away.) The
monastery lay on the holiest site in the world outside
Bethlehem and Jerusalem. It was blessed with imperial

protection, and it belonged to Christendom as a whole — not simply to eastern Orthodoxy. Inevitably it grew rich and began to amass priceless gifts.

In the seventh century the Pope of Rome gave Abbot John Klimakos a gift of woollen bedding for fifteen beds, and money to buy feather mattresses. Later, in the thirteenth and fourteenth centuries, the Popes protected the monastery, conferring on it privileges which they confirmed in Papal bulls. The abbot had now become a bishop, gradually extending his jurisdiction over the neighbouring dioceses of Pharan and Raithou. Soon he would become an archbishop, elected (as today) by the monks and consecrated by the Patriarch of Jerusalem. He became spiritual leader of the smallest independent church in the world. One happy result of this independence was that the church of Sinai took no part in the great schism of 1054, which split the Orthodox churches of the east from the Catholic churches of the west. Latin monks continued to live in the monastery — most of them from France — building their own chapel and using their own service books. Between the fourteenth and the sixteenth centuries, French, Dutch, German, and English pilgrims visited St Catherine's and carved their coats-of-arms on the monastery walls. And the crusaders built great wooden doors to the narthex of Justinian's church.

Pilgrims came, as ever, for a variety of reasons to Mount Sinai. Some were attracted by the remarkable legends of the place. In the seventh century they came to see monks like Fr Orontius, who could burn incense in his hand (and had lost a finger doing so). They also came seeking peace or pardon. In the ninth century two brothers from Brittany who had murdered their uncle were ordered by King Lothair to visit Rome, Jerusalem, and Sinai, chained together. They spent three years on Sinai, and returned by way of Rennes, where one brother died.

Still the monastery increased in wealth. In 1203 the
Archbishop of Crete gave the monks property there worth
400 ducats a year. When the Venetians captured Crete in
1204, Doge Pietro Ziani confirmed the monks in their
property, as did successive Doges until Venice lost the
island in 1645. In the thirteenth century the Popes confirmed the monks in their possessions in lands conquered
by crusaders. Soon St Catherine's came to own vineyards,
hospitals, woods, pasture, churches, houses, bakeries, and
trading rights, in such diverse places as Raithou, Alexandria, Jerusalem, Jaffa, Laodicea, Antioch, Damascus, Constantinople, Crete, Pharan, and Cyprus.

At the same time the monastery was building up and
preserving its unmatched collection of icons. At first sight
it is strange to find such a wealth of Christian art — over
2000 icons in all — on Mount Sinai. The earliest Christians
took very seriously the second of the ten commandments
given to Moses on that mountain: 'You shall not make
yourselves a carved image or any likeness of anything in
heaven above or on earth beneath or in the waters under
the earth; you shall not bow down to them or serve them'.
In one sense an icon seems to break that commandment,
for it is a picture of earthly beings to be reverenced in
worship.

When he preached in Athens, the Apostle Paul told the
Greeks that, 'since we are the children of God, we have no
excuse for thinking that he looks like anything in gold,
silver or stone that has been carved or designed by a man'.
In Ephesus, Paul and two of his supporters caused a riot,
when they threatened the livelihood of a silversmith called
Demetrius by attacking idols. Demetrius employed many
craftsmen to make shrines to and statues of the goddess
Diana. Paul argued that such gods, made by human hands,
are not gods at all.

Faithful to this Jewish tradition, the early Christians

were careful not to fall into the errors of their pagan opponents by making images of God the Father or Jesus. But as Christianity escaped more and more from its Jewish origins and took on many of the aspects of Greek religion, it became easier to forget this early purity. In the fourth century AD, Christian writers mention that images of the Virgin Mary, as well as of Jesus and his apostles, were appearing in churches.

Many Christians bitterly opposed this new development. A bishop called Epiphanius, who came from Salamis, is reported in the fourth century as tearing down an image painted on a curtain. Later, Eastern Christians would not only smash existing icons but even kill each other in the controversy over them.

In the year 726 the Emperor Leo III banned all image worship. His ban met opposition. When his officers attempted to destroy an icon which hung over the entrance to the imperial palace, they were prevented by a murderous mob. But four years later Leo decreed that all images should be destroyed. So began the iconoclast controversy, which lasted nearly 120 years. Monks especially opposed the attempt by a lay emperor to decree what should happen in churches. Popes Gregory II and Gregory III protested, but Leo was relentless. He exiled monks who opposed his views on icons. Throughout the Christian world vast numbers of images of Christ, his mother and his apostles were destroyed. In 754 Leo's successor, Constantine V Copronymius called a synod at Hiera, which was attended by 338 church fathers and approved of iconoclasm. A holy recluse, Stephen the Younger, who tried to promote a movement opposing the decision of this synod, was put to death. The Emperor Constantine humiliated monks and finally put to death the Patriarch of Constantinople, who was lukewarm in promoting iconoclasm.

The defenders of icons fought back. Their arguments in defence of the images were curiously theological ones. The great Council of Chalcedon in 451 had declared that Jesus possessed two natures, one divine and the other human. Defenders of icons claimed that they depicted only the human nature of Jesus. They were not images of the divine. John of Damascus, living in the safety of Moslem Palestine in the seventh century AD, asked why, if the Son of Man appeared in human form, his human form could not be painted on wood.

These arguments prevailed at a Council of Nicaea in AD 787. But only fifty years later, when the Empress Theodora (widow of the Emperor Theophilus) confirmed the decision, was the iconoclastic controversy over.

In the meantime, many thousands of icons had been destroyed. Remarkably, the monastery of St Catherine escaped the whole turmoil. The capitulation of Egypt to Islam, agreed by the Patriarch of Constantinople in 642, kept the monastery out of the reach of the iconoclastic Christian world. Here the production of icons continued. The monastery's existing icons were protected from the rest of the Christian world by its powerful Moslem conquerors.

In the ninth century the monastery became holier still, when the monks discovered on the mountain-side the body of St Catherine, miraculously transported there from Alexandria. Catherine, the rich daughter of a king, is said to have attacked the Emperor Maximian for his paganism. The emperor brought fifty learned men to convert her from Christianity. To his dismay she converted them. Some say that Maximian wanted to commit adultery with Catherine and that her refusal angered him quite as much as her uncompromising Christianity. He decided to put her to death. However, the spiked wheels on which she was to be broken broke themselves. When she was

71

beheaded, it is recorded that milk flowed from her veins instead of blood.

What is certain is that the body found by the monks on Mount Sinai and today still reverenced in the monastery included bones which oozed oil. The monks would collect this oil, which was enormously prized by pilgrims. Oil continued to flow from the saint's bones for many years. When the truce between the Sultan and the Christians enabled Magister Thietmar to visit the monastery, he was shown the body of St Catherine, still exuding oil. He came away with a few precious drops. So did Henry II of Brunswick, who visited the monastery in 1330, and perhaps also brought back to Europe a small bone from the saint's body.

The fame of St Catherine brought increasing fame — and therefore wealth — to the monastery. The closest ties were with France. In 1229 King Louis built a church dedicated to St Catherine in Paris. The Dukes of Normandy treated the monastery with great generosity. The monks gave a finger of their patron saint to Rouen and soon were visiting that city each year to collect gold and silver in support of their mother house. European knights guaranteed the safety of pilgrims to Mount Sinai. The crusader knights themselves stayed there, eating in the great refectory and carving their coats of arms on the lintels of its doors.

The ending of the crusades brought some stability to the Middle East and better relations between Christians and Moslems. Many courtly westerners were able to visit Sinai in comparative ease. In the fourteenth century, as well as Henry II of Brunswick, Philip of Artois, Duke Albert of Austria, Augustinian monks from Verona and a Florentine named Frescobaldi (who tells us there were 200 monks living in and around the monastery) all visited Mount Sinai. The journey was still arduous. *En route*, Bishop

Hugo of Verdun died of fatigue in the desert.

A German visitor named von Baldensel crossed the desert on a horse, though he had to hire camels and their owners to carry his food and corn. He noticed the absence of lice, flies, and fleas on the holy mountain, as well as the great number of lamps hanging in Justinian's chapel. The monks in their turn were amazed at the sight of a horse so near to St Catherine's. Von Baldensel spent much time kneeling before the head and bones of the saint herself, who at that time was seated upright in a marble chair, covered in a red, gold-embroidered cloth. On his return to Europe he published a best-selling account of his visit, which was translated into French by Jehan Le Long d'Ypres, an enterprising monk of St Bertin de Saint Omer.

A similarly successful account of a visit to the monastery was published by the Italian notary Nicolas de Martoni. Nicolas had, by his own account, a terrible journey across the desert. On his arrival he was rewarded by having his feet soaped and washed by the abbot himself, in the monastery refectory before supper, while the other monks chanted canticles in Greek. This, Nicolas reported, was the community's rule. It is a rule which has now lapsed, according to my experience.

A journey to Mount Sinai was costly as well as arduous. Men and women rich enough to visit St Catherine's were also in a position to support it lavishly. In the fourteenth century the monastery maintained, as well as its many Dschebelijah servants, over 400 monks. These included Georgians and Arabs. They served over 100 small chapels, some inside the monastery walls, some spread around it. They drew income from their many possessions elsewhere. But they also seem to have been able to call on the west for money whenever they needed to do so. When the Turks took Constantinople in 1453 and then moved on to

Sinai, they claimed from the monks a tribute of 700 ducats a year. The monks turned to Europe for help. King Louis XI of France promised 2000 ducats annually, and Queen Isabella of Spain 500 ducats.

The monastic life is based on prayer and meditation, but it also centres around books — Bibles, liturgies, lives of the saints, homilies, psalters, and so forth. The monks of Mount Sinai soon began producing their own. Because so many different monks lived there at various times, these books were needed.

The renown of the monastery meant that the monks were often given precious volumes, as well as being wealthy enough to buy them — hence the presence in the monastic library today of those volumes older than St Catherine's itself. Some volumes betray Moslem influence. Others contain brilliantly illuminated sermons by the fathers of the church, many of these in the rich decorated style of Constantinople artists. The privations of the desert fathers seem to have coalesced in the minds of the monks with the sufferings of the Old Testament Job, who is depicted in manuscripts in St Catherine's sitting in a pit, scraping at his boils with a stone — an example of patience under misery and humiliations. The library contains writings by famous monks of St Catherine's, especially the abbot John Klimakos. Other manuscripts contain pagan works and include the writings of Homer and Aristotle as well as books by explorers and navigators.

In the ancient world the scroll was the usual form of writing. The book (or *codex*) was known to the Romans but rarely used by them. Dr Michael Clanchy of the University of Glasgow has observed that the early Christians on the other hand 'seem to have positively favoured the book format, because it distinguished their scriptures from those of the Jews and pagans'. These early Christians also favoured the use of papyrus rather than parchment, because 'papyrus may have been too closely associated in the minds of early Christians with the pagan lore of antiquity which they were determined to supersede'.

Michael Clanchy concludes that 'Christianity can thus be said to have invented the parchment book'. The invention was officially blessed in 332 when the Emperor Constantine ordered fifty vellum Bibles in codex form from the famous 'Scriptorium' of Eusebius of Caesarea who lived and worked in the city of that name, near modern Haifa in Israel, during the fourth century. These Bibles were to be presented to the principal churches of the empire. In some way that we can no longer trace, one of these fifty precious volumes almost certainly found its way into the monastery of St Catherine on Mount Sinai and lay there for centuries, unknown to the outside world.

On his visit to the monastery in 1836 Alexandre Dumas uncannily sensed that the library contained some hitherto undiscovered treasure among 'the vast number of manuscripts which the monks never open'. Dumas added that the value and importance of this library would not be known 'until some young and enterprising scholar from Europe will shut himself up for a year or two in the midst of these dusty volumes'.

On 11 May 1844 some Bedouin arrived in Cairo and offered to take the twenty-nine year old Constantin Tischendorf to Mount Sinai. 'I had good advice,' wrote the German scholar, 'and took care not to offer them too much money.' He offered 140 piastres for each of the three camels, take it or leave it. Unfortunately for Tischendorf, the Bedouin decided to leave it and sped away. The Austrian consul in Cairo persuaded them to return, and Tischendorf made a better offer: 480 piastres for four camels, to carry himself, along with a dragoman and three Bedouin servants.

So they set off across the desert. The heat was insupportable. Tischendorf's straw hat with its long green veil frightened the camels. Once it blew off and he feared he would die of heat. For over a day his servants searched for it. Finally the hat was retrieved and the little caravan continued on its way. Because of the burning sun they started out each day before dawn. From ten o'clock in the morning until five in the afternoon they rested in their tents. Then for another six hours they rode again. Tischendorf felt as if he were in a Turkish bath. At night he slept under the stars, not in his tent, his baggage and a loaded gun by his side and a Bedouin on guard.

Tischendorf did not take to the people they met *en route* for Mount Sinai. The women, he observed, 'fully believe in the evil eye'. To his annoyance, mothers repeatedly covered up their children when he was looking kindly at them. And although they had sufficient provisions, including water carried in earthenware jugs on one of the camels, the little party needed to press on continually. They waded across the Red Sea. They spent a night under the immense rocky walls of Ras Abu Zemnia. Then they took the lonely path between majestic mountains and across the plain of Markha, until they came to the Sinai Mountains.

On the twelfth day the party reached the wide plain of Raha, above which rises the bare northern rock of Sinai. Soon Tischendorf saw what he later described as the monastery's 'superb garden, which, with its cypresses, pomegranates, and orange trees, peers most refreshingly from the grey stone walls'. The travellers made their camels run to the foot of the fortress of St Catherine. At ten o'clock the basket was let down to them. Tischendorf had obtained two letters of introduction from the sister house in Cairo, but one of these, he judged, was less warm than it ought to have been. He suppressed it, and put only the more favourable letter into the basket. It was drawn up into the monastery. And then the monks let down the rope, this time with the crossbar attached to it. Tischendorf and his party were drawn up. He was at last on the verge of the most momentous discovery of the Christian centuries.

At first his impression was one of sheer relief. 'How striking it is,' he wrote, 'in the midst of the barren desert, cheerless with its sand and rock, suddenly to abide within these hospitable walls — in these well-arranged and ornamental pleasure grounds and chambers, surrounded by men of serious aspect, with long beards and black gowns.' As he wrote to Angelika from the safety of the monastery, he had lived on little more than hens and pigeons, rice, cheese, and some tea and coffee. They had pitched tents by day, but by night their only protection were furs, sheepskins, and a great woollen cover. Everywhere he could hear howling wolves and see the spoor of tigers, wild boars, and hyenas. The monastery of St Catherine was an oasis after such privations and dangers. 'I feel as if I were going towards a great and marvellous feast,' he had told Angelika in December. Now he had arrived.

CHAPTER III

Early Success

Ever since 1842, Tischendorf later recalled, it had occurred to him to ask 'whether it was not probable that in some recess of the Greek or Coptic, Syrian or Armenian monasteries, there might be some precious manuscripts, slumbering for ages in dust and darkness'. In St Catherine's monastery on Mount Sinai lay precisely such a manuscript, though one far more precious and rare than even Tischendorf could have dared hope for.

Alas, Tischendorf soon began to despise the monks who for centuries had guarded and preserved this document. His attitude was one regrettably shared by very many nineteenth-century Protestant visitors to this remote outpost of Greek orthodox monasticism. To examine and understand them helps to explain Tischendorf's later treatment of his Greek hosts.

In 1877, for example, an American professor of Biblical literature, Philip Schaff, reached the monastery. He had not enjoyed his journey there, nor had his wife and daughter or the four other companions who went with him. 'The romance of camp life among the wild Bedouin lies in anticipation and reminiscence, rather than actual experience', he recalled. 'The journey is a weariness to the flesh from beginning to end.' He soon decided that the inhabitants of Mount Sinai were little better than superstitious fools. Their surroundings, he wrote, 'are replete with silly legends which disturb the gravity of a Protestant traveller'. He saw the rock on which Moses supposedly broke the tablets of the Law, the rock too from which he summoned water, and a mould of the golden calf which the faithless Israelites had worshipped, 'although', he commented, 'it has no more resemblance to a calf than to any other animal'. As for the monks themselves, he decided that, 'They lead a simple, temperate, idle, monotonous, and stupid life'. He agreed with such European savants as Dean Stanley and Professor Palmer that they erred in 'not converting the Arabs or contributing to the geography, history or geological knowledge of the East'. A self-confessed Protestant such as Philip Schaff never spotted that the rationale of the Christian monk might involve other, quite different aims.

In Sinai, on top of Gebel Musa, Schaff met 'two heroic English ladies', a Miss Brocklehurst and a Miss Booth. Near the very end of the nineteenth century, two yet more intrepid British ladies, Mrs Agnes Smith Lewis and her twin sister, Mrs Margaret Dunlop Gibson, visited the monastery. Their journey, too, was hazardous enough. They had accidents. Their tents blew away. They suffered thirst. 'Our path ran through the limitless desert, over very stony ground, where a few tufts of sapless heath or of spiky thorns enticed our camels to stop and nibble.' The Archbishop of Sinai had treated them extremely courteously in Cairo. He 'gave us a most kind reception,' they recalled, 'especially after he had read a letter to the monks written by the Vice-Chancellor of Cambridge University, and remarked its interesting seal'. Yet in spite of the welcome given to them both in Cairo and in the monastery on Mount Sinai, these two ladies — who were

79

Presbyterians — secretly despised their hosts. 'The gradual degeneracy of the occupants' of the monastery, wrote Mrs Lewis, 'might almost be traced in their style of building, run up to suit temporary wants' since the time of Justinian.

Although they shared the same religion, the cultural gap was too great to be bridged between these westerners and the monks of the Near East. John G. Kinnear, describing his visit to the chapel of the burning bush in 1839, criticized the monks for displaying 'a great deal more fuss and ceremony about admitting us, than reverence after we were in'. Mrs M.E. Rogers, describing the monastery for Sir Charles W. Wilson's *Picturesque Palestine* (one of the many travel books popularizing the Orient) described how she 'saw a monk calling to prayer by hammering a bent piece of metal on a rope'. Neither she nor John Kinnear give the slightest indication that the monks might have insights into prayer and reverence not shared by visitors from the more civilized west.

Agnes Lewis did, in fact, try to join in the worship of the monastery; but she didn't like it. Her sister shared her distaste. 'There was some very fine singing,' they admitted, 'but far too many repetitions of *Hagios o Theos* and *Kyrie Eleison*. It was the last of their services we attended.'

A climb to the top of Mount Sinai by the two sisters brought a horrifying cultural/religious clash between their Christian ways and those of the monks. On their way up the mountain, they saw some monks in procession. The two ladies, with customary British politeness, said 'Good morning' and decided to shake hands with the prior. The prior for his part not unnaturally supposed that they wished to join in the act of worship. He therefore sprinkled holy water over the two Presbyterians and then held up the cross so that Mrs Lewis might reverence it. Although a monk who was following in the procession cried, 'Her form of worship is different from ours', the prior still held up the cross, insisting, 'Adore it'. Agnes Lewis kissed it, and then proclaimed, 'I adore the Saviour, who died upon the cross'. Later she brooded about whether or not she had done the right thing. She concluded she had been right, if only because the prior was a simpleton. 'Had I done otherwise,' she concluded 'I should have thrown the poor Hegoumenos [prior] into a state of great perplexity; he would have thought me an atheist, for his intellect was not capable of understanding my notions.' Even so, she vowed such an occurrence would be the last: 'it was a lesson to me never again to approach a Greek ecclesiastic when walking in procession.'

In short, these visitors made scarcely any attempt to enter into the minds, culture, and worship of a group of Christians whom they basically despised. Mrs Lewis and Mrs Gibson took their own religious superiority for granted. They complacently observed how puzzled were the monks that their visitors did not fast at the prescribed Christian times. And yet, ironically enough, the monks obviously relished their company, loved to be with them, and did all they could for their British guests.

It was Agnes Lewis and Margaret Gibson who acted as guides for Mrs Bensley and her party on their journey to Sinai in 1896. Mrs Bensley witnessed a remarkable scene that both revealed the affection felt by the monks for Agnes Lewis and also her own revulsion for the oriental Christians. On their arrival inside the monastery, 'A stout, red-faced monk, in the plain black garb of the Greek priesthood (rather greasy in this case), rushed forth with loud shouts of merriment, and fell on the neck of Mrs Lewis, with whom he had made friends during the previous winter. He patted her affectionately, he felt her garments, he made her sit by his side with his arm round her shoulders. A lively conversation then followed in modern Greek, of which we understood nothing, but frequent bursts of laughter showed it to be of a very pleasant nature.'

This delightful scene revolted Mrs Bensley. She feared the same thing might have to happen to her. She put down her lady companion's familiarity to a desire to gull the monk into showing the party some of the monastery's treasures. 'The good old man had to be propitiated,' she conceded, 'yet we did not relish the thought that we might have to submit, in our turn, to similar familiarities.'

Mrs Bensley treated all orientals, not simply Greek monks, with the same disdain. She apparently believed that the inhabitants of Cairo would be taken in by a street conjurer in a way impossible for Europeans. 'I do not know who admired him most,' she confessed, 'the Arabs, who believed him to be a great magician inspired by Allah, or we, who had never seen such skill and cleverness as he displayed in these inexplicable tricks.' But of course Mrs Bensley had no evidence whatsoever to suppose that the watching Arabs believed that a street conjurer was really producing chickens from his mouth and serpents from his ears.

This western feeling of superiority is what enabled visitors to Mount Sinai less honest than Mrs Lewis, Mrs Bensley, and their parties so shamelessly to try to cheat the monks out of their inheritance. In 1896 Mrs Bensley observed how carefully the monks protected their books, all of them properly shelved, and the manuscripts kept separately in large chests. Yet she still felt able to make fun of what she described as their 'so-called' library.

Today we can, perhaps, derive a certain humour from the failure of these westerners to appreciate the resources of Christian spirituality displayed by Orthodox monks. No doubt the monks themselves made their own judgments, charitable or not, on their western visitors. But

82

Tischendorf's judgments were unusually harsh. In every monastery he visited, seeking ancient manuscripts to bring back to Europe, he reported that his advice was requested by men with sore eyes, 'many of whom were hastening towards total blindness'. He added: 'If there be a mode of life which leads directly to blindness, it is certainly that of these monks'.

Tischendorf did not spare the monastery of St Catherine on Mount Sinai such censure. He could not accept the right of those who lived there to follow their own profession and not that of a nineteenth-century German savant. 'If . . . these monks had filled their lives with serious intellectual occupation,' he wrote, 'even such a monastic life could have been fruitful and full of blessing.' Unfortunately, from Tischendorf's viewpoint, they fell far short of the achievements of the University of Leipzig. 'There are here . . . no lecture halls, where a host of eager young disciples might sit at the feet of their masters in the quest of truth: there are no monks versed in the art of penmanship as in the olden days, who by their beautiful writings enriched the world's wealth.' In short, the monks of Mount Sinai, withdrawn from the world and Greek orthodox in religion, were neither medieval scholars nor Lutheran reformers. 'No great thinkers have peopled the corridors and galleries of the spacious monastic buildings,' Tischendorf judged; 'no cells are here where mental struggles are fought, such as Luther's in Erfurt. The whole life of the monastery is empty as a burnt-out crater.'

Soon Tischendorf was reading all kinds of malice and evil into the features of his hosts on Mount Sinai. 'The present superior of the Monastery,' he wrote, '. . . , notwithstanding the delicacy of his features, bears the strongest expression of duplicity in his glance.' Such was the generally received opinion of obscure Greek Orthodox monks among western Protestants in nineteenth-century

Europe that Tischendorf had not the slightest compunc-
tion about publishing these views once he returned from
the East. Moreover it never seems to have occurred to him
that his own behaviour with regard to the monks' greatest
treasure might be far more duplicitous than anything he
could have descried in their superior's features. For his aim
was to discover their Biblical treasures and, if he could, to
take them away with him.

Religious life on Mount Sinai, said Tischendorf, 'has
deteriorated into a daily burden of prescribed and ungra-
ciously observed devotions, and to a meagre bill of fare
according to detailed rules for fast days'. Soon he was
attributing to the monks positive hypocrisy over their
religious way of life. For example, Tischendorf believed
— erroneously in fact — that the rule of St Basil, which
the monks followed, forbade wine at all times. He therefore alleged that 'the crafty monks, so the Abbot or
Archimandrite himself told me, have discovered that no
rule forbade distilled liquor'. To avoid breaking the rule,
Tischendorf alleged, the monks distilled a palm brandy
and drank that. He superciliously observed, 'It is unfortunately the only product of the "spirit" which they can take
credit for'. My own experience in St Catherine's monastery does not accord with Tischendorf's slur. The monks
are very willing to provide their guests with a certain *Cru
des Ptolémés*, which, though not comparable to the great
Crus of France, nonetheless is very definitely a kind of
wine. And they are willing to drink a little of it themselves, though not on those specific days when this is
proscribed by the rule of St Basil.

The awkward truth is that this great German Christian
scholar soon grew to hate the monks of Mount Sinai to an
astonishing degree. Only eight days after he had arrived at
the monastery of St Catherine, he wrote to Angelika, 'Oh,
these monks! If I had the military strength and power, I

should be doing a good deed if I threw this rabble over the walls. It is sad to see how man can carry his baseness and wretchedness into the lofty grandeur of this mountain world'. He continually described them as 'ignorant'. The Greek servant they provided for him was a 'half-witted fellow'. Their library was 'a poor place, to which no-one in the monastery paid much attention.' The new room in which they kept some of their books and manuscripts was 'pathetic'. It was perhaps this hatred of these despised monks that enabled Tischendorf to steal from them their greatest treasure.

And yet in the midst of all this hatred of his Christian brethren Tischendorf maintained his pious Lutheran ways. On Whitsunday 1844 he sat on top of Mount Sinai, and then sent to Angelika a copy of the prayer he self-consciously recited there: 'Oh that the Holy Spirit would permeate me with its eternal power'.

Two monks, however, did earn a good word from Tischendorf. One was Gregorios, the venerable guest-master, who forty years earlier had been a soldier. Daily he practised firing Tischendorf's double-barrelled rifle at a tile hung on the monastery wall. The other, more important friend for Tischendorf's purposes, was Kyrillos, the librarian. Through Kyrillos the German scholar was to make the greatest discovery of his career.

Tischendorf believed that Kyrillos inhabited the monastery unwillingly, brought by force 'for some unexplained act of insubordination towards the patriarch'. He liked the librarian, who was in his middle forties, and found him an 'honest, well-informed, serious, benevolent man'. In Tischendorf's view the librarian and Gregorios the guest-master were the only two of the monks to show any interest in the manuscripts of St Catherine's monastery. Kyrillos allowed the German scholar to take manuscripts from the library and examine them in his own rooms.

85

At that time books and manuscripts were kept in three separate rooms in the monastery. In one of these, in May 1844, Tischendorf discovered what he described as 'the pearl of all my researches'. According to his own account:

> I perceived in the middle of the great hall a large and wide basket full of old parchments; and the librarian, who was a man of information, told me that two heaps of papers like these, mouldered by time, had been already committed to the flames. What was my surprise to find amid this heap of papers a considerable number of sheets of a copy of the Old Testament in Greek, which seemed to me to be one of the most ancient that I had ever seen.

Altogether Tischendorf claimed to have discovered 129 (or 130, his accounts vary) parchments of the Greek Old Testament. Kyrillos gave him forty-three of them — 'all the more readily,' says Tischendorf, 'as they were destined for the fire'. But the abbot of the monastery refused to let him have the rest. Tischendorf suggested that his own too lively interest in the manuscript had roused their suspicions as to its value. 'It would seem', he wrote, 'that before the year 1844 no-one in the monastery had taken particular notice of these sheets of parchment, or to have any idea of their value.' He was allowed to note the contents of the parchments the monks wished to keep. 'I transcribed a page of the text of Isaiah and Jeremiah,' he wrote, 'and enjoined on the monks to take religious care of all such remains as might fall their way.' Taking his precious forty-three parchments with him, he left the monastery and returned to Cairo.

Now this story, told by Tischendorf long after the event, entirely fits in with his general desire to depict the monks of St Catherine's as little better than idiots. It was repeated in countless journals and newspapers throughout the Christian world. In the twentieth century the same story has been told by Tischendorf's son-in-law (Ludwig

Schneller, in 1927) and by his granddaughter (Hildegaard Behrend, in 1956). It appears in the account published by the British Library of the greatest manuscript in their possession, the Codex Sinaiticus, which Tischendorf brought from the monastery of St Catherine in 1859, fourteen years after his first visit.

It seems to me hardly likely to be true. Quite apart from the fact that the forty-three parchments he supposedly rescued from a basket of rubbish are in remarkably good condition, the highly suspicious circumstances under which Tischendorf took the Codex Sinaiticus from the monks in 1859 made him (as we shall see) desperate to prove that the original owners of the manuscript were unfitted to keep it.

What is more, Tischendorf nowhere acknowledged the devotion of the monks of St Catherine's in preserving this manuscript over so many centuries. No-one in fact knows how the manuscript, written before St Catherine's monastery was founded, came into their possession. We do know that before it did so, it was once treasured in the library of Caesarea, one of the greatest of the ancient world, comparable to those in Alexandria and Jerusalem. Among the forty-three parchments brought back by Tischendorf from Mount Sinai are notes by a scribe named Pamphilius, who attempted to correct the manuscript. Pamphilius wrote that he based his corrections on a famous Biblical work, the *Hexapla* of Origen, which was kept in the library at Caesarea.

Almost certainly, then, the parchments Tischendorf found on Mount Sinai had once been at Caesarea, where Pamphilius corrected them. Now Caesarea was taken by the Arabs in 638. It is a reasonable conjecture that the great Biblical manuscript was saved and taken by refugees to Sinai. Whether this happened immediately or after many years of wandering is impossible to judge. But by the time

Tischendorf got hold of the forty-three parchments, they had certainly been cared for by the monks of St Catherine's for something like 1000 years — and perhaps more.

By January 1845 Tischendorf was back in Leipzig. As well as visiting Mount Sinai and collecting his precious forty-three parchments, he had on his journey sought ancient manuscripts in the Coptic convents of the Libyan desert, in Jerusalem, Bethlehem, and the convent of St Saba on the shores of the Dead Sea. His searches had taken him to Nazareth, to Smyrna and the island of Patmos, to Beirut, Constantinople, and Athens. Finally, on his way home he had visited the great libraries of Vienna and Munich.

In return for the expenses of his travels, Tischendorf gave all he had discovered to King Frederick Augustus II of Saxony. Then, according to his son-in-law Ludwig Schneller, 'He immediately developed an astonishing activity with a view to making these manuscripts available to human knowledge'.

This is very far from the truth. Tischendorf had not the slightest intention of letting anyone else into his secrets. Even at the height of his fame, he displayed a quite extraordinary viciousness towards any scholar whose reputation might diminish his own standing in the eyes of the world. One such rival was the British Biblical scholar Samuel Prideaux Tregelles. Tischendorf questioned his probity, just as he had accused the monks of Mount Sinai of hypocrisy. Tregelles, he held, was a pious humbug, 'always acting so piously, always bandying talk of "God" and "God's word" around, without scorning to use the most spiteful weapons of this world'. In truth, there is little doubt that in the mid-1840s Tischendorf himself behaved precisely in this way with regard to the publication of his new discovery. He planned to tell the world only enough to forward his own reputation, without giving any other scholar an opportunity of joining in the spoils.

In 1846 Tischendorf published his brilliant edition of the forty-three parchments, under the title *Codex Frederico-Augustanus*. But what is most remarkable about this edition is that nowhere in it does Tischendorf reveal either where he found the manuscript or that he had left over eighty parchments behind. Ludwig Schneller attempted to excuse this deliberate omission by appealing to German national pride. 'If, in particular, the English had got to know the place,' he wrote, 'they would have gone there straight away to buy the treasure with lavishly spent English money, and have it taken to the British Museum in London.' In truth Tischendorf intended to try to buy the treasure himself. So in his edition of the forty-three parchments he simply described its provenance as from the east, specifying somewhere in the neighbourhood of Egypt. He asked his friend Dr Pruner-Bey, physician to the Viceroy of Egypt, to approach the monks and buy the rest.

Dr Pruner-Bey failed. He wrote to Tischendorf, 'The monks of the monastery have, since your departure, learned the value of these sheets of parchment, and will not part with them at any price'.

Tischendorf was now made extraordinary professor at Leipzig. He published an account of his travels in the east which managed to describe his visit to St Catherine's monastery without mentioning anything of the manuscript he had discovered there. This account did, however, stress the disagreeable nature of the monks, in Tischendorf's view. (He even objected to their harmless pastime of duelling with sticks, which Tischendorf found particularly abhorrent in that sacred place.) He was now publishing learned work after learned work, and his European reputation was rapidly growing, but he was determined to return to Mount Sinai and, if he could, bring back the missing parchments.

At the end of 1852 he set off again. His loving Angelika was left behind once more, this time with children to look after. On 21 January 1853 she wrote to him how moved she was to go into his study, where on the writing-desk were her beloved husband's hat and a birthday poem about him, written by his son Paul. Two days later she was writing again how difficult it was to bear his absence, but she added speedily that his own hardships must be even more difficult to bear. And indeed this second journey was hard. Tischendorf was dogged with storms all the way from Alexandria to Cairo.

What was worse, he came back from Mount Sinai virtually empty-handed. This time two Germans, a married couple, accompanied him to the monastery. Strangely, the monks could not (or would not) produce the eighty-six or eighty-seven parchments that Tischendorf had seen nine years earlier. They seemed, he said, to have forgotten all about them. All he could find was a tiny fragment from the same collection of parchments, in another roll of papers, apparently being used as a bookmark. Written on both sides, and containing eleven lines of the first book of the Bible, this fragment convinced Tischendorf that the whole manuscript originally contained the complete Old Testament. But he now feared that the greater part of it had been long since destroyed.

In spite of his gloom over the possibility of recovering the rest of the manuscript from Mount Sinai, Tischendorf's phenomenal energy had not deserted him on his second trip to the east. Elsewhere — in Cairo, Alexandria, Jerusalem, Laodicea, Smyrna, Constantinople, and Mount Athos — he had discovered sixteen *palimpsest* manuscripts (that is, manuscripts in which old writing has been erased to make room for new), many important Greek uncial manuscripts, as well as Coptic, Syrian, and Arabic parchments and papyrus fragments. He decided to call the oldest of the palimpsests he had discovered Codex Johannes, after the Crown Prince of Saxony. 'Praise the Lord!', he asserted. 'I must believe I am about His work, since He so much blesses me.'

Amid increasing fame, he continued to publish editions of his discoveries, as well as producing new, improved editions of the Greek New Testament. By the end of his life he had collated the texts of twenty-three manuscripts, edited and published the texts of seventeen notable codices, and provided the scholarly world with no fewer than twenty editions of the Greek New Testament.

But his failure to obtain the whole of the monastery's elusive manuscript rankled throughout the late 1840s and the 1850s. What made matters worse for Tischendorf were reports that others had seen and examined the precious document. Major Macleod, a Scots army officer, saw it in 1845. Worse from Tischendorf's point of view was the news that a Russian scholar, Porphyrius Uspensky, had been shown the whole manuscript (with the exception of Tischendorf's forty-three parchments) in 1845 and again in 1850.

Uspensky was by no means so great a scholar as Tischendorf, and did not fully recognize the antiquity of the manuscript. Nonetheless, he knew it was an important find. In 1857 he observed that 'this manuscript, whatever it is, is perhaps the oldest in all the Orthodox church, and by its antiquity unique'.

Tischendorf did not learn that Uspensky had seen the coveted manuscript until August 1859. The notion that someone else was the first to discover it roused him to a fury. In a letter to his Scottish friend Dr Samuel Davidson of Glasgow, Tischendorf wrote that the 'heresy-seeking' Russian's 'lack of judgment' had led him to draw up a pamphlet, 'The Disputes over the Sinai Bible' [*Die Anfechtungen der Sinaibibel*], 'which lays about it with a flail'.

But for the time being he returned home almost at peace with himself. At least no-one else had found the manuscript. He drew consolation from the other documents found in Cairo, Alexandria, Jerusalem, Laodicea, Constantinople, and the monastery of Mount Athos in Macedonia. 'In spite of the failure of my greatest ambitions,' he wrote to Angelika, 'I have nevertheless been crowned with grace and mercy far beyond my expectations.'

Yet the story remains puzzling. Tischendorf published the fragment of Genesis chapter 24 that he had found in St Catherine's, as well as much else. His reputation was now formidable. The Vice-Chancellor of Cambridge University, after meeting him in 1855, wrote, 'He's not an old man, and yet he has produced the output of a century'.

The puzzle is that this man, who had found nothing he had hoped for on his second visit to Mount Sinai, was determined to go there a third time. Was it, as his son-in-law and granddaughter both suggest, that he really did suppose some other scholar — perhaps even an Englishman! — had managed to buy the remaining parchments from the monks, and slowly came to think this might not be the case when no publication of it was forthcoming?

At any rate, Tischendorf began to make preparations for his last and outstandingly successful visit to the monastery of St Catherine on Mount Sinai. It was, he believed, his last chance. He was growing older and soon would not be able to stand the rigours of the journey. And this time he sought the help not of the Saxon Ministry of Public Worship and Education, which had financed his two previous trips, but of the most powerful figure in the whole of Orthodox Christendom: the Tsar of Russia.

CHAPTER IV

The Discovery of the Codex

Tischendorf promised the Russian minister in Dresden, Prince Wolkowsky, that if commissioned by Tsar Alexander II, he would go to the east and give to his Imperial Majesty all that he could bring back. The Russian minister of culture in St Petersburg supported the scheme. So did the Tsarina and her mother. Alexander II agreed, and in January 1859 Tischendorf once again set sail for Egypt.

By the end of January he was in the monastery. By his own account, he 'devoted a few days in turning over the manuscripts of the monastery, not without alighting here and there on some precious parchment or other'. But of his old discovery, he saw nothing.

On 4 February he told his Bedouin to prepare to leave for Cairo three days later. That evening he took a walk with the young Athenian steward of the monastery and then went for some refreshment in the steward's cell. Then the steward said that he too had read the Greek version of the Old Testament, and he took down from the corner of his cell a bulky parcel, wrapped up in a red cloth, and laid it before Tischendorf.

Tischendorf took it to his own rooms. It contained not

simply the eighty or so leaves he had seen in 1844. Altogether he held in his hands 346 parchments, all in the same handwriting and from the same volume. 'I was beside myself with joy', he wrote to Angelika. He was amazed to see not just the Old Testament, but also the whole of the New. 'It is the only such manuscript in the world', he told his wife. 'Neither the Codex Vaticanus nor the London Alexandrinus contains the whole New Testament, and the Sinai Codex is undoubtedly older than both. This discovery is a remarkable occurrence and a great one for Christian knowledge', he continued. He added, 'Naturally, no-one in the monastery really knows what is contained in the manuscript.'

As he read on Tischendorf was astounded to discover that the Sinai Codex contained the whole of a very early Christian letter, the epistle of Barnabas, 'of which a considerable part, till this moment, was considered lost in the Greek original'.

'I had tears in my eyes,' he told Angelika, 'and my heart was beating as never before.' Then he picked up another page and saw the title, 'The Shepherd'. He immediately recognized this as the visionary book written in the second century AD by a Christian called Hermas. Tischendorf felt deeply moved. 'Had I not always said, that I go in the name of the Lord in search of treasures which will bear fruit in his church?'

Tischendorf was now faced with a problem. Entirely by his own efforts the world would be given an extraordinary enrichment of Christian knowledge, but only if he could take the manuscript away with him. Moreover, he had also promised to bring back everything he could find and give it to the Tsar. Tischendorf therefore tried to bribe the young steward to let him keep the codex.

The steward refused. Even if he had wished to deceive his fellow-monks, he had no choice, since he had borrowed the codex from the sacristan of the monastery, Skevophylax Vitalios, in order to show it to Tischendorf. Tischendorf therefore now embarked on the remarkable piece of duplicity which was to occupy him for the next decade, which involved the careful suppression of facts and the systematic denigration of the monks of Mount Sinai.

First Tischendorf asked the monks whether he might take the codex to their sister monastery in Cairo, in order to copy the whole manuscript. The sacristan Vitalios disagreed. Tischendorf decided to appeal to the abbot of St Catherine's. But the abbot was in Cairo, *en route* to Constantinople, where he and all the abbots of the sister monasteries of St Catherine's were gathered to elect a new archbishop in place of the one who had recently died at the age of ninety. The matter was causing some difficulty for the monks, because any new archbishop had to be consecrated by the Patriarch of Jerusalem, who was refusing to accept the favoured choice of the assembled abbots. With the Bedouin Sheik Nasser, Tischendorf set off for Cairo in the hope of reaching the abbot of St Catherine's before he left for Constantinople. They reached Cairo in seven days, and he persuaded the assembled abbots to agree to the plan. Sheik Nasser set off back to collect the codex from St Catherine's, and did the return trip in an incredible twelve days. Tischendorf was allowed to take eight pages at a time to his Cairo lodgings, in order to copy out the whole manuscript.

For two months, in stifling heat, Tischendorf busied himself with copying the manuscript. He enlisted the help of a German doctor and a German pharmacist, who both knew Greek. They copied the text. Tischendorf proofread their copy. The whole document consisted of 110,000 lines. To these Tischendorf brilliantly added the alterations of later correctors — 12,000 altogether.

On top of this astounding feat of scholarship, Tischendorf still found time to write to his wife and children. 'Be good children,' he wrote in February, 'which will please me when your mother writes to tell me about you.' And he signed his letter, 'Your father, who loves you. Cairo, in Egypt, where the people are brown, dark brown and totally black, and many children go naked in winter and summer'. After finishing the transcript of the codex from Mount Sinai, he went elsewhere seeking more manuscripts for Christianity and Tsar Alexander II, until the end of July. On his return, he devoted himself to the problem of getting the Sinai codex out of the hands of its owners and into the hands of the Tsar.

In his favour was the continuing dispute over the election of the new archbishop of Sinai. If Tischendorf could enlist the support of the Tsar for the monks' favoured candidate, perhaps they would then be willing to let him take the precious manuscript to Russia. According to Tischendorf's own account, in Cairo he suggested to the monks of St Catherine's that they might wish to present the codex to the Tsar. But, he alleged, 'the monks of Mount Sinai, although willing to do so, were unable to carry out my suggestion', because an archbishop was required to ratify the suggestion, and no archbishop was available.

In his later writings Tischendorf suggested that he and the monks of St Catherine's had frequently discussed the notion of presenting the codex to the Tsar. The evidence does not bear this out. On 24 February 1859, he gave the monks a note agreeing to return the codex within a month and a half. Only a month later, on 30 March, did he write to Angelika of his plan to persuade the monks to let him take the manuscript to Russia as a gift for the Tsar. Nor did he in fact manage to persuade them to do this. In spite of visiting Constantinople in support of the future

96

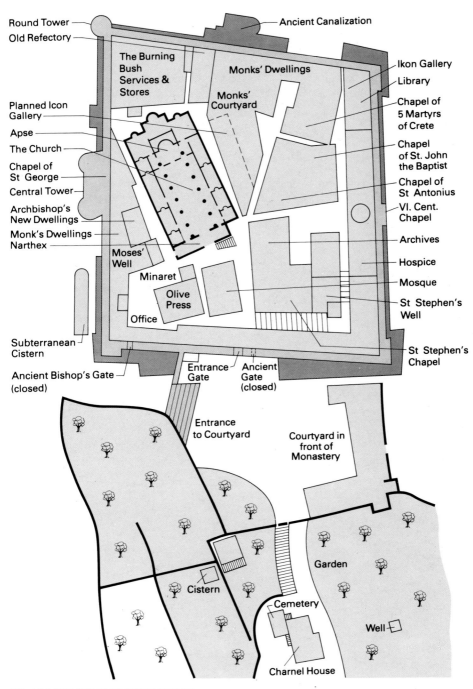

Round Tower
Old Refectory
Ancient Canalization

The Burning Bush Services & Stores
Monks' Dwellings
Monks' Courtyard

Ikon Gallery
Library
Chapel of 5 Martyrs of Crete

Planned Icon Gallery
Apse
The Church
Chapel of St George
Central Tower
Archbishop's New Dwellings
Monk's Dwellings
Narthex
Moses' Well
Minaret
Olive Press
Office
Subterranean Cistern
Ancient Bishop's Gate (closed)

Chapel of St. John the Baptist
Chapel of St Antonius
VI. Cent. Chapel
Archives
Hospice
Mosque
St Stephen's Well
St Stephen's Chapel

Entrance Gate
Ancient Gate (closed)

Entrance to Courtyard

Courtyard in front of Monastery

Cistern
Garden
Cemetery
Well
Charnel House

PLAN OF ST CATHERINE'S MONASTERY AT MOUNT SINAI

Opposite: *This aerial view of St Catherine's monastery clearly shows the oasis outside the formidable walls of the monastery.*

Above: *The bell tower of St Catherine's with, to the right, the minaret of the mosque which is used by the monks' Islamic servants.*

Above: *This icon from St Catherine's shows Moses receiving the Tablets of the Law on Mount Sinai.*
Left: *The great doors of the monastery church were made of cypress wood, intricately carved, early in the twelfth century.*

Opposite: *The interior of the church, which was built for the monks of St Catherine's on the orders of the Emperor Justinian in the sixth century.*

ΟΛΕΓΕΤΑΙΕΡΜΗΝ
ΟΜΕΝΟΝΔΙΔΑΣΚΑ
ΛΕΠΟΥΜΕΝΕΙΣΔΕ
ΓΕΙΑΥΤΟΙΣΕΡΧΕΣ
ΚΑΙΙΔΕΤΕΗΛΘΟΝ
ΟΥΝΚΑΙΙΔΟΝΠΟΥ
ΜΑΙΝΕΙΚΑΙΠΑΡΑ
ΤΩΕΜΙΝΑΝΤΗΝΗ
ΜΕΡΑΝΕΚΕΙΝΗΝ
ΩΡΑΗΝΩΣΔΕΚΑΤΗ
ΗΝΑΝΔΡΕΑΣΟΑΔΕΛ
ΦΟΣΣΙΜΩΝΟΣΠΕ
ΤΡΟΥΕΙΣΕΚΤΩΝΔΥ
ΟΑΚΟΥΣΑΝΤΩΝΠΑ
ΡΑΙΩΑΝΝΟΥΚΑΙ
ΑΚΟΛΟΥΘΗΣΑΝΤΩ
ΑΥΤΩ
ΕΥΡΙΣΚΕΙΟΥΤΟΣΠ
ΤΟΣΤΟΝΑΔΕΛΦΟΝ
ΤΟΝΙΔΙΟΝΣΙΜΩΝΑ
ΚΑΙΛΕΓΕΙΑΥΤΩΕΥ
ΡΗΚΑΜΕΝΤΟΝΜ
ΣΙΑΝΟΕΣΤΙΝΜΕ
ΘΕΡΜΗΝΕΥΟΜΕ
ΝΟΝΧΣΗΓΑΓΕΝ
ΑΥΤΟΝΠΡΟΣΤΟΝ
ΙΝΕΜΒΛΕΨΑΣΑΥ
ΟΙΣΕΙΠΕΝΣΥΕΙ
ΜΩΝΟΥΙΟΣΙΩΑΝ
ΝΟΥΣΥΚΛΗΘΗΣΗ
ΚΗΦΑΣΟΕΡΜΗΝ
ΕΤΑΙΠΕΤΡΟΣ
ΤΗΕΠΑΥΡΙΟΝΗΘΕ
ΛΗΣΕΝΕΞΕΛΘΙΝ
ΤΗΝΓΑΛΙΛΑΙΑΝΚΑΙ
ΕΥΡΙΣΚΕΙΦΙΛΙΠ
ΚΑΙΛΕΓΕΙΑΥΤΩ
ΔΙΑΛΙΠΠΟΣΑΠΟΒΗ
ΣΑΙΔΑΝΤΗΣΠΟΛΕ
ΩΣΑΝΔΡΕΟΥΚΑΙΠ
ΤΡΟΥΕΥΡΙΣΚΕΙΦ
ΛΙΠΠΟΣΤΟΝΝΑ
ΝΑΗΛΚΑΙΛΕΓΕΙΑ
ΟΝΕΓΡΑΨΕΝΜΩ
ΕΝΤΩΝΟΜΩΚΑΙ
ΠΡΟΦΗΤΑΙΕΥΡΗ
ΚΑΜΕΝΙΝΥΝΤ

ΙΩΣΗΦΤΟΝΑΠΟ
ΝΑΖΑΡΕΤΕΙΠΕΝ
ΑΥΤΩΝΑΘΑΝΑ
ΕΚΝΑΖΑΡΕΤΔΥΝΑ
ΤΑΙΑΓΑΘΟΟΝΤΕΙΝΑΙ
ΛΕΓΕΙΑΥΤΩΦΙΛΙ
ΠΟΣΕΡΧΟΥΚΑΙΙΔΕ
ΙΔΕΝΟΙΣΤΟΝΝΑ
ΘΑΝΑΗΛΕΡΧΟΜ
ΝΟΝΠΡΟΣΑΥΤΟΝΚ
ΛΕΓΕΙΠΕΡΙΑΥΤΟΥΝΑ
ΘΑΝΑΗΛΑΓΕΛΑΙ
ΘΩΣΕΙΣΑΡΑΗΛΕΙΤΙ
ΕΝΩΔΟΛΟΣΟΥΚΕ
ΣΤΙΝΛΕΓΕΙΑΥΤΩ
ΝΑΘΑΝΑΗΛΠΟ
ΜΕΓΙΝΩΣΚΕΙΣ
ΑΠΕΚΡΙΘΗΟΙΣΚΑΙ
ΕΙΠΕΝΑΥΤΩΠΡ
ΤΟΥΣΕΦΙΛΙΠΠΟΝ
ΦΩΝΗΣΑΙΟΝΤΑ
ΥΠΟΤΗΝΣΥΚΗΝ
ΙΔΟΝΣΕ
ΑΠΕΚΡΙΘΗΝΑΘΑ
ΝΑΗΛΚΑΙΕΙΠΕΝ
ΡΑΒΒΕΙΣΥΕΙΟΥΙ
ΘΥΣΥΕΙΟΒΑΣΙΛΕΥ
ΤΟΥΙΗΛ
ΑΠΕΚΡΙΘΗΙΣΚΑΙ
ΕΙΠΕΝΑΥΤΩΟΤΙΕΙΠ
ΣΟΙΟΤΙΕΙΔΟΝΣΕΥ
ΠΟΚΑΤΩΤΗΣΣΥΚΗ
ΠΙΣΤΕΥΕΙΣΜΕΙΖ
ΝΑΙΟΥΤΩΝΟΨΗ
ΚΑΙΛΕΓΕΙΑΥΤΩ
ΑΜΗΝΑΜΗΝΛΕ
ΥΜΙΝΟΨΕΣΘΑΙ
ΟΥΡΑΝΟΝΑΝΕΩ
ΓΟΤΑΚΑΙΤΟΥΣΑΓ
ΓΕΛΟΥΣΤΟΥΘΥΑ
ΝΑΒΑΙΝΟΝΤΑΣΚ
ΚΑΤΑΒΑΙΝΟΝΤΑΣ
ΕΠΙΤΟΝΥΝΤΟΥΑΝ
ΘΡΩΠΟΥΚΑΙΤΗΗ
ΜΕΡΑΤΗΤΡΙΤΗΓΑ
ΜΟΣΕΓΕΝΕΤΟΕΝ
ΚΑΝΑΤΗΣΓΑΛΙΛΑΙΑ
ΑΣΚΑΙΗΝΗΜΗΤΗ

ΤΟΥΙΥΓΕΚΕΙΕΚΑ
ΘΗΔΕΚΑΙΟΙΚ
ΜΑΘΗΤΑΙΑΥΤΟ
ΤΟΝΓΑΜΟΝΚΑ
ΕΤΕΡΗΣΑΝΤ
ΟΙΝΟΣΟΤΙΙ
ΕΠΙΔΕΛΕΓΕΙΗΜ
ΤΟΥΙΥΠΡΟΣΑΥ
ΟΙΝΟΣΟΥΚΕ
ΛΕΓΕΙΑΥΤΗΟΙΣ
ΜΟΙΚΑΙΣΟΙΓΥ
ΟΥΠΩΗΚΕΙΗ
ΜΟΥ
ΛΕΓΕΙΗΜΗΤΗΡ
ΤΟΙΣΔΙΑΚΟΝ
ΟΤΙΟΑΝΛΕΓΗ
ΠΟΙΗΣΑΤΕ ΗΟ
ΔΕΕΚΕΙΝΟΙΝΑ
ΑΠΙΑΙΕΞΚΑΙΤΟ
ΘΑΡΙΣΜΟΝΤΩ
ΟΥΔΑΙΩΝΧΩ
ΣΑΙΑΝΑΜΕΤΡΗ
ΑΣΟΝΤΡΕΙΣΚΑ
ΓΕΙΑΥΤΟΙΣΟΙΣ
ΜΙΣΑΤΕΤΑΣΥ
ΥΔΑΤΟΣΚΑΙΕΓΕ
ΣΑΝΑΥΤΑΣΕΩ
ΝΩΚΑΙΛΕΓΕΙΑ
ΤΟΙΣΑΝΤΛΗΣΑ
ΝΥΝΚΑΙΦΕΡΕ
ΑΡΧΙΤΡΙΚΛΙΝ
ΔΕΗΝΕΓΚΑΝΟ
ΩΣΔΕΕΓΕΥΣΑΤΟΟ
ΤΡΙΚΛΙΝΟΣΤΟΥ
ΟΙΝΟΝΟΓΕΓΕΝΙ
ΝΟΝΑΛΟΥΓΚΗ
ΠΟΘΕΝΕΣΤΙΝ
ΔΕΔΙΑΚΟΝΟΙΗ
ΔΕΙΣΑΝΟΙΗΝ
ΚΟΤΕΣΤΟΥΔΩ
ΦΩΝΕΙΤΟΝΝΥ
ΟΝΟΑΡΧΙΤΡΙΚ
ΝΟΣΚΑΙΛΕΓΕ
ΑΝΘΡΩΠΟΣΠ
ΤΟΝΤΟΝΚΑΛΟ
ΝΟΝΤΙΘΗΣΙΝ
ΟΤΑΝΜΕΘΥΣΩ

Left: *A page from the Codex Sinaiticus, the mid-fourth century text of the Bible brought back by von Tischendorf from Mount Sinai and now in the British Museum.*

Above: *A monk works in the modern library of St Catherine's monastery, which contains over 3,000 ancient books and manuscripts.*

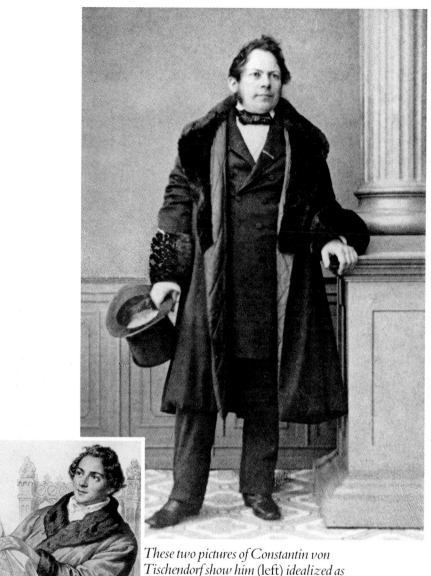

These two pictures of Constantin von Tischendorf show him (left) idealized as the great Biblical scholar and (above) in a photograph as the determined explorer.

archbishop Cyril, and in spite of the help he managed to elicit from Prince Lobanov, the Russian ambassador to Turkey, the most the monks would agree to was that Tischendorf could take the manuscript to Russia not as a gift but as a loan, in order to produce a published facsimile of the whole. To achieve even this took much time and effort. Tischendorf returned to Cairo on 24 September. 'The monks and archbishop then warmly expressed their thanks for my zealous efforts in their cause,' he wrote, 'and the following day I received from them, under the form of a loan, the Sinai Bible, to carry it to St Petersburg, and there to have it copied as exactly as possible.'

Tischendorf clearly hoped that at some later date the monks would agree to let the Tsar of Russia keep the manuscript. He had brought from Prince Lobanov a letter supporting that suggestion. But the letter makes absolutely clear that the proposed gift had not yet been made. Dated 22 September 1859 (10 September, old style), it reads:

> Monsieur Tischendorf has told me that the venerable confraternity of Mount Sinai has proposed to offer through him an old Biblical manuscript in homage to his Imperial Majesty the Tsar Alexander II. Since this offer cannot be made officially until the newly-elected superior is recognized by the Sublime Porte, Monsieur Tischendorf desires to take the said manuscript as a loan to St Petersburg for the time being, there to check a copy with the original while it is being printed. In supporting this desire of Monsieur Tischendorf, I declare that, if it is judged possible to agree to this, this manuscript remains the property of the confraternity of Mount Sinai, until such time as the superior in the name of that confraternity has officially offered it to His Imperial Majesty. It goes without saying that if unforeseen circumstances prevent the confraternity from putting this intention into effect, the manuscript would be returned without fail.

This letter Tischendorf delivered to the monks. In some of his accounts of the transaction, he quotes it. Never once did he refer to his own letter to the monks, dated 28 September 1859, which remained hidden in the monastery of St Catherine until it was discovered there in 1960, along with a handful of other vital letters, by Professor Ihor Sevcenko.

The letter, in Tischendorf's own hand, is written in bad Greek, and was probably drawn up with the help of a Cairo notary. So important did the monks of Mount Sinai consider this letter on its discovery in 1960 that they put it on permanent exhibition in the monastery under glass. However, as the ink began to fade, the letter was replaced with a photocopy (with the right-hand side partly sliced off), under which is attached a not very competent translation. What Tischendorf wrote is as follows:

> I the undersigned, Constantin von Tischendorf, sent at present to the East by orders of Alexander, Tsar of All Russias, testify by the present letter that the Holy Con-fraternity of Mount Sinai, in accordance with the letter of His Excellency Ambassador Lobanov, has handed over to me, as a loan, an ancient manuscript of both Testaments, being the property of the aforementioned monastery and consisting of 346 folia and a small fragment. These I wish to take with me to St Petersburg in order that I may compare the original with the copy made by me when that is printed. This manuscript is entrusted to me under the conditions laid down in the aforementioned letter of Mr Lobanov, dated 10 September 1859, numbered 510. I promise to return it, undamaged and in a good state of preservation, to the Holy Confraternity of Mount Sinai at its first request.

Then Tischendorf left Cairo, and the monks of Mount Sinai never saw their codex again.

He returned to Europe triumphant. By way of Leipzig, he reached St Petersburg. By his own account, on 19

November 1859, 'I presented to their Imperial Majesties, in the Winter Palace at Tsarkoe-Selo, my rich collection of old Greek, Syriac, Coptic, Arabic, and other manuscripts, in the middle of which the Sinaitic Bible shone like a crown'.

Tischendorf's account makes no mention of the fact that the Sinaitic Bible was, strictly speaking, not his to present to Alexander II and the Tsarina. He proposed that the manuscript be published. The Tsar agreed to pay for it, requesting that publication coincide with the celebrations for the thousand-year jubilee of the Russian monarchy in the autumn of 1862.

The request made enormous demands even on a scholar of Tischendorf's extraordinary abilities. Scarcely more than two years were available for the work. The text of the Bible in the codex was written entirely in *uncials*, that is, in capital letters. It contained neither chapter headings nor any division into verses or paragraphs. The whole manuscript had been written without punctuation, with no spaces between words. To it had been added a vast number of corrections and emendations. But Tischendorf was a genius.

For a facsimile edition of the codex, Tischendorf would have to supervise the production of many different typefaces. He counted, for example, seven different sizes of the Greek letter *omega* in the whole manuscript. Nevertheless, he set to work with a will. He refused the Tsar's invitation to stay in Russia, and supervised the work from Leipzig, making three visits to St Petersburg in the twenty-seven months the project took to reach completion. It was a phenomenally short time to produce the four magnificent folios in which the edition finally appeared. During that time Tischendorf refused all other invitations. His friend Dr Samuel Davidson passed to him an invitation to attend a meeting of the distinguished British Association. Tischendorf thanked him, and turned the invitation down. 'All my time belongs to the great work which you know about', he wrote to Davidson. 'I have to give my all to see to the publication of the four folio volumes by the autumn of 1862. My labours will be interrupted only by a journey to St Petersburg at the beginning of May, where I must produce a report and make preparations.'

Tischendorf did, however, spare the time to show the codex to King William of Prussia in Berlin. He also — to his great regret, as we shall see — allowed a rival scholar, Samuel Prideaux Tregelles, to examine it for a few days in Leipzig. But his industry was endless. He arranged for a firm of papermakers in Leipzig, Ferdinand Flinsch and Co., to produce a fine paper of the same colour as the parchment of the codex. He copied exactly the uneven spaces between the uncial letters of the original. Red letters appearing in the text, along with the numerous little signs spread throughout it, were all to be faithfully reproduced.

Then, to Tischendorf's rage, almost as soon as his momentous discovery was made public, the claim was made that the entire codex was a forgery. The claim was made by one of the greatest forgers of the nineteenth century, the Greek scholar Constantine Simonides, who said he had written the manuscript himself. Simonides had pursued a bizarre career selling both genuine documents as well as forged ones. During a stay in England between 1853 and 1855 he failed to sell his forgeries to Sir Frederick Madden of the British Museum one day, and then turned up the next day selling genuine manuscripts. He did successfully sell thirty-one forgeries to the noted and gullible English collector Sir Thomas Phillipps.

In July 1855 he prosecuted a successful piece of business in Tischendorf's own university. He had discovered three genuine leaves of a Greek copy of the *Shepherd of Hermas* in the monastery of St Gregory on Mount Athos. While there he copied six other leaves from the same document, and then offered them as genuine to the University library in Leipzig.

Now, just as Tischendorf was about to produce his magisterial folio edition of the Codex Sinaiticus, Simonides claimed to have forged the whole manuscript during a stay on Mount Athos in 1840. Simonides even produced a Greek monk named Kallinikos, who was willing to testify that he had witnessed the forgery. Moreover Simonides was sufficiently skilled at calligraphy for many to find his claim highly plausible. He asserted that his uncle Benedict had suggested he make the forgery and present it to the Tsar; but tiring of this idea, he stated that instead he had handed the document to a former archbishop of Sinai. In this way the forged codex, Simonides claimed, had reached the monastery of St Catherine and eventually fallen into the hands of Tischendorf.

As A.J. Farrer, the twentieth-century expert on literary forgeries, observed, 'The implication that Tischendorf had mistaken a manuscript of the nineteenth century for one of the fourth century naturally roused that irascible theologian to a condition of fury'. Tischendorf knew that Simonides was taking a humorous revenge after a previous episode. When he had tried to sell the forged copy of the *Shepherd of Hermas* in Germany, Tischendorf had exposed him. In a letter to the Syriac scholar, the Revd William Cureton, Tischendorf expressed his amazement that although some scholars had thanked him for this, others had wanted the whole affair kept quiet, out of shame at being tricked by Simonides. Now he raged at Simonides' malice. 'With the many articles about the Simonides swindle,' he complained to his friend Davidson, 'I have nowhere seen, by the way, that anyone proved how Simonides came to his extraordinary idea concerning the authorship of the Codex Sinaiticus.' Was it that his fellow-scholars were *still* smarting at being tricked by Simonides until Tischendorf proved them all wrong? Maybe, he suggested to Davidson, the Berlin professors were so filled with vanity that they would never come to a proper appreciation of his own critical skills. Hardly anyone, he lamented, spotted that fact that 'the impudent cheat Simonides' behaved so maliciously to him simply 'because I revealed in such a devastating fashion his frauds'.

In fact a good number of scholars did see this, including the hapless Tregelles. Tregelles even generously wrote that he was 'as absolutely certain of the genuineness and antiquity of the Codex Sinaiticus as of his own existence'. (Such generosity did not make Tischendorf treat Tregelles any better. Later scholars found that whenever in his editions of the Bible Tischendorf used information discovered by Tregelles, he omitted to mention its source!) And though Codex Sinaiticus was obviously not a forgery, doubts about its status sowed by Simonides delayed its impact on Biblical scholarship. Because of Simonides, Codex Sinaiticus took longer to make its proper mark on the Christian world.

But nothing could stifle the impact of Tischendorf's monumental edition of the codex. Just after Easter 1862 the twenty-two books of the Old Testament and twenty-nine of the New, together with the letter of Barnabas and the Shepherd of Hermas, appeared in three folio volumes, the printer's ink (mostly brown) exactly corresponding with the original. Twenty copies were printed on genuine parchment, for presentation to royalty.

At the beginning of October 1862 Tischendorf set off for St Petersburg, together with thirty-one crates carrying 1232 folios of his edition of the codex. They weighed 130 hundredweight. On 10 November, at Tsarkoe-Selo, he handed over the first copies to the Tsar and Tsarina. The codex itself was put on exhibition in the Imperial Public Library.

Two hundred and twenty-three copies were presented by the Tsar to the great libraries of the world. (One of these, ironically, went to the monastery on Mount Sinai, where it is still on display, in place of the original.) The remaining folios were given to Tischendorf himself, to sell for as much as he could get.

Tischendorf was now world-famous. 'Nearly all the European courts showered so many orders and distinctions on him,' wrote his son-in-law, 'that they could never have found room on one man's chest.' Oxford and Cambridge Universities honoured him with their highest degrees. The Pope wrote him an autograph letter declaring, 'I would rather have discovered this Sinaitic manuscript than the Koh-i-noor of the Queen of England'. The King of Saxony made the university professor a Privy Councillor.

'These honours pleased him,' said his son-in-law, 'but they were only of secondary importance to him. The promotion of the science of theology and the good of the Christian community were first and foremost in his life.'

Tischendorf would of course have been less than human not to have delighted in these honours. Sending a photograph of himself to the wife of his Scots friend Samuel Davidson, he wrote, 'a picture of me in my grand ceremonial clothes does not yet exist: as soon as it is made, I will send one too'. He also sent a picture of his two youngest children, adding that Alexandra, his youngest daughter, was godchild of the Grand Duchess Alexandra Constantin of Russia, the sister-in-law of the Tsar.

Now, it might be thought, was the time for the codex itself to return home to Mount Sinai. In dedicating his great edition to the Tsar in 1862, Tischendorf had written, 'This relic from the time of the first Christian emperor has

lain like a holy treasure at the foot of the mountain on
whose summit Moses once saw the glory of God and
received from God's hands the Tables of the Law'. These
Tables of the Law contained the specific injunction, 'Thou
shalt not steal'. But the title of Tischendorf's edition,
Codex Sinaiticus Petropolitanus, indicated (by its last word,
'Petropolitanus') that some people — including Tischendorf and the Tsar himself — might be more pleased if it
were allowed to remain in St Petersburg.

The monks of St Catherine's, however, were by no
means agreed that this should be the case. A letter
discovered by Professor Sevcenko in the monastery indicates their annoyance as early as 1859 at rumours in Cairo
— put about perhaps by Tischendorf himself — that they
intended to give the manuscript to Alexander II. The
archbishop, Cyril, in whose cause Tischendorf had worked at that time, had now secured his election. But he
showed no signs of being willing or able to persuade his
fellow-monks to donate their most precious document.

Tischendorf was now in a quandary. He had given to
the Tsar something that, at that moment, he had no right
to give. As a result he had received acclaim, honour, and
money (though, as his letters to Samuel Davidson reveal,
he would have received more money had the agent
charged with selling his copies of the 1862 folios not
continually undersold them!). He had carefully concealed
as much as he could of the original arrangements for
taking the great codex to Russia. Yet his appeals to
Archbishop Cyril, asking the monks to ratify his gift of
the manuscript to Alexander II, fell on deaf ears.

His anxieties were reflected in the Russian court. After
its triumphal exhibition, the manuscript from Mount Sinai
was placed in the keeping of the Russian ministry of
foreign affairs, as an indication of its uncertain ownership.
But Tischendorf's troubles were nothing compared with

those of Archbishop Cyril, whose promotion he had sought precisely to get hold of the codex. On 21 January 1867, the internal quarrels of the monastery which were certainly in part due to the fact that Cyril had allowed their most precious possession to be alienated, led the monks to depose their archbishop. Even after his deposition, Cyril continued to insist that he had only loaned the codex.

Tischendorf was now thoroughly alarmed. Suspicions were being voiced by his enemies that he had even 'stolen' the manuscript. Indeed, the Russian ambassador to the Sublime Porte, Prince N.P. Ignatieff, who had now taken over negotiating with the monks of St Catherine's, quite openly used such words in speaking and writing about the Sinai Bible.

Tischendorf sped to Russia once again. In spite of his failing health, he offered to go yet a fourth time to Mount Sinai. Ignatieff would have none of it. Tischendorf, who had created the misunderstanding in the first place, was not now to go to Sinai again as the Russians' representative and at their expense. The deposition of Cyril gave the ruthless ambassador a chance to obtain the gift of the Codex Sinaiticus without Tischendorf's further intervention. The Russians agreed to recognize Cyril's rival Kallistratus as archbishop, provided Kallistratus would co-operate with them in the matter of the codex. Ignatieff cynically advised the Russians to offer the monks 'a sum of money — as little as necessary — so as to give us the right to affirm that we bought the Bible and didn't steal it'.

Kallistratus agreed. He persuaded at least some of his fellow-monks ('a delegation', as Tischendorf's grand-daughter has it) to sign over the precious manuscript to their Imperial Majesties, the Tsar and Tsarina. In return the monks were given 9000 Russian roubles (worth about £1350 at that time) and some Imperial decorations.

Now, and only now, did the Tsar finally honour

Tischendorf for the gift of the codex. Yet, in spite of this fact that he had been, so to speak, elbowed out of the negotiations by Prince Ignatieff, the German scholar was happy to take credit for the whole affair. On 27 May 1869, he wrote to Samuel Davidson from Leipzig a long, hitherto unpublished, self-congratulatory letter:

> Shortly I will write a Mémoire about the final definitive acquisition of the Codex Sinaiticus by the Russian government. The Tsar took this opportunity of raising me to the hereditary Russian nobility — for in 1868 I started the completion of the matter personally in St Petersburg, and in March of *this* year followed the real presentation by the Sinai monastery to the Tsar.

It is fascinating to discover Tischendorf designating 1869 as the date of the 'real' presentation to Alexander II of the precious manuscript which he himself had presumed to present to the Tsar and Tsarina on 19 November 1859.

Tischendorf was delighted with his hereditary honour. It was the equivalent of being knighted in Britain, he explained. He quoted to Davidson the wording of the official citation: 'in recognition of your exceptional services to knowledge in general, and in particular of your successful efforts to enable Russia to possess the oldest manuscript of the Bible'. The appointment was dated 7 May (old style 25 April) 1869. The codex was brought out of the vaults of the ministry of foreign affairs and once again put on exhibition in the Imperial Public Library.

We have evidence of Tischendorf's extreme relief and joy at the successful accomplishment of his work. Towards the end of his life he was visited by an American theologian, Philip Schaff, who was Professor of Biblical Learning at Union Theological Seminary, New York. He described Tischendorf as 'the happiest theologian I ever knew. He never got over the satisfaction and delight of discovering what would immortalize a man of far less learning and merit than Tischendorf.' Professor Schaff expressed the general admiration of Tischendorf. 'His indomitable perseverance in the search and subsequent publication is almost without parallel in the history of literature.' Of the Codex Sinaiticus, Schaff asserted that, 'The monks were ignorant of its very existence. It took a German scholar to find it out and rescue it from probable ruin'.

Yet Schaff found in Tischendorf a man still anxious to justify his behaviour with regard to the codex and the monks of Mount Sinai. Schaff visited him twice, in Leipzig and in Ludwigshafen, and each time Tischendorf recounted his own version of the story. Schaff recalled that, 'Tischendorf said he had recommended the Tsar to give a great deal to the monks, as well as a new costly shrine for St Catherine's bones'. The German scholar showed Schaff two letters from Archbishop Kallistratus, full of flowery compliments, and saying that Codex Sinaiticus was given to the Tsar as a testimony of the monks' eternal devotion.

Philip Schaff also provides evidence of the unhappy effect Tischendorf's behaviour produced among the monks themselves. After his visit to Mount Sinai in 1877, he observed that, 'It is not impossible that patient research in the library may result in some other literary discovery, although of far inferior importance'. He added, 'It would be worthwhile for a Biblical or patristic scholar to spend some weeks in the Convent for the purpose. But their experience with Tischendorf has made the monks very cautious and suspicious'.

In fact, from the beginning many of the monks of Mount Sinai were deeply dissatisfied with the whole affair. They have remained so to this very day. It is perhaps not surprising that one of Tischendorf's rivals, the Russian Uspensky, reported their dissatisfaction as early as

107

1860. The famous German traveller Georg Ebers observed in 1869 that even Kallistratus was annoyed — though this was probably due to the fact that the Russian roubles had not yet arrived!

Irritation continued to rankle. In 1875 Pericles Gregoriades, professor in the theological school of the Holy Sepulchre, Jerusalem, managed to gain access to the library of St Catherine's. He reported that, 'The exploits of Tischendorf seem to have made the monks so suspicious of western scholars, that they have hitherto refused permission to anyone to ransack their shelves, and I therefore felt as if I had accomplished a daring feat this year when at Sinai I persuaded the Archbishop to let me undertake the task'. In 1906 Professor C.R. Gregory of Leipzig visited St Catherine's and came back emptyhanded. This was, perhaps, only right, because he was not only Tischendorf's successor in his professional chair but had also, in successive editions of Codex Sinaiticus, consistently defended his predecessor's behaviour.

Philip Schaff even reported that the monks had begun to deny that the Tsar ever paid them a penny. They said they had refused the money, and (in vain) asked for the return of the codex, which had been loaned and then stolen from them. As we shall see, even now — as a result of Tischendorf's duplicity in 1859 — the monks of Mount Sinai cling with extraordinary tenacity and secrecy to their many remaining treasures.

Constantin von Tischendorf does not disappear from this story. We shall again come across his irascibility, his ruthlessness, and his sheer brilliance. But the disputes of the 1860s were beginning to take their toll of him, as was his colossal enterprise in producing the first publication of the codex in so short a time. He published indefatigably; and until 1869 he suffered the hidden strain of knowing that his negotiations with the monks of Mount Sinai

108

might at any moment result in disaster. On 14 May, 1864, he told his friend Samuel Davidson, 'for the last few days I have been visited by a nervous pain in my temples which has kept me from my work'. Professor Radius, his medical adviser and friend for thirty years, demanded that he rest from all new great works, especially in view of his tremendous effort over so many years. In 1870 he suffered a serious illness from which he did not fully recover for a long time. Then, on 5 May, 1873, 'in the midst of undiminished, happy work' (according to his son-in-law, Ludwig Schneller), he suffered a devastating stroke from which he never fully recovered. He learned to speak and walk again. He tried to write with his left hand. But over a year he made no real improvement. Then he began to suffer stroke after stroke. On 7 December, 1874, he died, aged nearly sixty. He was buried in St John's cemetery in Leipzig.

In his will he had written 'I have aimed above all things at truth. I have bowed to truth throughout, I have never formed my opinion by the applause on my right or my left'. His father had once told him, 'To fight in love for right and truth is more than knowledge'. To Tischendorf himself, perhaps, fighting for religious truth and knowledge became more important than charity or what was morally right.

He summed up his own greatest achievement thus: 'that Providence has given to our age, in which attacks on Christianity are so common, the Sinaitic Bible, to be to us a full and clear light as to what is the real text of God's Word written, and to assist us in defending the truth by establishing its authentic form'. That was a fair summary; but the ultimate authentic truths established by the Sinaitic Bible were to turn out far differently from what Tischendorf himself ever imagined and very far from what he had hoped for.

Meanwhile the Codex continued its wanderings. The Russian Revolution of 1917 led to the execution of the Tsar and his family, and the introduction of an officially atheist regime in Russia. The financial problems of the Soviets led them to release for sale in the west a considerable number of precious manuscripts — so many, in fact, that the flood of hitherto inaccessible volumes was in danger of destroying the western market in rare books.

In 1931 the British antiquarian bookseller Maurice L. Ettinghausen led a deputation of three to Moscow, to persuade the Russian authorities that it was folly to try to sell, say, three or four copies of a first edition of Homer all at once. Ettinghausen made friends with the head of the Russian department for the exchange of books, who happened at that time to be a Hungarian. He was introduced to the Vice-Commissar for Foreign Trade, who had been Quartermaster General of the Red Army. And in the former Imperial Public Library, to one side, on a dusty lectern, he saw a square leather box, with a leather cover lettered 'Codex Sinaiticus Petropolitanus'.

As a joke, Ettinghausen told the Vice-Commissar for Foreign Trade that if he ever needed money, he should tie Sinaiticus up in a brown-paper parcel and send it to Ettinghausen in London. The Vice-Commissar said he had never heard of the manuscript.

Two years later the Hungarian head of the department for the exchange of books was in London. In the autumn of 1933 he came to see Ettinghausen and asked him if Codex Sinaiticus was worth a million pounds. Maurice Ettinghausen replied that he did not know, but if ever the Russians wished to sell the codex, he would be prepared to find a buyer in the west. A few weeks later the Russian cultural attaché in Paris, Comrade Ilyin, informed Ettinghausen that the Soviet government was prepared to sell the codex for £200,000. Ettinghausen immediately informed

110

Sir Frederic Kenyon of the British Museum.

Then the bargaining began for the most precious Bible in the world. On behalf of the British Museum Sir Frederic offered £40,000. Comrade Ilyin lowered his price to £100,000. Consulting the Prime Minister, Ramsay MacDonald, and the Archbishop of Canterbury, as trustees of the Museum, Sir Frederic raised his bid to £60,000, and then agreed to pay £100,000. In December the British Government announced the sale, guaranteeing half the price, provided that the British public would subscribe the other half.

The speed of the transaction was amazing. On 27 December 1933 the manuscript arrived in London by train. The Russian Trade Delegation brought the leaves to Bush House in the Strand. From there Maurice Ettinghausen, two detectives from Vine Street Police Station, and Miss Margaret Lane of the *Daily Express* newspaper, took them by taxi to the British Museum in Bloomsbury. When they arrived Ettinghausen was astonished to see a vast crowd of men and women waiting in the great square outside the Museum's main portals and stretching out into the street. As he got out of the taxi, carrying the great Bible, all the men in the crowd took off their hats.

The manuscript was immediately put on show inside the Museum. Huge crowds came to look at these darkish vellum pages with the unremarkable ink and the remarkable text. 'Never before in the course of its long history', observed the *British Museum Quarterly* of 1934, a trifle superciliously, 'can the British Museum have witnessed an apparently unending stream of visitors waiting patiently to file past a manuscript the austere and unadorned pages of which can be read by very few of those who come to do homage.'

As scholars began to look at the great codices of the Bible, they gave to each of them a letter, for convenience

111

of reference. Codex Alexandrinus in the British Museum is assigned 'A'; Codex Vaticanus in Rome is 'B'; Codex Ephraem in Paris is 'C'; Codex Bezae in Cambridge is 'D'; and so on. Tischendorf could not bear to have his own great codex assigned a letter of the alphabet that came later than these, so he began again with the Hebrew alphabet, and gave to Sinaiticus the first letter, '*Aleph*'. Now Codex Sinaiticus became 'British Museum Additional Manuscript 43725'. But almost all scholars continue to refer to it as '*Aleph*'.

Incredibly, the Russians had sent the manuscript before being paid for it. The British Treasury ordered full payment two weeks after the codex arrived. The government in the end did not need to pay half of the agreed purchase price. The British public subscribed over £53,000.

'There was no country in which the transfer of the Codex to a permanent home in England was not welcomed', wrote Ettinghausen over thirty years later. This was quite untrue. The United States, for one, had been keen to buy the codex, but Britain pipped her at the post. Many in Germany were peeved that the manuscript discovered by one of their greatest *savants* should not have returned to add to their national glory. And the monks of Mount Sinai were exceedingly annoyed.

It is difficult to argue that the Soviets had no right to sell the codex and the British none to buy it. As Caspar René Gregory wrote, the affair of selling it to the Russians had been 'regularly brought to a business-like close'. There is some doubt as to whether all the confraternity of Mount Sinai had ever agreed to the sale; but it is certain that the monks there received 7000 roubles and their fellow-monks in Cairo received 2000. The monks accepted the money and gave receipts which, as late as 1907, were in the hands of the Russian Government.

But many felt it wise to fudge around the shadier aspects of Tischendorf's deal. Gregory mocked unnamed 'envyers' of Tischendorf who were alleged to have suggested that he slipped the codex into his breast-pocket in February 1859 and vanished unseen from the monastery. 'Try to slip into your pocket unseen three hundred and forty-six leaves of parchment which are forty-three centimetres long and thirty-seven centimetres broad', said Gregory bitingly.

He made a further point:

> On the 28th of September 1859 Tischendorf did not take it away from the monks at Cairo by stealth, with or without the necessary and necessarily gigantic breast-pocket. For it was given to him in all due form by the head monk in the presence of the others who were at Cairo, and in the presence of the Russian consul, who of course, made an official minute of the whole proceedings. The monks delivered over the manuscript to Tischendorf in order that he should take it to Leipzig and publish it, and then present it to the Russian emperor in the name of the monks.

Now, as we have seen, this last sentence is simply not true. Gregory, moreover, made out that the monks were extremely pleased, not to say absurdly flattered by the useless honours bestowed upon them by Tsar Alexander II. Decorations, wrote Gregory, 'are valued in the East even more highly than they are in the decoration-loving circles in Western Europe, and the monks received a number of these decorations'. By the time he wrote these words, Gregory had already visited Mount Sinai and come away empty-handed. To insult those who had once possessed the great codex and who refused to let him take away any more of their treasures was entirely congenial to Tischendorf's successor. 'An Eastern monk', he opined, 'thinks he is doing an enormous day's work if within twenty-four hours he does as much as an ordinary European would do in twenty minutes.' If there was any delay in concluding the transfer of the codex to the Tsar, it was chiefly the fault, Gregory alleged, of the monks of Mount Sinai themselves.

Others were less devious than Gregory in judging the rights and wrongs of the transfer of Codex Sinaiticus from St Catherine's monastery to St Petersburg. Even so, in 1933 and afterwards, accounts of the affair, though usually truthful, rarely contain the whole truth. Maurice Ettinghausen recorded that, 'In consideration of a promotion in the Church for the head of the monastery, plus a number of Russian decorations and the sum of 9000 roubles (£1350), Tischendorf was allowed to take the manuscript himself to Russia and place it, on 19 November 1859, in the hands of Tsar Alexander II'. Even today the inscription in the case where Codex Sinaiticus is displayed in the British Library records simply: 'The manuscript was discovered in 1859 by the German Biblical Scholar Constantine Tischendorf in the Greek Monastery of St Katherine on Mount Sinai, and subsequently presented by the monks to the Emperor of Russia'.

The British now treated the manuscript with impressive love and care. In particular, two scholars of the department of manuscripts at the British Museum, H.J.M. Milne and T.C. Skeat, worked brilliantly and indefatigably at examining the codex. They proved, as we shall see, that Tischendorf was correct about the last verse of St John's Gospel and incorrect in supposing that four scribes had originally produced the manuscript.

And it was decided to rebind Codex Sinaiticus. Douglas Cockerell was given the job and concluded it with great skill and considerable taste. He obtained a large number of oak boards and left them for three months — to eliminate any possible twisting — before choosing the ones he needed to bind the precious document. Alum-tawed goatskin was used to cover the boards, and the manuscript

114

was bound in two volumes, with gold lettering on the spine and a fine, simple design to ornament the leather. Thus bound it lies on display today.

CHAPTER V

The Significance of the Codex

In spite of his ruthlessness, no-one has ever doubted that Tischendorf was an incomparable Biblical scholar. As his son-in-law observed, 'The same purpose had inspired other learned men before him: Bengel, Wettstein, Bentley, Lachmann, and others. But what they had commenced with somewhat inadequate means, Tischendorf all but brought to perfection, and far surpassed their work'. I would agree with the introduction of the first English translation of Tischendorf's essay *When were our Gospels written?* that 'As a critic and decipherer of ancient manuscripts he was without a rival, and to his other services in this important department of sacred literature he added one which, alone, would reward the labour of a lifetime, in the discovery of the Sinaitic Manuscript'.

Not content with bringing the codex to the scholarly world, Tischendorf was determined to expound its significance. He believed that he had at last found a witness to the pure, uncorrupted text of Holy Scripture, and above all of the New Testament. The original text of the New Testament Tischendorf was convinced came from the hands of the Apostles themselves. Copied and recopied and multiplied during fifteen centuries, their original words had, he knew, 'in many passages undergone such serious modification of meaning as to leave us in painful uncertainty as to what the Apostles had actually written'. Now, with the discovery and publication of the text of the codex from Mount Sinai, a solution was at hand.

In 1862 therefore Tischendorf brought out not only three folio volumes of the text but also a fourth containing his own commentary on and exposition of the whole. His phenomenal eyesight and his insight into early palaeography enabled him to identify no fewer than four different scribes of the original text, even though their handwriting was extremely similar.

In fact we now believe that only three scribes copied down the original text of the codex. These scribes had taken sheepskin, much scraped and rubbed down and ruled on it with a pointer to keep the lines of their writing straight. Then they had written out the Bible — in many if not all the books by dictation, for two of the three scribes made *phonetic* spelling mistakes. The third scribe, who spelled almost perfectly, wrote most of the New Testament, and some scholars have conjectured that this was copied from a written original, not taken down by dictation. But as this same scribe also wrote — with no spelling mistakes — most of the history and poetic books of the Old Testament, the theory is unproven.

A second scribe, who spelled fairly well, wrote the prophetic books of the Old Testament as well as the *Shepherd of Hermas* in the Codex Sinaiticus. And a third scribe, who spelled atrociously, wrote out Tobit, Judith, the first half of IV Maccabees, the first two-thirds of the Psalms, and six pages of the New Testament (including the first five verses of the Book of Revelation).

From time to time the readers, not the scribes, made errors. At I Maccabees, chapter 5, verse 20, for instance, the text should read that Judas Maccabaeus took 8000 men to the land of Gilead. The reader, not sure of the number, called out 'either six or three thousand'. The scribe wrote down, 'either six or three thousand'.

Codex Sinaiticus lacks much of the Old Testament, and originally must have contained about 790 leaves; 242 of the leaves found by Tischendorf contain parts of the Old Testament. A further 147½ contain the New Testament, as well as the *Letter of Barnabas* and part of the *Shepherd of Hermas*. And herein lies the initial great importance of the codex. Codex Sinaiticus is the only known complete copy of the Greek New Testament in uncial (that is, rounded capital) script.

Secondly, along with Codex Vaticanus, it is one of our two earliest copies of the whole Greek Bible (that is to say, the New Testament in its original Greek and the Old Testament in the Greek translation of the third century BC which the rabbis later condemned as unauthentic Scripture). 'There is no original document of this kind,' Tischendorf declared, 'which can present more valid proofs of its ancient nobility.'

The ancient form of the letters, the fact that no large initial letters thrust out into the edge of the page, the rarity of punctuation, the short titles and subscriptions to the various books are reasons why scholars, beginning with Tischendorf himself, deduced that the codex must be a very early production of the Christian era. But scholars also knew that the codex could not have been written much before the middle of the fourth century AD. A scribe whose handwriting is contemporary with those who wrote the codex added in the margins of the four gospels a series of numbers devised to locate parallel passages of the life of Christ. These numbers were devised by the great theologian Eusebius of Caesarea to refer to a series of tables he drew up (or 'canons', as they are called), listing these parallel gospel passages. Now Eusebius died around the year AD 340. Because his canons are included in Codex Sinaiticus, the manuscript obviously cannot pre-date him.

All these considerations still point to a phenomenally early date for this great Biblical manuscript — perhaps around AD 340.

No-one has yet been able to prove with any certainty *where* Codex Sinaiticus was written. It cannot have been written in St Catherine's monastery, where Tischendorf found it, since the monastery was not built when the manuscript was written. But one plausible and attractive suggestion is that the original home of the manuscript was Caesarea itself. The suggestion is supported by two remarkable errors in Codex Sinaiticus. At Acts chapter 8, verse 5, all other biblical manuscripts tell us that Philip went down to Samaria. The scribe of Codex Sinaiticus, for no good reason at all, wrote that he went down to Caesarea. Again, Matthew chapter 13, verse 54, in all other manuscripts, says that Jesus went 'to his own town'. The scribe of Codex Sinaiticus wrote that he went 'to Antipatris'. Antipatris is a town thirty miles south of Caesarea.

None of this is conclusive proof that Codex Sinaiticus did originate there, and another origin for Codex Sinaiticus has been suggested. When Constantine the Great decided that Christianity could be one of the permitted religions in his empire, he put his authority behind a powerful boost to the spread of that religion. Christianity, like Judaism, is a 'religion of the book', that is, a religion based on sacred scriptures. As we have already seen, in the year 331 Constantine ordered Eusebius of Caesarea to arrange for the production of fifty manuscripts of the Bible, 'written legibly on fine parchment . . . by professional scribes'. Eusebius, who ran a 'Scriptorium' at Constantinople, responded with alacrity to this move by the emperor to preserve and spread the Scriptures. It has

119

been suggested that both Sinaiticus and Vaticanus are two of the codices produced by him on the emperor's orders. Indeed, Tischendorf believed that one of the scribes of Codex Sinaiticus also worked on Vaticanus. And certainly the hands in the two volumes are strikingly similar. But again, no proof has so far been produced of this hypothesis about the origin of the codex.

What we can say, however, is that Codex Sinaiticus is part of that peaceful conquest of the Roman Empire by Christianity in the fourth century AD. It represents the triumph of the codex form over papyrus rolls containing only one or two books of the Bible. It gave a great impetus to those who wished to find connections — real or imaginary — between the Old and New Testaments, especially to those Christians who wished to find prophecies of Jesus's life, death, and resurrection in the Old Testament.

Not surprisingly, others before Tischendorf had devoted themselves to purifying the Biblical text by means of Codex Sinaiticus. And after the codex was written, later correctors laid hands on it and for several centuries made alterations and notes on that text too. As he studied the codex, the eagle-eyed Tischendorf counted 14,800 such corrections made by nine separate correctors.

These correctors had devised conventional signs to indicate what they believed was the true text. For instance, a row of dots alongside part of the text indicated that the corrector believed that section ought to be deleted, because it was not in the original text of the Bible.

Fascinatingly, we can sometimes discover where the corrector's information came from. In that part of the Sinai manuscript which Tischendorf left in Leipzig, a scribe wrote at the end of the Book of Esther the following words:

Collated with an exceedingly ancient copy, which was

corrected by the hand of the holy martyr Pamphilus; and at the end of the same ancient book, which began with the first Book of Kings and ended with Esther, there is some such subscription as this, in the hand of the same martyr: 'Copied and corrected from the *Hexapla* of Origen, corrected by himself. Antoninus the Confessor collated it; I, Pamphilus, corrected the volume in prison through the great favour and enlargement of God; and if it may be said without offence, it is not easy to find a copy comparable to this copy.' The same ancient copy differed from the present volume in respect to certain proper names.

This pedigree is long. The *Hexapla* of Origen had taken that scholar and theologian twenty years to compile. In six columns he had assembled material from the Greek version of the Old Testament. One column contained the Hebrew text, but transliterated into Greek letters. Another contained what Origen himself considered to be the perfect text. This volume became the greatest treasure of the library of Christian books at Caesarea.

Origen finished his *Hexapla* in the year AD 245. Later Antoninus the Confessor worked on it. Then Pamphilus, who was the teacher of Eusebius and an outstanding scholar, corrected Antoninus's work during his imprisonment in the years of persecution. Finally, an unknown scribe used Pamphilus's work to add corrections to the codex from Mount Sinai.

Now the fabulous textual wealth of Codex Sinaiticus was made available to the Christian world in Tischendorf's great edition, which he supplemented shortly before his death by a major two-volume edition of the text of the New Testament. Even today this edition remains an indispensable work of reference for scholars of the Greek text, for Tischendorf presented an amazingly extensive mass of information setting out evidence for and against various readings of the existing manuscripts.

His insights were brilliant — so brilliant that not

everyone was bold enough to accept them. One suggestion made by Tischendorf on the evidence of Codex
Sinaiticus, rejected by many of his contemporaries and
vindicated by later scientific techniques, shows his genius
at its most remarkable.

On the evidence of his eyesight alone, Tischendorf
decided that the last verse of St John's Gospel (John 21,
verse 25) was a later addition to the original text of Codex
Sinaiticus. The verse reads, 'There were many other
things that Jesus did; and if all were written down, the
world itself, I suppose, would not hold all the books that
would have to be written'. Tischendorf claimed that this
verse was written with a greater delicacy than the rest. He
insisted that the shape of the letters was slightly different.
He added that the ink used was a little lighter in colour for
this verse than for the rest. (The scribes re-filled their pens
on average every one-and-a-half lines as they wrote the
Codex Sinaiticus; but Tischendorf said he had never seen
precisely that colour of ink elsewhere in the whole manuscript.)

At the time most scholars disagreed with his judgment
about this verse. But long after his death, twentieth-
century science proved Tischendorf to have been absolutely right. When the Codex Sinaiticus was examined
under ultra-violet light, it was discovered that the Gospel
of John did in fact originally end at chapter 21, verse 24.
After this verse, the scribe added a small tail-piece, and the
words, 'The Gospel according to John'. Later on, another
scribe erased the tail-piece and these words, writing over
them our present verse 25.

As Tischendorf revealed such astounding skill, the
codex remained in Russia, apparently permanently. For
ten years European scholars had been privileged to assess
its importance. Tischendorf resented their 'interference'.
He also bitterly regretted, for example, allowing Tregelles

to see the manuscript when it was in his Leipzig home, especially as Tregelles, on the basis of those few days, ventured to disagree with some of Tischendorf's own conclusions. Tregelles, for instance, claimed there was no difference between the various bits of handwriting in the original manuscript and that therefore only one scribe had worked on it, whereas Tischendorf had detected four different hands. Again, Tregelles refused to accept that John chapter 21, verse 25, was not originally part of Codex Sinaiticus. A sufficient explanation of the difference between that verse and what went before, he thought, was that the scribe had simply taken a fresh dip of ink.

Now Tregelles was a remarkable self-taught scholar. Born in a Quaker family in Falmouth in 1813, he became first a Plymouth Brother and then a Presbyterian. Debarred from university (as were all non-Anglicans in England at that time), he had worked for six years in Neath Abbey Iron Works in Wales. At the age of twenty-five he had decided to devote himself to the study of the text of the Bible. To train himself he had spent five months in Rome in 1844, studying the Codex Vaticanus. (The Vatican authorities, in their customary fashion at that time, would not allow him to transcribe a single word of the document, though Tregelles occasionally made notes on his finger nails.) He soon became a formidable scholar. The University of St Andrews gave him an honorary degree of Doctor of Laws. The government gave him an annual civil list pension of £100 in 1862 and doubled this in 1870. He died in 1875.

Tischendorf responded to Tregelles's views on the Codex Sinaiticus with an astonishing viciousness. In reviews and published works he attacked the British scholar's conclusions. But it is his private letters to Samuel Davidson that reveal the passionate nature of the disagree-

123

ment between these two men of God. In their differences, Tischendorf wrote, 'it is simply impossible for me to be wrong'.

It seemed as if, having brought the Codex Sinaiticus to the notice of scholarship, Tischendorf now regarded it as his own private possession. He was obliged to write to Tregelles about the codex, but he told Davidson 'I fortunately didn't give anything away'. And because he had so generously allowed Tregelles to examine the manuscript, he was mortified when the British scholar presumed to disagree with Tischendorf's own views about it.

Tregelles, he said, had been 'naïve and malicious' enough to regard the last verse of St John's Gospel as originally part of the Codex Sinaiticus even though Tischendorf declared it was not. 'It took even me a long time to see that the closing sentence was in another hand', wrote Tischendorf. But, he went on, after he had convinced himself of the true state of affairs and clearly demonstrated it for everyone else to see, it was 'laughable' for Tregelles to seek to impress on people a different point of view. If Tregelles tried to pursue the matter further, he declared, 'it will come down about his head, as he deserves'. After all, he complained, Tregelles had spent no more than 'four or five days in my house — most of the time collating the Catholic Epistles' (that is, the two New Testament letters attributed to St Peter, the three attributed to St John, and the letter of St Jude).

Tischendorf did not think Tregelles fit to determine the true text even of those parts of the codex that he had examined. When his edition of the Catholic Epistles was published, Tischendorf wrote to Samuel Davidson, 'You will have perfectly seen how much Tregelles disgraced himself in his discoveries in the Catholic Epistles. Every single correction is nothing more than a sin of haste on his part'.

124

Tischendorf was perhaps all the more hostile to Tregelles because deep down he suspected that the scholarship of his rival approached his own heights. (As Professor Owen Chadwick observed in his history of the Victorian church, 'European scholarship came to think the works of Tregelles almost as important as the discoveries of Tischendorf'.) But *anyone* who studied in Tischendorf's field, whether Old Testament or New Testament, was liable to come under the German's lash. When a scholar called Lagarde published an edition of the book of Genesis, Tischendorf described the unfortunate man as 'a most impudent and imprudent person'. In this book, wrote Tischendorf, Lagarde 'allowed himself to be really impertinent towards me, for which I will cane him according to his deserts'.

What were these godly men so viciously fighting about? It was the attempt to establish the very words of God himself — spoken, they believed, to the men and women of the Old Testament, spoken directly through Jesus, and spoken through Jesus's followers under the influence of the Holy Spirit. By discovering and transcribing the Codex Sinaiticus from St Catherine's monastery Tischendorf believed he was dissolving the mists of centuries and revealing these words afresh. Small wonder that he considered his gifts to Christianity incomparable. Of Tregelles he wrote, 'What cut off in the strongest way my Plymouth rival's justification for competing with me are the extraordinary enrichments of textual knowledge which the Lord imparted to Christian scholarship through me'.

Tischendorf's achievement in presenting Codex Sinaiticus to the scholarly world did not satisfy him. He wanted to uncover the secrets of Codex Vaticanus too. The Vatican's reluctance to let anyone see it was no match for the determination and ruthlessness that had enabled

Tischendorf to rob the monks of Mount Sinai of their most precious possession.

In 1866 he paid a visit to Rome with the intention of making a definitive edition of the text of Codex Vaticanus. Earlier in his career, during the reign of Pope Gregory XVI, Cardinal Mai had frustrated his attempt to make a thorough study of the manuscript. Now Pope Pius IX put obstacles in his path. There was, he asserted, no need for Tischendorf to examine Codex Vaticanus, for Roman Catholic scholars were already engaged in a definitive edition of the document.

Tischendorf, however, managed to obtain permission to consult such parts of ancient manuscript as might bear on passages of special interest or difficulty in Holy Scripture. Once inside the Vatican, he instantly started to copy out the whole codex. After eight days he was discovered. By now he had copied nineteen pages of the New Testament and ten of the Old. For this flagrant breach of his agreement, Tischendorf's permission to see Codex Vaticanus was withdrawn. With his customary resourcefulness under difficulty, he now persuaded Carlo Vercellone, the Roman Catholic scholar who was actually preparing the official edition of Codex Vaticanus, to let him examine the manuscript for a further six days. This enabled Tischendorf to bring out his own edition the following year, anteceding Vercellone's. When the Roman Catholic edition appeared in 1868, Tischendorf savaged it in reviews. When the Roman Catholics protested, Tischendorf replied in a pamphlet entitled *Responsa ad Calumnias Romanas* (A Reply to Roman Lies).

The Catholic scholarly world was naturally enough disturbed to be so much at odds with the leading Protestant expert on the text of the Bible. In May 1869 the head of the Vatican Library, Cardinal Petre, urgently begged Tischendorf to 'disarm'. Tischendorf was not ready to do so. He told his friend Samuel Davidson that 'first of all the Romans must start behaving decently'.

Some later scholars have gone so far as to maintain that Tischendorf's publication in 1867 of Codex Vaticanus was as much of a 'discovery' as that of Codex Sinaiticus, because Vaticanus had remained virtually inaccessible in Rome for 400 years. But Tischendorf continued to favour Codex Sinaiticus as the greatest of all Biblical treasures.

His faith in this codex was shared by others. In Britain the Authorized Version of 1611 still captivated many, even those who suspected its inaccuracies. Right or wrong, it had become a sacred text.

> Throw no shadow on the sacred page,
> Whose faults, if faults, are sanctified by age,

wrote John Ruskin. The Authorized Version had enshrined sacred Scripture in a language of unique beauty and force. But scholars and serious churchmen were now well aware that it was inaccurate. Even so, when the authorities in the Church of England agreed to a revision, they decreed that the new translation must 'introduce as few alterations as possible . . . consistently with faithfulness'. Nonetheless, this project gave an urgency to the study of the Greek New Testament, and in particular to the work of two great Cambridge scholars, Brooke Foss Westcott (who later became Bishop of Durham) and Fenton John Anthony Hort.

Westcott and Hort were learned, solid, conservative, brilliant scholars. They were willing to spend hours in the drudgery of collating texts, poring over dictionaries of ancient languages and scouring early manuscripts. Some, therefore, found them dull. According to one story, there was a dense fog once in London which, the Dean of St Paul's remarked, 'is commonly attributed to Dr Westcott having opened his study window in Westminster'. But Westcott and Hort, though no radicals in their conclusions, were willing to ask new questions. 'I would give a man a degree', Westcott once told a group of Cambridge dons, 'for asking twelve good questions.' In short, Westcott was a thoroughly conservative scholar who was not afraid of looking at radical problems. His temperament was matched by that of his fellow-scholar Hort.

When Westcott became Bishop of Durham the *Durham University Journal* described him in words that could equally have applied to his colleague Hort, as 'Before all things a Biblical student, bringing to the text of the Bible all the habits and resources of most accurate linguistic scholarship, along with a reverential affection to which no detail, however slight, was insignificant; unsurpassed in his command of all the statistics of text and matter, yet never mastered by them, never mechanical nor dry; . . . . free from all verbal or mechanical ideas of inspiration, yet treating every syllable of Scripture with a reverent care which no maintainer of verbal inspiration could excel'.

And these two men revered Codex Sinaiticus. Alongside Codex Vaticanus, it was the basis of their great Greek text which undergirded the nineteenth-century revision of the English Bible. They believed that the combined witness of Vaticanus and Sinaiticus 'should be accepted as true readings until strong internal evidence is found to the contrary'. They insisted that no readings based on these two great manuscripts 'can be safely rejected absolutely, though it is sometimes right to place them only on an alternative footing'.

Not everyone agreed with these two Cambridge professors of divinity; but those who disagreed were chiefly slightly bizarre. (More than *slightly* bizarre was Dean J.W. Burgon of Chichester, who described Sinaiticus and Vaticanus as being among '*the most scandalously* corrupt copies extant'.) As Caspar René Gregory justly observed of Codex Sinaiticus, 'Many scholars have felt it necessary to decry the text of this manuscript. That is wrong. Tischendorf may well have rated his great find a trifle too high. He would have been more than human if under the circumstances he had not done it, seeing that he for three years ate, drank, and slept this manuscript. Had he lived, he would surely here and there have modified his predilection for its readings. But it is, nevertheless a very exceptional manuscript'.

As witness to the authentic words of Holy Scripture Westcott and Hort marginally preferred Codex Vaticanus over Sinaiticus. But here, too, Caspar René Gregory had some astute words of comment. 'It used to be the fashion to say that the Sinaitic manuscript was very badly written, was full of clerical errors, and therefore less trustworthy. And the Vatican manuscript was supposed to be very correctly written. When, however, the Vatican copy came to be better known, it was found that in this respect there was not much choice between the two.'

What really outraged men like Dean Burgon was principally that, however learnedly Codex Sinaiticus was edited, it revealed a text of the Bible that again and again differed from what they had revered and loved as Holy Writ. Take, for example, the Lord's Prayer. Generations of Englishmen had been accustomed to the version, in Luke chapter 11, verses 2 to 4:

> Our Father which art in heaven,
> Hallowed be thy name.
> Thy kingdom come,
> Thy will be done, as in heaven, so in earth.
> Give us day by day our daily bread.
> And forgive us our sins; for we also forgive every one
> that is indebted to us.
> And lead us not into temptation; but deliver us from
> evil.

They learned to accept this as an alternative to the more familiar version in Matthew chapter 6, verses 9 to 13.

Now they were presented with an even more truncated version. The Lord's Prayer of Codex Sinaiticus reads simply:

Father, Hallowed be thy name,
Thy kindgdom come.
Thy will be done, as in heaven, so upon earth.
Give us day by day our daily bread.
And forgive us our sins, as we ourselves also forgive
every one that is indebted to us.
And bring us not into temptation.

Codex Vaticanus even omitted the words, 'Thy will be done, as in heaven, so on earth'. For generations, it would seem, men and women had repeated spurious words, fondly believing that they came from the lips of Jesus himself. Moreover, even the more familiar version in Matthew was suspect. The Matthean ending to the Lord's prayer, 'For thine is the kingdom, and the power, and the glory, for ever. Amen', likewise was absent from Vaticanus and Sinaiticus.

Some well-loved stories also disappeared in the text so carefully and long preserved on Mount Sinai. The eighth chapter of St John's Gospel, in the received text, contains the story of a woman who had been caught committing adultery. The scribes and the Pharisees wish to stone her to death, following, as they say, the law of Moses. Jesus says, 'He that is without sin among you, let him first cast a stone at her'. One by one the woman's accusers slip away, until she and Jesus are alone together. Then he asks her, 'Where are your accusers? Has no-one condemned you?' She answers, 'No-one, my Lord'. Jesus responds, 'Neither do I condemn you. Go, and sin no more.'

We now know that some ancient manuscripts transfer this story elsewhere in the New Testament, to the Gospel of Luke. In some manuscripts the scribes have indicated that they doubt its authenticity. *It nowhere appears in either Vaticanus or Sinaiticus.*

The evidence of the manuscript from Mount Sinai was proving more and more difficult to digest. In the received text, Luke chapter 24, verse 51, tells how Jesus left his disciples after his resurrection. He blessed them, was parted from them, 'and was carried up into heaven'. Sinaiticus omits the final clause. As the textual critic C.S.C. Williams observed, if this omission is correct, 'there is no reference at all to the Ascension in the original text of the Gospels'.

Persistently and disturbingly, the codex from Mount Sinai omits cherished sentences of Holy Scripture. In Matthew chapter 17, the disciples of Jesus fail to cast out a devil from an epileptic. Verse 21 in the received text gives Jesus's explanation that such a healing requires much prayer and fasting. Codex Sinaiticus omits the explanation. Again, the received text of Mark's gospel begins with the words, 'The beginning of the Gospel of Jesus Christ, the Son of God'. Codex Sinaiticus omits 'the Son of God'. In Luke's Gospel, the received text of chapter eleven contains the following words, attributed to Jesus: 'You know not what manner of spirit you are of. For the son of man is come not to destroy men's lives, but to save them'. Neither sentence occurs in Codex Sinaiticus.

As if this were not enough to shock those schooled on older versions of the gospels, Codex Sinaiticus even minimizes some of the punishments in store for the wicked, according to the traditional texts. St Mark's Gospel, chapter 9, for instance, describes hell as a place 'where the worm dies not, and the fire is not quenched' (a description taken from the last verse of the Old Testament prophet, Isaiah). Codex Sinaiticus omits the words.

Scholars like Tischendorf, Westcott, and Hort were not, however, daunted by what they found. All three, and many like them, had sufficient faith that what they were doing ultimately would uncover divine truth. Even so, they made assumptions about the transmission of the text of Holy Scripture which Codex Sinaiticus ought to have led them to abandon.

One was that all scribes and theologians had been as scrupulously honest about the text as they were. Tischendorf, Westcott, and Hort believed that the alterations in the Biblical witness had all occurred accidentally. Scribes had misread words, perhaps. Or they had misheard them. Occasionally they would have mistranslated from the Hebrew. They might have subsconsciously harmonized differences between the gospels. But they would never have deliberately altered anything in Holy Writ. Tischendorf found it difficult to understand 'how scribes could allow themselves to bring in here and there changes, which were not simply verbal ones, but materially affected the meaning' of a passage. He did not understand, he wrote, why they 'did not shrink from cutting out a passage or inserting one'. In short, he felt they surely must have had the same reverence for the original words of the Scripture as he had.

Westcott and Hort were equally adamant that all alterations must have happened by accident, not by design. In their introduction to their edition of *The New Testament in the Original Greek*, they wrote, 'It will not be out of place to add here a distinct expression of our belief that even among the numerous unquestionably spurious readings of the New Testament there are no signs of deliberate falsifications of the text for dogmatic purposes'.

Codex Sinaiticus could have proved them wrong, not so much because its own text has been corrupted in this way, as because it contains many texts which later scribes were theologically motivated to delete or change.

For example, in the first chapter of Mark's Gospel we are told of a leper who says to Jesus, 'If you will, you can make me clean'. Codex Sinaiticus continues, Jesus, 'angry, stretched out his hand and touched him, and said, "I will; be clean" '. Later manuscripts, perceiving that to attribute anger to Jesus at this point made him appear, perhaps, too human, alter the word 'angry' to 'moved with compassion'.

In Matthew's Gospel Codex Sinaiticus contains another suggestion about Jesus which conflicted with the theological views of later Christians and was therefore suppressed. Speaking (in Matthew chapter 24) of the day of judgment, Jesus, according to Codex Sinaiticus, observes that 'of that day and hour knoweth no-one, not even the angels of heaven, neither the Son, but the Father only.'

Other ancient manuscripts also contain the words 'neither the Son'. But the suggestion here that Jesus might not be on the same level of knowledge as God was unacceptable to later generations of Christians, and the phrase was suppressed.

At this point even Hort was momentarily tempted to suspect a theologically motivated suppression, admitting that the omission of these words 'neither the Son' can indeed be explained 'by the doctrinal difficulty which they seem to contain'.

Even more strikingly, because Codex Sinaiticus was worked over by correctors long after it was first written, one can actually see this process of alteration for doctrinal reasons at work. Two examples make this abundantly clear. In both cases later correctors have objected to the text as preserved by the great codex. The first example concerns Jesus praying on the Mount of Olives.

According to the text of Codex Sinaiticus, St Luke's Gospel records that 'there appeared unto him an angel from heaven, strengthening him. And being in agony, he prayed more earnestly; and his sweat became as it were great drops of blood falling down upon the ground'. This text, with its suggestion that Jesus needed the support of an angel, and that before his arrest and trial he was in agony, is not to be found in the Vatican codex. Codex Sinaiticus clearly shows that the debate about them affected later scribes. One of them has placed dots beside the text, indicating that it ought to be deleted. A yet later scribe has carefully tried to erase these dots.

Equally revealing is the way the correctors of Codex Sinaiticus dealt with words attributed to Jesus on the Cross by St Luke's Gospel. Jesus's prayer, 'Father, forgive them, for they know not what they do', is deleted by a corrector. J. Rendel Harris believed that the text was deliberately cut out by those Christians who believed God could never have forgiven the Jews for the death of Jesus. Had not the destruction of Jerusalem shown this? Here, on the other hand, Hort still maintained that the text had disappeared for entirely innocent and accidental reasons. 'Wilful excision on account of the love and forgiveness shown to the Lord's own murderers', he wrote, 'is absolutely incredible.'

Rendell Harris, writing in the first decades of this century, believed that Hort had been quite wrong about the probity of earlier Christians when it came to transmitting texts. 'To Hort the scribes were all angels, as far as theology was concerned', he wrote. Rendell Harris believed that Hort's great authority in these matters had actually set back a proper understanding of the way we have inherited our text of the Bible. 'If he said that there were no dogmatic falsifications (though the text is actually reeking with them)', Rendell Harris observed with some sharpness, then other scholars judged that 'there was no need to pursue the subject further.'

It must not be supposed from these examples that Codex Sinaiticus invariably supports an 'unorthodox' view of Jesus. On the contrary. In the genealogy of Jesus given by St Matthew, for instance, Codex Sinaiticus is (unlike some other manuscripts) one that carefully supports the doctrine of the virgin birth of Jesus, ending the list of his ancestors with the words, 'Jacob begat Joseph, the husband of Mary of whom was born Jesus, who is called Christ'.

Often, too, the additions to the text which are found in later documents but *not* in Sinaiticus are merely harmless, and indeed sometimes positively useful additions. Two such examples may be cited from St John's Gospel. In chapter 4 a woman of Samaria is asked by Jesus for a drink. She answers 'How do you, a Jew, ask a drink from me, a woman of Samaria?' Later scribes add an explanation to the original authentic text: 'for the Jews have no dealings with the Samaritans'.

Similarly in chapter 5 of John's Gospel, Jesus comes across a great many sick persons lying by a pool. A later scribe has added an explanation not found in Codex Sinaiticus: 'for an angel went down at a certain season into the pool and troubled the water: whosoever then first after the troubling of the water stepped in was made whole of whatever disease he had'.

One of the most delightful, and innocuous later changes to the text as preserved by Codex Sinaiticus, concerns the parable of the prodigal son, which is recorded in Luke's Gospel in chapter 15. In this parable, Jesus tells of a young man who persuades his father to give him his inheritance early, and then goes away and wastes it all. Starving, looking after pigs for a living, the young man repents. He decides to return home and say to his father, 'I have sinned against heaven and in your sight. I am no more worthy to be called your son. Make me like one of your hired servants'. And, in Codex Sinaiticus, he does precisely this. He finds, however, that his father has long looked out for him and welcomes him, as if he were returned from the dead, as a beloved son.

Now the delightful change in later manuscripts is that the son, himself so unexpectedly welcomed by his father, prudently omits to offer himself as a hired servant!

Yet in the end all the textual changes discovered as a result of the heroic labours of Tischendorf and his fellow scholars remained disturbing. And in one point twentieth-century theologians have found the witness of Codex Sinaiticus extremely disturbing indeed. The issue concerns the central doctrine of the Christian faith itself: the resurrection of Jesus Christ.

CHAPTER VI

The Resurrection of Jesus

Tischendorf had hoped to find a manuscript of the New Testament which would, as he wrote, 'approach very nearly to the original text as it came from the hands of the Apostles'. Now, he claimed, 'such a manuscript is before us in the Sinaitic copy' of the Scriptures. Destructive theologians like Strauss and romanticists like Renan could no longer destroy the faith of others. 'He who has made shipwreck of his own faith and who lives only after the flesh, cannot endure to see others trusting their Saviour', Tischendorf proclaimed scornfully. 'Do not, then, let yourself be disturbed by their clamour, but rather hold that you have, the more firmly because others assail it.'

But here arose an extraordinary paradox. The Codex Sinaiticus, the manuscript which in Tischendorf's view approached most nearly to the text of the Gospels as they were originally written, revealed an extraordinary omission. According to Sinaiticus, the Gospel according to Mark, unlike the other three Gospels, contains no account of the appearance of Jesus to his disciples after his resurrection.

According to Mark, chapter 16, three women — Mary of Magdala, Mary the mother of James the disciple, and

Salome — bring oils to anoint the dead body of Jesus as it lies in his tomb. A huge stone had been placed over the entrance to this tomb, and the three women wonder who will roll it away for them. They are astonished to find it already rolled away. Entering the tomb, they see a youth wearing a white robe sitting on the right-hand side. They are dumbfounded, but the youth says 'Fear nothing'. He tells them that Jesus of Nazareth, who was crucified, is not there, because he has risen.

Then the youth gives the three women a message for Jesus' disciples: 'He will go before you into Galilee and you will see him there, as he told you.' But, oddly enough, the women do not hand over this message. According to St Mark's Gospel, as contained in Codex Sinaiticus, 'they went out and ran away from the tomb, beside themselves with terror. They said nothing to anybody, for they were afraid'.

There, according to Codex Sinaiticus, the Gospel of Mark comes to an end. It does not so end, of course, in the Authorized Version of the English Bible, nor in the received text of any of the orthodox Christian churches. Their versions all continued with a further twelve verses:

> Now when he was risen early on the first day of the week, he appeared first to Mary Magdalene, from whom he had cast out seven devils. She went and told them that had been with him, as they mourned and wept. And they, when they heard he was alive, and had been seen by her, disbelieved.
>
> And after these things he was manifested in another form to two of them, as they walked, on their way into the country. And they went away and told it unto the rest: but they did not believe them either.
>
> And afterwards he was manifested unto the eleven themselves, as they sat at meat; and he upbraided them with their unbelief and hardness of heart, because they did not believe those who had seen him after he was risen.
>
> And he said to them, 'Go into all the world, and preach

the gospel to the whole creation. He that believes and is baptized will be saved; but he that disbelieves shall be condemned. And these signs shall follow those who believe: in my name they will cast out devils; they shall speak with new tongues; they shall pick up serpents, and if they drink any deadly thing it shall in no way hurt them; they shall lay hands on the sick, and they shall recover.'

So then the Lord Jesus, after he had spoken to them, was received up into heaven, and sat down at the right hand of God. And they went forth and preached everywhere, the Lord working with them, and confirming the word by the signs that followed. Amen.

Now if the text of Codex Sinaiticus truly represents what came from the hand of the person who wrote this Gospel, these twelve verses, Mark 16, verses 9 to 20, are as spurious as the text of the three heavenly witnesses exposed by Richard Porson. Far from defending the traditional gospel story, Tischendorf's great discovery had exposed a yet more alarming addition to the original text.

The scribe who brought Mark's Gospel to an end in Codex Sinaiticus had no doubt that it finished at chapter 16, verse 8. He underlined the text with a fine artistic squiggle, and wrote, 'The Gospel according to Mark'. Immediately following begins the Gospel of Luke.

Tischendorf was far too good a scholar to alter any of this, in presenting Codex Sinaiticus to the world. His great edition of the Greek New Testament according to the codex (*Novum Testamentum Sinaiticum*, published by F.A. Brockhaus of Leipzig in 1863) faithfully ends the gospel with the words 'for they were afraid'. But to Tischendorf this discovery was nothing like so great a problem as it would become for later scholars and believers. Principally this was because Tischendorf did not believe that Mark was the most important Gospel writer. St Mark, in Tischendorf's opinion, was not an eyewitness of what he set down but a friend of eyewitnesses. His

Gospel, though important, was therefore secondary to the witness of those evangelists who had been eyewitnesses, namely Matthew and John.

Tischendorf followed the tradition dating back to the early church that Matthew wrote the first of the Gospels (hence its position in the whole Bible, before the other three). Clement of Alexandria, who lived around the year AD 200, says that the earliest gospels are those that give Jesus' family tree, and there is no family tree in Mark. Origen, writing in Alexandria in the third century AD, said that the first gospel was written, in Hebrew, by Matthew. St Augustine, writing in Africa around the year AD 400, asserted that Matthew wrote first, in Hebrew, and that Mark copied him, in Greek.

So long as Matthew was seen as prior to Mark — so that Mark's gospel appeared to be no more than an abbreviation of his more important predecessor — the apparent lack of any appearance of the risen Jesus in Codex Sinaiticus was regarded as some kind of accident. Scholars presumed that Mark knew of the resurrection appearances recorded in Matthew.

But slowly, by brilliant detective work, scholars became convinced that the earliest Gospel was almost certainly Mark. No-one quite knew how to assign a precise date to John's Gospel; but of Matthew, Mark and Luke it gradually became clear that Mark was written first.

Tischendorf's revered predecessor Karl Lachmann had already advanced one of the decisive arguments for saying that Mark wrote first. In 1835 he examined the order of events in all three gospels. He discovered that the order is the same only when Matthew and Luke agree with the order of Mark. When either Matthew or Luke disagrees with Mark, they disagree with each other too. Matthew and Luke, although they diverge from Mark's order, never agree with each other against Mark. In short,

Mark's order is basic to the other two. Mark's order is always supported either by Luke or Matthew — Luke in the first part, Matthew in the second. And where Luke and Matthew agree with each other in the sequence of events, this agreement begins and ends with the pattern of events in Mark.

To this powerful demonstration that Matthew and Luke used and copied Mark, other scholars added further proofs. The two later Gospels often use the exact language of Mark — even amounting to little or insignificant verbal parallels. Fifty-nine per cent of Matthew's language repeats Mark's words. Fifty-five per cent of Luke's language is likewise derived from Mark (a percentage rising to sixty-nine when Luke is quoting the actual words of Jesus). Again, the content of Mark's Gospel is almost entirely duplicated in the other two. Of Mark's 661 verses, 610 are paralleled in either Matthew or Luke, or both of them. Mark's Gospel can be divided up into eighty-eight separate paragraphs. Only three of these are not to be found in the other two Gospels.

Sometimes the words and constructions used by the writers of the three first Gospels tally to such an extent that it becomes impossible to maintain that they could have been written independently of each other. Rare words occur in precisely the same context in all three. Sometimes an odd construction is also repeated, even though its sense is far from clear. For example, in Mark chapter 2, verses 10 and 11, Jesus appears to start talking to the scribes and then breaks off in mid-sentence to address a paralysed man. This same oddity appears in Matthew and Luke.

Now so long as it was assumed that Mark was the copyist rather than Matthew or Luke, the status of these two evangelists as reporting eye-witness testimony of the events they describe was not necessarily in doubt. But

141

once scholars began to assume that Matthew and Luke had themselves been dependent on Mark, the notion that their Gospels are based on the evidence of Jesus' actual disciples became harder to maintain. If St Matthew had been an eye-witness of the ministry of Jesus, why should he copy from someone like Mark, who was not? It would not be surprising for a later follower of the Christian way of life to abbreviate the Gospel of a disciple (as St Augustine believed Mark abbreviated Matthew). But would a disciple have any need to copy from a later follower?

In any case, Augustine's suggestion does not stand up to analysis. For the story in Mark is almost always *more* detailed than that in Matthew. For instance, when Mark describes how Jesus fed 5000 persons, he uses 194 words, whereas Matthew uses 157. This is scarcely abbreviation. It is Matthew who abbreviates, not Mark. And sometimes, as he abbreviates Mark, we can see Matthew making mistakes.

Here lies one of the most powerful arguments for the priority of Mark. Sometimes Matthew even gets a story wrong while incidentally revealing that he is basing his account on the true facts — as recounted by Mark. One of the most striking examples of this is to be found in the way both evangelists tell the story of the murder of John the Baptist.

Mark's version of the story is fairly complicated and also filled with the kind of mixed motives that lead weak rulers to make tragic mistakes. In this case the weak ruler is the tetrarch Herod. Herod had married the wife of his brother Philip, whose name was Herodias. John the Baptist condemned the marriage as unlawful. Mark tells us that Herod feared John, knowing him to be a righteous and holy man, and therefore kept him safe. When he heard John, he was much perplexed; yet, says Mark, he heard him gladly. John the Baptist's enemy was Herodias, and she forced her husband to have him executed, even though, as Mark tells us, Herod 'was exceedingly sorry'.

This famous story is recounted in Mark, chapter 6, verses 17 to 29. Matthew tells the same story in chapter 14, verses 3 to 12. As elsewhere, his narrative is shorter than Mark's. And he makes Herod an enemy of John the Baptist from the start. Herod, Matthew alleges, wanted to put John to death, but held back for fear of the people who looked on the Baptist as a prophet.

Herodias' plot against John, involving the dancing of her daughter who claimed as her reward the head of John the Baptist on a platter, ought to have pleased the tetrarch. But at this point Matthew slips up. Herodias' daughter dances; she publicly claims her reward; then, says Matthew (reverting to Mark's story), Herod was sorry; but because he did not wish to be humiliated before his guests, he sent and had John the Baptist beheaded in prison.

Matthew, setting out to produce a more elegant version of Mark's story, ends up with a blunder, an inconsistency. And this happens often enough. Moreover, throughout their gospels Matthew and Luke can be seen to be refining Mark's style. Summing up the whole discussion in 1924, the British scholar B.H. Streeter declared that 'the primitive character of Mark is shown by (a) the use of phrases likely to cause offence which are omitted or toned down in the other Gospels; (b) roughness of style and grammar, and the preservation of Aramaic words'.

Among other elements of Mark's Gospel toned down by Matthew and Luke are his criticisms of the disciples of Jesus. We can even see that Mark was willing to write down episodes and remarks that might cast doubt on some of the claims made for Jesus himself, in a way that his fellow evangelists later rejected. An example occurs in chapter 10 of Mark's gospel. A stranger runs up to Jesus and, kneeling before him, asks, 'Good Master, what must I do to win eternal life'. Mark says that Jesus replied, 'Why do you call me good? No-one is good except God alone'. Matthew, recounting the same story, was clearly anxious in case Jesus' reply suggested that he was not himself also the sinless Son of God. So Matthew chapter 19, verse 17, alters Jesus' reply to 'Why do you ask me about what is good?' Here the evangelist is clearly correcting Mark's account, for theologically motivated reasons. It is quite inconceivable that Mark could have altered Matthew's version, the other way.

The fact seems to be (in John Fenton's words) 'that the three later evangelists found [the Gospel of] Mark unsatisfactory in some respects and tried to replace it with books that would be more acceptable to the readership for which they wrote'. One example Fenton points to is the way they carefully modified any implied criticism of Jesus' mother in Mark. Mark recounts that Jesus' family set out to arrest him, assuming him to be mad. The story is dropped by the later evangelists. 'Mark's theology', John Fenton observes,

> might be described as a negative and existential. The good news is not that the disciples have been made wise or strong; not that they were or are saints — neither Peter, nor James, nor Mary his mother; it is not that Jesus healed people, or that there is any present glory. It is strictly good news of *God*, not of men; just as the Son does not know the day or the hour, so he does not know in the end that what is happening to him is God's will. God will send the Son of Man to gather the elect; if he had not shortened the time no human being would be saved. Wait for him, and endure the coming tribulation, without the comfort of examples of faith for support.

Once we assume that Mark was written first and used by at least two of the other evangelists, we are forced to ask whether or not they, so to speak, watered down what he had to preach. John Fenton makes no bones about this. Mark's theology, he asserts, 'was too stark and rigorous for the Church, and the revisions that were made by Matthew, Luke and John were adaptations to meet the weakness of human nature'.

If the later evangelists found Mark's treatment of Jesus' mother and the disciples too negative for them to reproduce, they must have felt even more strongly impelled literally to 'flesh out' his teaching about the resurrection of Jesus. Everywhere in his Gospel Mark presupposes that Jesus is alive. But unlike the other evangelists, he did not feel the need to depict him walking about or eating and drinking after his crucifixion. Not only do Matthew, Luke, and John feel this need. Other Christians decided to supplement the harsh ending of Mark himself. The extra twelve verses we have already quoted were probably added by a presbyter named Aristion in the second century. They were known to the early church father Irenaeus, and probably also to Justin Martyr, who lived in the first half of that century.

But they clearly did not find favour everywhere. It is fascinating to find the early church providing other spurious endings to the text of Mark's Gospel as we know it from Codex Sinaiticus. So from the fourth century onwards, some manuscripts offered a shorter conclusion:

> But they [the three women] briefly reported to those in the company of Peter all that they had been told. And after this Jesus himself appeared to them, and sent out by means of them, from the east to the west, the holy and imperishable message of eternal salvation.

St Jerome also tells us of another addition to the tradition. After verse 14 in the longer spurious ending to Mark, some texts added the words:

> And they excused themselves, saying 'This age of lawlessness and unbelief is under Satan, who does not allow the

145

truth and power of God to prevail over the unclean things of the spirits. Therefore reveal your righteousness now.' Thus they spoke to Christ. And Christ replied to them, 'The term of years of Satan's power has been fulfilled, but other terrible things draw near. And I was delivered over unto death for those who have sinned, so that they may return to the truth and sin no more, in order that they might inherit the spiritual and incorruptible glory of righteousness which is in heaven'.

One revealing feature of this spurious passage is that some of its phrases occur nowhere else in the New Testament, let alone in Mark who is alleged to have written it down. And here, as well as in the shorter spurious ending to Mark, occur words nowhere else used by the evangelist in his Gospel. Although the passage quoted by St Jerome also occurs in a manuscript of the New Testament now known as Codex Washingtonianus, it is certain that neither this, nor the longer and shorter attempts to provide an ending for Mark after chapter 16, verse 8, are authentic. The ending of the oldest of our canonical gospels remains that discovered by Tischendorf on Mount Sinai in 1859.

Yet scholars continued to resist this frightening conclusion. Quite apart from minimizing its impact by continuing to defend Matthew and Luke as older than Mark's Gospel, they believed they had a cast-iron reason for supposing that no book could end in the way Codex Sinaiticus ends Mark.

Mark ended, they contended, half-way through a sentence. The Greek words with which Codex Sinaiticus concludes Mark's Gospel are *ephobounto gar*, 'for they were afraid'. Codex Sinaiticus prints them:

ephoboun

to gar.

Now this is certainly an odd kind of sentence in Greek.

And its oddness persuaded many scholars that the evidence of Codex Sinaiticus was wrong. No Greek sentence was ever written, they asserted, with such an ending. So B.F. Westcott and F.J.A. Hort, in their brilliant edition of the Greek New Testament, although they accept the greatness of Tischendorf's manuscript, nevertheless do not put a full stop at the end of *gar*, but indicate that they believed that the original manuscript of Mark's Gospel continued the sentence. 'It is incredible that the evangelist deliberately concluded . . . a paragraph with *ephobounto gar*,' wrote Hort. In 1896 J.C. Du Buisson asserted emphatically, 'No writer of Greek would have ended a paragraph with the words *ephobounto gar*; no historian would have concluded his work with a minute detail of an unimportant incident; no Evangelist would have closed the joyful account of the Resurrection with words which strike a note of unmitigated fear.' Professor F.C. Burkitt added his voice to the rest. 'Not only the narrative, the paragraph, the sentence, are each left incomplete, but even the subordinate clause seems to hang in the air', he wrote, adding, 'In no case would the Gospel have originally ended with *ephobounto gar*.'

It is indeed unusual to find Greek clauses or sentences, let alone paragraphs, ending with the word *gar*. Unfortunately for those scholars unwilling to accept the evidence of Codex Sinaiticus, it is by no means impossible. And once those scholars had made their dogmatic statements, other scholars naturally set about trying to prove them wrong. They succeeded.

Sentences were discovered in Homer, in Aeschylus, and in Euripides ending with the word *gar*. And not only that: the Greek version of the Old Testament was also found to contain such sentences (at Genesis chapter 18, verse 15, and chapter 45, verse 3; and at Isaiah chapter 29, verse 11). As a scholar of Trinity College Cambridge, Richard

Rusden Ottley, wrote magisterially in 1926:

> It seems, then, that neither Homer, nor the tragedians, nor
> the translators of the Old Testament into Greek, saw any
> objection to ending a sentence with *gar* if they had occasion
> to do so. The occasions, and consequently such sentences,
> are not very numerous; but that is all. Without wishing to
> suggest, or attempting to demolish, any theory as to the
> ending of St Mark's Gospel, I merely wish to point out
> that a sentence ending with *gar* is not without precedent.

In truth, Codex Sinaiticus was being cumulatively vindicated.

To assume that Mark simply did not tell of any
appearance of Jesus bodily risen from the dead is undoubtedly startling in the traditional context of Christian
belief. As Thomas Arnold wrote a few years before
Tischendorf reached the convent on Mount Sinai, 'I know
of no fact in the history of mankind which is proved by
better and fuller evidence of every sort' than the resurrection of Jesus. Quoting that dictum, the English scholar
J.S. Lawton observed that 'The Gospel tradition must be
accepted or rejected as it stands, with its combination of
stress both upon the empty tomb and the appearances'.
But it had now become clear that the very earliest Gospel
tradition stressed only the empty tomb and ignored
altogether any supposed appearances.

Tischendorf would have been horrified that his greatest
discovery had led to this conclusion. In 1972, a century
after his death, a learned scholar (P.W. van der Horst)
could still write in the *Journal of Theological Studies* that 'A
gospel without an appearance of the risen Lord is strange
indeed'. No-one doubted that the author of Mark's Gospel
believed that Jesus was somehow still alive. But whether
this conviction depended on the belief that Jesus had also
'bodily' appeared after death to his followers was now an
open question.

BOOK II

CHAPTER VII

Fragments

The exploits of Constantin Tischendorf brought to the monastery of St Catherine on Mount Sinai greater fame than at any time since the Middle Ages. More and more westerners sought out its literary treasures. But Tischendorf's behaviour had also made the monks far less willing to welcome these predatory scholars. Mrs Agnes Lewis, whose gaiety, affection for the monks, and personal charm enabled her to win over these men whose suspicions were certainly justified, records that until the visit to Mount Sinai of the distinguished English scholars Rendel Harris and Dr Bliss in 1889, the monks greatly distrusted western scholars and 'had been unwilling to allow all their treasures to be examined'. Yet soon another remarkable manuscript was discovered.

Rendel Harris was willing to use his influence to help other visitors to the monastery. When Professor Bensley journeyed there in 1892, Rendel Harris gave him a letter of recommendation to the librarian of the monastery, Fr Galakteon. Galakteon was overjoyed. 'The world is not so large after all,' he exclaimed, 'when we can have real friends in such distant lands.'

In spite of the impertinent slights of the European

visitors, Galakteon was a learned man who entered into scholarly correspondence with such noted European Biblical experts as F.C. Burkitt. He was willing to co-operate with those who genuinely sought new insight into the Scriptures through the monastic treasures of which he was chief guardian.

He became particularly friendly with Mrs Lewis, and as a result the second greatest literary treasure of the monastery was revealed to the western world. This time, however, the monks took care not to let it out of their possession.

The treasure in question was the Codex Syriacus, the oldest translation of the Gospels into any language, now proudly displayed at the entrance to Justinian's chapel on Mount Sinai. Since the theft of the Codex Sinaiticus, it is the monastery's most important literary possession. Agnes Lewis and Margaret Gibson photographed it, along with many other documents, on their visit to St Catherine's in 1891. Not surprisingly, they failed to spot its significance, since the translation, made into Syriac in the fifth century AD, had been partly erased in the seventh or eighth century and the parchment reused. The two women returned to Cambridge and showed their photographs to Professor R.L. Bensley and F.C. Burkitt of Trinity College. The two men pored over the photographs during the long vacation, and spotted that the Codex Syriacus was a palimpsest. They immediately determined to go to Mount Sinai to examine, and if possible transcribe, the manuscript in person.

Enlisting the support of Rendel Harris, they reached Cairo at the beginning of 1892. Their guides were the redoubtable Mesdames Lewis and Gibson. In Cairo they were introduced to the Archbishop of Sinai. He 'did not seem personally oppressed by his sanctity', observed Mrs Bensley. 'We found a jovial, easy-tempered man, who shook hands with us, treated us to coffee and sweets, and at once ordered his secretary to prepare our letters of introduction to his vice-regent in the convent on Mount Sinai.' Professor Bensley showed the archbishop a recently published edition of the apocryphal *Gospel of Peter*, a papyrus of which had been found near Cairo. 'Four gospels quite enough for me,' exclaimed the archbishop, but to Bensley's annoyance decided to keep the volume as a present. In return he made arrangements with the Towara tribe of Bedouin for the British visitors to pass through their territory *en route* for the monastery.

They took ten days to reach St Catherine's, ten days which included a complete rest on 5 February, because that was a Sunday. Their puzzled dragoman prepared them Sunday dinner, which they ate in a tent surmounted by the Union Jack. Arriving at the monastery, they found there forty or fifty monks, and were welcomed, in a few words of fluent French, by the steward, Nicodemus. Mrs Bensley was surprised to find this 'handsome, intelligent man' among the monks, because in her opinion Sinai was 'a kind of reformatory where monks from other countries are sent to expiate their offences in solitude and privation'. Although she found that all the monks were 'ever respectful and kind' towards their visitors, Nicodemus, who spoke three or four languages with ease, seemed to her 'somewhat out of place among his simple and ignorant brethren'. She concluded that he must have been there on a passing visit, to put the place in order!

The monks did everything possible to aid their scholarly guests. They fed them on compressed dates, rice, quince-jam, and a delicious kind of date wine. Daily they brought armfuls of new manuscripts to their visitors. Mrs F.C. Burkitt, who had accompanied her husband, copied out old Arabic texts. Agnes Lewis and Margaret Gibson listed all the Arabic and Syrian manuscripts in the monastery, in preparation for the checklist to be published by Cambridge University Press. They learned that the archbishop planned a new library for the monastery's manuscript possessions. Mrs Lewis made a note to send him a special box to contain the Codex Syriacus. (She did in fact have one made in Cambridge, of Spanish mahogany with a glass lid, and sent it to Mount Sinai, but I discovered no trace of it there.)

But their most important work was the transcription of around 300 pages of the Codex Syriacus. At first Professor Bensley tried to work on the manuscript inside the monastery; but Mrs Lewis persuaded the monks to allow them to take it to their tent outside the great walls, where the light was perfect.

For three hours at a time one of the three men, Burkitt, Bensley, and Rendell Harris (who had hurried out to Sinai to join them) transcribed the palimpsest document, while the other two sharpened pencils, refilled inkstands and reached for Bible or Syriac dictionaries. 'Slowly but steadily,' Mrs Bensley remembered, 'letter upon letter, and line upon line, by the help of sharp glasses and chemical agents, the long-lost gospels were brought to light.' To other visitors to Mount Sinai, the British team must have seemed a bizarre sight, with the Union Jack flying over their tent. Thirty or so Russian pilgrims came, ate with the monks in the great refectory, stayed a week in the monastery guest chambers, and stared curiously at the scholars from Cambridge. A group of hunting sportsmen called, found the tent empty, and left their calling cards. Not unnaturally, the monks themselves were intensely curious at the work of the scholars; and equally typically, Mrs Bensley put this down to their alleged stupidity. 'The monks, when they passed through our grounds to their lower plantations and gardens,' she noted, 'looked wondrously at these wizards from the North, who paid so much attention to the yellow parchments which their owners could neither read nor appreciate.'

The party from Cambridge had intended to go on to Jerusalem, but when the time came for them to leave, the whole of the Codex Syriacus had not been fully transcribed. They decided to stay on and finish the work. The monks generously sent two Dschebelijah and a camel to Cairo, to obtain further provisions for feeding their guests. 'Two hundred miles to the nearest grocer's shop,' commented Agnes Bensley. Finally, the work was accomplished. In 1894 Cambridge University Press published *The Four Gospels in Syriac transcribed from the Sinaitic Palimpsest*. The palimpsest itself remained on Mount Sinai.

The Cambridge scholars proved conclusively that Codex Syriacus dates from the fifth century AD. The precious palimpsest was therefore, like Codex Sinaiticus, older than the monastery that had preserved it for so many centuries. And the Cambridge scholars were disturbed to find that Codex Syriacus agrees with Codex Sinaiticus in omitting the resurrection appearances of Jesus from the end of St Mark's Gospel.

Yet their edition of Syriacus was a magnificent achievement, making all the more remarkable the cultural blindness which made so many western visitors to Mount Sinai, such as Mrs Bensley and Mrs Lewis, unable properly to appreciate the great courtesy of their hosts. On the one hand they provided evidence of the monks' welcome to their scholarly visitors. 'For the great English professor,' wrote Mrs Bensley, the archbishop always showed 'a decent kind of reverence.' He gave each of the Cambridge visitors a little box of resin from the tarfa tree — traditionally equated with the 'manna' of the Old Testament — and a small golden ring with the monogram of St Catherine's. Yet simultaneously they denigrate and deride the holy fathers.

155

At the same time, many visitors reveal their own cultural limitations. 'Perhaps in our eyes the impressive beauty of the chapel is a little marred by the grotesque old pictures, chiefly of apostles and martyrs, that abound on the walls,' wrote Mrs Bensley, 'but the monks admire it all the more for these pious additions, many of which are, moreover, long-cherished presents from illustrious pilgrims.' These 'grotesque old pictures' were of course part of the most remarkable collection of Christian icons in the world. Other western visitors shared Mrs Bensley's blindness. Sir Gardner Wilkinson, describing the great church of the monastery in 1843, observed that 'many bad pictures of saints ornament and disfigure the walls'.

The monks were, perhaps, fortunate when visitors did not recognize the value of what they saw on Mount Sinai. The more perceptive were often all the more ready to take away the monastery's treasures. The Russian Porphyrius Uspensky, visiting St Catherine's in the mid-nineteenth century, spotted the value of the icons and took four of them back with him to Russia. These, now in Kiev, are four of the seven oldest surviving icons in the world. The other three are still in the monastery on Mount Sinai.

So is Codex Syriacus. Its discovery in St Catherine's monastery foreshadows the remarkable discoveries of 1975. But for a time the monastery's fame as the home of these astounding documents of the early Christian church was overshadowed by other discoveries — some of them mere fragments of parchment, but all of them revolutionizing our insights into the beliefs and environment of our first Christian forefathers.

The rediscovery of Egypt which had led to such a great influx of visitors to Mount Sinai in the nineteenth century, led also to the foundation in 1882 of the British Egyptian Exploration Fund. One of its founders and chief benefactors, Amelia Edwards, bequeathed a chair of Egyptology to University College, London, and (following her wishes) Flinders Petrie was appointed first professor. His indefatigable work began to open up that part of the world to other scholars. The Oxford scholars B.P. Grenfell and A.S. Hunt began excavation on the western edge of the Nile Valley at Behnesya, the site of ancient Oxyrinchus.

Oxyrinchus was an ideal site to seek for new Biblical manuscripts, and Grenfell and Hunt were not disappointed. That 'stately and populous city', as Gibbon called it became an extremely influential centre of Christian orthodoxy. The inhabitants were devoted to charity. Its bishop controlled twelve churches and ruled 10,000 females and 20,000 males of the monastic profession at the time of St Antony. In the late nineteenth century, B.P. Grenfell and A.S. Hunt, excavating the rubbish heaps of this once famous Christian city, discovered countless papyrus fragments of early Christian texts. Their very first excavation produced at least 300 Greek texts. They constructed special containers to hold this excavated wealth. Even today some of the texts are still in these containers, and will not be deciphered and published until well into the twenty-first century.

But in Oxyrinchus the scholars perceived one particular text of great significance; a papyrus containing a series of sayings by Jesus, resembling but not identical to sayings in the canonical gospels.

We now know, from a find at Nag Hammadi on the Nile, seventy-five miles north of Luxor, that the Oxyrinchus papyrus discovered in 1897 was part of a *Gospel of Thomas*, written perhaps in the year AD 140 or earlier. This gospel consisted of 114 sayings of Jesus, as well as a prologue stressing their importance and attributing their preservation to Didymus Jude Thomas, one of Jesus' twelve disciples.

The gospel discovered at Nag Hammadi, which is now

157

in the Coptic Museum in Old Cairo, was almost certainly not written by St Thomas Didymus. In earlier times this would automatically have disqualified it from consideration by orthodox Christians, since they only reckoned canonical texts written by genuine apostles, not texts attributed to them. But today scholars do not hold that Matthew and John were written by the disciples of those names. They even hold that some letters in the New Testament attributed to Paul (*Hebrews*, for instance) are not in fact by him. Apostolic authorship can no longer be the test of genuine Christian authority. The Gospel of Thomas, containing as it does many quite new sayings by Jesus, as well as many with traces of Aramaic (the language he spoke) adhering to their text, can no longer be automatically ignored by the orthodox.

During the early Christian centuries dozens of gospels appeared, some bizarre, others deeply moving and inspiring. Some deal with the infancy, childhood, and early manhood of Jesus. Others purport to tell of his experiences in Hades before his resurrection.

But what excited many scholars even more than these finds was the possibility of supplementing the witness of the great codices — Sinaiticus, Alexandrinus, and so on — to the text of the New Testament by means of even earlier texts: fragments of Holy Scripture written on papyrus and preserved over the centuries.

In ancient Egypt papyrus grew plentifully in the shallow waters of the Nile. A papyrus stalk would be split open; its pith was cut into strips, and these were beaten across each other. Then the smoother side was used for writing (though scribes, having used up the better side, often moved over to the rougher one). Separate sheets of papyrus, glued together, made a roll, which was wound round a spindle to form what scholars call a 'rotulus'. At the most such a roll stretched no more than about three metres (almost ten feet) in length. For this reason no rotulus could possibly contain a whole Bible. The Gospel of Luke and Luke's later history (the Acts of the Apostles) would have taken a roll each.

To read such a roll was no simple task. With one hand the reader would hold the spindle. With the other he would unroll a little of the papyrus. The text was therefore written in thin columns, rather like a modern newspaper. For this reason, among others, the codex proved much more popular, for folding pages, sewn together in the middle, could accommodate a much wider text (and fine parchment could more readily be used on both sides). It has also been argued that Christians who might at any moment during the Diocletion persecution need to flee or at least conceal their religion, might find a codex easier to hide inside their sleeves.

Not surprisingly, of the eight Christian fragments of the Bible dating from the second century that have been discovered in Egypt, all of them once belonged to codices. The oldest Biblical text of all, now displayed in John Rylands University Library, Manchester, consists of four torn fragments which for centuries helped to wrap up an Egyptian mummy. Discovered in 1936, they are said to date from the second century *before* Christ on the basis of their handwriting. Through them we have access to a few verses of the fourth book of the Old Testament — Deuteronomy — in ancient Hebrew.

The oldest fragment of the New Testament is also to be found in John Rylands Library. No bigger than the palm of a man's hand, the papyrus contains a few verses from the Gospel of John (chapter 18, verses 31 to 33, 37 and 38). It has been dated as originating in the first half of the second century AD; and this is probably the most important fact about the fragment, for it proves that John's Gospel must have been written and in wide circulation far

159

earlier than many scholars previously believed.

The John Rylands Library fragment of St John's Gospel is part of a valuable collection of papyrus fragments obtained by the American Chester Beatty in Egypt in 1930. It includes two fragments of Matthew and John, six leaves of Mark, seven of Luke, and thirteen of Acts, as well as fragments of the letters of St Paul and the Book of Revelation. Next the University of Michigan obtained a great deal more of Paul's letters, written on papyrus at the beginning of the third century AD, as well as thirty-two leaves of Revelation containing chapter 9, verse 10, to chapter 17, verse 2. Then the Bodmer Library in Geneva obtained yet more papyrus fragments from Upper Egypt, including over fourteen chapters of the Gospel of John.

But in spite of the hopes of many explorers and scholars, these discoveries — important though they are — have not replaced the great codex of Mount Sinai and its fellow codices. Our surviving Greek New Testament manuscripts dating from before Codex Sinaiticus was written amount to barely twenty items, most of them fragments, all of them from Egypt. They contain parts of the four canonical gospels and much of the Biblical writings of St Paul, as well as part of Acts and about a third of the book of Revelation. No trace of nine New Testament books survives in any third-century manuscript. Sadder still, only rarely do two manuscripts of this date overlap. As a result the opportunity presented by codices Sinaiticus and Vaticanus for comparing, say, their witness to the ending of Mark's Gospel is not offered to us by the earlier fragments.

There are in fact far more passages from the Gospel of John preserved in these early fragments than from any other book of the New Testament. The papyrus in the Bodmer Library, Geneva, once consisted of something like thirty-nine sheets of papyrus folded to make a codex

Above: *This mosaic on the apse of the monastery church shows the Transfiguration of Christ with, on either side of Jesus, Moses and Elijah, and the Saints Peter, James, and John at His feet.*

Right: *A detail of the apse mosaic. Previous page: David Roberts's mid-nineteenth century lithograph of St Catherine's monastery, with Mount Sinai rising in the background.*

Right: *Mosaics from San Vitale in Ravenna showing* (above) *the Empress Theodora and the Emperor Justinian.*

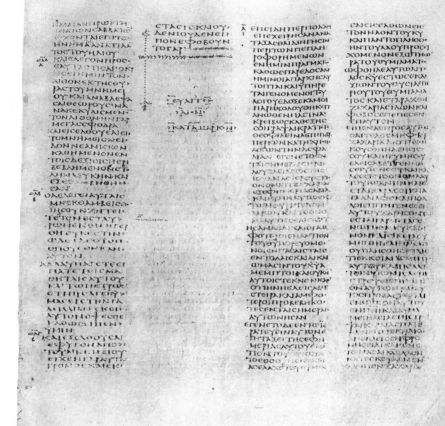

Above: *The ending of St Mark's Gospel according to Codex Sinaiticus, where it contains no account of an appearance of the Risen Jesus.*

Opposite (top): *Codex Syriacus, also from St Catherine's, is the oldest translation of the Bible into any language and (below) icons from St Catherine's of Moses (left) and John the Baptist.*

Above: *This icon from the monastery depicts St Catherine and her wheel.*
Right: *Jesus Christ, depicted in one of the five oldest surviving icons in the world, now at St Catherine's monastery on Mount Sinai.*

Opposite: *Fr Paulos, a monk at St Catherine's who studied theology at Athens University before joining the community at Mount Sinai.*

Overleaf: *This twelfth-century icon from St Catherine's monastery depicts St John Klimakos's famous ladder to heaven (see page 13).*

of 156 pages. Today we possess seventy-five leaves and another thirty-nine fragments. Scholars vary in dating these pieces of papyrus, some putting them around the year AD 200, others arguing that the codex was written even as early as the first half of the second century.

Dating from maybe two centuries before Codex Sinaiticus was written, we can read in the Bodmer papyrus a remarkably intact text of the early part of John's Gospel, petering out into little more than fragments for the last part. And when this text was published, it was seen to support that of Codex Sinaiticus far more than any other of the great intact codices.

The witness of the great codices has thus been supplemented, not replaced, by newly discovered fragments. The revolutionary nature of Codex Sinaiticus with regard to Jesus' resurrection was not yet properly acknowledged. The world of Biblical scholars and Christians awaited the next great finds.

CHAPTER VIII

The Dead Sea Scrolls and the Gnostic Gospels

If, then, the fragments of papyrus discovered by diligent Biblical archaeologists do not match the revelations brought by Constantine Tischendorf, the post-World War II discovery of the Dead Sea Scrolls undoubtedly does so. Early in 1947 two young shepherds were looking after a flock of goats and sheep at the foot of the cliffs bordering the Dead Sea near Qumran. One of their animals went astray. Searching for it, a shepherd threw a stone into a cave-like opening in the rock. It shattered something inside the cave.

The two shepherds were at first frightened and sped away. On their return, one of them climbed into the cave, to discover decayed rolls of leather in an elongated jar. The first of the Dead Sea Scrolls had been found.

Eventually, by the hands of Bedouin tribesmen, these reached dealers in Bethlehem, and through them the notice of the Syrian Orthodox metropolitan of Jerusalem, who bought one of the scrolls. Another was acquired by the Hebrew University. In April 1948 the American School of Oriental Research, Jerusalem, made a public announcement about the whole find. But by now the first of the Arab-Israeli wars was under way. Other excavations were delayed until mid-February of the following year — when no fewer than seventy more documents were discovered.

Not for another two years or so did the scholars realize that the Bedouin shepherds had stumbled upon the centre of a group of Essenes, who had lived around Qumran for two centuries or so before AD 68. The Roman historian and chronicler Pliny the Younger (AD 61–c.113) had mentioned such a group, living between Jericho and En Gedi. These scrolls might well have come precisely from the men and women he was describing.

Essenes became a self-contained, spiritually separatist group of pious Jews about 150 years before the birth of Jesus. Part of the Jewish nationalist revival under the Maccabeans, they increasingly looked towards the last day, waiting — like other Jews at that time — for the coming of the Messiah. Like the early Christians, the Essenes met together for a common meal which antici-pated the banquet of the chosen ones of the Messiah. They quoted the same Old Testament texts as did the Christians who sought to recognize the Messiah. Their decision to separate themselves from the rest of Judaism was based explicitly on such texts as that of Isaiah chapter 40, verse 3: 'In the desert prepare the way of the Lord; make straight in the desert a highway for our God' — exactly the text cited by John the Baptist preaching in the wilderness of Judaea at the time of the coming of Jesus.

Now Bedouin and scholars vied with each other to find new scrolls from the region of the Dead Sea. Bedouin provoked scholars to renewed activity, after they had found a second cave near the first in February 1952. The following month the scholars explored over 200 caves, and in one were rewarded by the find of two oxidized rolls of beaten copper, inscribed with twelve columns detailing treasures of ancient Israel and their supposed hiding places in Palestine. The Bedouin persisted in their own efforts and later that year discovered more caves with fragmentary scrolls. In January 1956 they found some beautifully preserved scrolls in a previously unopened cave.

As the excavations continued the scholarly world found itself in possession of texts of the Old Testament, commentaries on books of the Old Testament, hitherto unknown documents (such as one recounting the war between the children of darkness and the children of light), fragments of Job, indeed texts relating to every book but one of the Hebrew canonical Scriptures. Altogether the Dead Sea Scrolls comprise many thousands of texts and fragments.

The Biblical texts obviously are of immense importance in elucidating the Jewish Scriptures — the Old Testament of Christians. The non-Biblical texts, as well as providing a wealth of information about the particular sect who left them here just as the birth of Christianity was taking place, also have a tremendous significance for Christianity too. For the Essenes and the early Christians shared the same common theological stream. Phrases, words, ideas, notions of God found in the gospels can again and again find parallels in these writings discovered on the shores of the Dead Sea.

One such parallel proved especially startling. The Dead Sea Scrolls revealed that at one point in its short history the Essene community had been led by a 'teacher of righteousness'. This teacher may even have been associated with the Messiah himself, just as the early Christians identified Jesus with the Messiah. Moreover, the teacher of righteousness was apparently persecuted by a 'wicked priest', probably in the days of Alexander Jannaeus (that is, 103 to 76 BC). The question scholars differ in answering is whether or not this wicked priest put the teacher of righteousness to death — a view strongly supported by

164

some French scholars and hotly denied by others, partly on the evidence of the text of the scrolls and partly, no doubt, out of anxiety that parallels between the teacher of righteousness and Jesus are not pushed too far.

Whatever the parallels between this teacher of righteousness and Jesus, the uniqueness of early Christianity is undoubtedly diminished by the discovery of the Dead Sea Scrolls. Common themes and language, shared traditions and habits reveal that Christianity and the religion of the Essenes were both responding to the same religious impulses in contemporary Judaism. One who welcomed the possibility that the Dead Sea Scrolls might force Christians to abandon some of their claims to uniqueness was the American man of letters, Edmund Wilson, who declared: 'It would seem an immense advantage for cultural and social intercourse — that is, for civilization — that the rise of Christianity should, at last, be generally understood as simply an episode of human history rather than propagated as dogma and divine revelation'. He added that, 'The study of the Dead Sea Scrolls — with the direction it is now taking — cannot fail, one would think, to conduce to this view'.

Another writer, J.M. Allegro, who had helped in editing some of the scrolls, exaggerated when he observed that, 'The enthusiasm with which the scrolls were first greeted became somewhat chilled as their potentiality for undermining the uniqueness and originality of Christianity dawned on Christians, scholars and laymen alike'. His contention might more plausibly be made with regard to the discovery at Nag Hammadi on the Nile of thirteen books of early Christian Gnostic writings, translated into Coptic. The discovery of more and more early Christian texts, preserved through the centuries on papyrus or parchment, force us to make an even greater reappraisal of early Christianity and of Jesus

165

himself than have the Dead Sea Scrolls.

For instance, the very earliest papyrus fragment relating to Jesus which we possess is from a gospel identical with neither Matthew nor Mark, nor Luke nor John. On display today in the British Library, it consists of no more than two leaves and a small piece of a third, much mutilated. But its significance is far greater than its present size. This hitherto unknown gospel contains sayings of Jesus which can be equated with those in Matthew, Mark, Luke, and John, though the phraseology differs. But the mutilated fragment contains part of a miracle performed by Jesus on the banks of the River Jordan and nowhere else recorded in extant Christian literature.

This virtually unknown gospel, dating from the very first centuries of the Christian era but superfluous, so to speak, to the New Testament as we know it, forces us to ask what precisely we mean by 'authentic' and 'unauthentic' Holy Scripture. And it brings us immediately back to Tischendorf's discovery on Mount Sinai. For Codex Sinaiticus, which was obviously written to include the complete Bible, also contains two 'superfluous' books, the letter of Barnabas and (part of) the *Shepherd of Hermas.* What right have they to be there? And why were they excluded from later Christian Bibles?

Tischendorf himself was enthralled at seeing Barnabas among the parchment leaves as he examined them in his cell in St Catherine's monastery. The letter had been known for over two centuries to scholars; but the first four chapters were missing from all the Greek copies in Europe. The entire letter was known only in a corrupt Latin version. Now Tischendorf perceived that he had discovered all the text in its original Greek.

But having discovered and later brilliantly edited this unique text, Tischendorf never properly considered it on its own merits. For him, thenceforth, it was useful only as a means to defend the early date of the Gospel of Matthew. Barnabas, Tischendorf knew, was undoubtedly a very early Christian book. At one point in the first four chapters, the author cites St Matthew's Gospel, chapter 20, verse 16, and chapter 22, verse 14. In doing so, he uses the phrase, 'It is written'.

Now this abstruse, almost obscure point, indicated to Tischendorf and many other believers, that at a very early stage Matthew was being regarded as authoritative Scripture, put on the same pedestal as the Old Testament itself. This clearly — if true — marked an important stage in working out exactly how the early church came to define what was in the New Testament and what were excluded.

The problem was that this citation by Barnabas occurred in those chapters known only from the corrupt Latin translation. Could one accept that the original document said the same? Some said not, including the foremost German authority on the subject, Dr Karl August Credner of the University of Giessen. 'The disputed expression', wrote Credner in 1832, 'does not appear in the original Greek.' Sitting in his cell in St Catherine's monastery on 4 February 1859, Tischendorf scoured the pages of Barnabas, found the citation, and exulted that Credner was wrong.

But that is all he did with Barnabas. He never looked at the letter in its own right. The same was true of the *Shepherd of Hermas*. Tischendorf never asked himself why such books should be contained in Codex Sinaiticus, whose ancient authors clearly considered it to comprise the whole of the authentic Bible.

The 'canon' of Scripture, that is the list of books considered divinely inspired, so that they possess the authority of God for faith and life, naturally included for Jews the Scriptures we know as the Old Testament (though there was not entire agreement about these). The problem arose as books appeared about Jesus and the daily conduct and expectations of his followers. Initially local churches would possess perhaps only one gospel — and that might *not* be Matthew, Mark, Luke, or John — along with other writings attributed to Jesus' disciples or St Paul.

Alongside these we know there were accounts of the acts of Jesus' followers, and apocalypses. A letter claiming to be from Paul to the Laodiceans and a third letter to the Corinthians have been discovered. In 1924 Montague Rhodes James produced a fine edition of the apocryphal material then available. Much has been discovered since then. Of the great find at Nag Hammadi, scholars already knew of some treasures from the writings of early church fathers. Others — such as the *Letter of James* and the *Wisdom of Jesus* — were previously unknown. The *Acts of Paul*, written by a priest in Asia Minor around the year AD 180, had been lost until the Nag Hammadi find revealed it; but in the late second century the church father Tertullian reported that the work was extremely popular. He added that even so its author had been deprived of his orders.

In the early church Christians quoted many apocryphal works without necessarily distinguishing these from other 'authentic' scriptures. The test of date (that is the notion that earlier works, being closer to the time of Jesus, are more likely to be authentic than later works) will not suffice, when it is considered that, for example, II Peter, now in the canonical New Testament, was written later than the letter of St Clement, Bishop of Rome at the end of the first century AD. Some Christian writings were accepted in some parts of the Christian world and rejected elsewhere. A list dating from about AD 200 (the so-called Muratorian canon) rejects the letter to the Hebrews and observes that many objected to the Book of Revelation.

The 'Gospel of Peter' was in use in Rhossus in the last decade of the second century, sanctioned by Bishop Serapion of Antioch, who later banned it. Even in the fourth century, Eusebius of Caesarea notes that such letters as James, Jude, II Peter, and II and III John, now indisputably in the New Testament, were accepted only by some of the Christian churches.

In short, the canon of the New Testament was not something clear-cut, indisputably God-given, obvious to all right-thinking men and women. On the contrary, it evolved, sometimes obscurely, over many centuries. Sometimes the debates over various Christian books were seemly. At other times they involved clashes of personality and rival ambitions. Deliberate suppression of books led to the regrettable disappearance of much that we should like to be able to read today. In AD 494 Pope Gelasius I issued a decree condemning over sixty books and thirty authors. Montague Rhodes James was over-sanguine when he suggested that if a person would read apocryphal works side by side with the accepted New Testament, 'it will very quickly be seen that there is no question of anyone's having excluded them from the New Testament: they have done that themselves'. Rival factions in the church also excluded each other's scriptures.

It is possible to find startling and perhaps unacceptable texts in apocryphal Christian writings. Here are two from the *Gospel of Thomas*:

> Jesus said, 'Whoever does not hate his father and his mother in my way cannot be my disciple.
> Every woman who makes herself male will enter the kingdom of heaven.

Equally bizarre is a dialogue, from the same gospel, between Jesus and his disciples. The disciples asked him, 'When will you be revealed to us, and when will we see you?' Jesus replied, 'When you take off your clothing without shame, and like little children, put your clothes on the ground and tread on them. Then you shall see the son of the Living One and not fear'. One way of dealing with such passages is to declare them absurd and ignore them. But the canonical New Testament is not without bizarre elements, seen from a twentieth-century point of view. A wiser way, perhaps, is to look into the passages for their deeper meaning. This was the way of the early church. And one must add that it would not be difficult to find equally startling and at first sight unacceptable statements in the four canonical gospels, as well as in the *Gospel of Thomas*.

Soon, however, the quarrel between Christians and Jews in the early days of Christianity led to doubts about the status of some Christian writings. A Christian named Marcion, later deemed a heretic, believed that much early Christian literature had been 'corrupted' by Jewish ideas. He refused to accept any gospel other than that of Luke. He also accepted as authoritative ten letters of Paul, 'purified' of Jewish ideas.

Though Marcion's views were for a time immensely popular, many Christians disagreed with him, and the first steps at working out the list of authentic Christian writings arose among those who wished to oppose Marcion's list. St Irenaeus, Bishop of Lyons, who died around the year 200, argued (unconvincingly, to modern ears) that there must be four authentic gospels, not one, since there are four winds. Other Christians made their own lists of books which were divinely inspired and books which were merely useful Christian reading. But for many years there was debate and disagreement about the whole subject.

In fact, the first list by any person of authority in the church which contains all twenty-seven books of the New Testament as we have it today, was written as late as the year AD 367. In that year the Patriarch Athanasius of Alexandria told the bishops of Egypt that these twenty-seven books were to be regarded as canonical. Even so, he added two other books (one of them the *Shepherd of Hermas*) as useful for instructing beginners in the faith. And for another 400 years or so, many in the east refused to accept the last of Athanasius's canonical books, Revelation, as divinely inspired.

Codex Sinaiticus, written some years before the letter of Athanasius, clearly included two more books than the ones he was willing to consider canonical. Yet St Irenaeus had regarded the *Shepherd of Hermas* as inspired. Clement of Rome quoted it with approval. Origen described it as 'a writing which seems to me to be extremely useful and, as I think, is inspired'.

Barnabas was similarly esteemed. Tertullian says it was not universally accepted, but this was true of many canonical works at this time. Clement of Alexandria, Origen's learned teacher, quoted it approvingly often. As late as the sixth century AD the Codex Claromontanus gives a list of the books of the Old and New Testaments which omits the letter to the Hebrews but puts Barnabas between Jude and the Book of Revelation.

When Brooke Foss Westcott came to consider Barnabas in the nineteenth century, many had tried to reduce its importance by claiming that it was a late work, and therefore of little primary value concerning the beliefs of the earliest Christian community. Westcott rejected such views. 'The arguments which have been urged against the claims of the Epistle of Barnabas to be considered as a work of the first [Christian] age cannot be supported', he judged. He quickly added that, 'while the antiquity of the Epistle is firmly established, its Apostolicity is more than questionable'. Barnabas the Apostle was a Jew of Cyprus who became one of the earliest converts to the church. He introduced St Paul into Christianity, after the persecutor of Christians had been converted on the road to Damascus, and he accompanied Paul on his first missionary journey. Paul mentions this Barnabas in his letters; and the letter attributed to him certainly in some respects fits an author who was passionately concerned with the relationship between Christians and Jews.

Tertullian in fact believed that the man who wrote the letter of Barnabas also wrote the letter to the Hebrews which is now in the canonical New Testament. The letter of Barnabas is opposed to those persons who believe that the agreement between God and the Jews in the Old Testament still belongs to Jews as well as Christians. The Jews, it argues, soon lost God's favour by their idolatry. Before Moses could even descend Mount Sinai they were, Barnabas observes, worshipping a golden calf.

Barnabas also claims the Old Testament as a Christian rather than a Jewish document. He finds there symbols of the Cross and of Christian baptism. He argues that the Mosaic Law, the psalms, and the prophets all directly refer to Jesus.

Whether or not the letter was written by Paul's companion to some extent depends on when it was written. Some date it in the seventies of the first century AD, because Barnabas refers to obscure Old Testament prophecies which, he maintains, are being fulfilled in his own time. This dating is supported, for instance, by the fact that the letter quotes a prophecy of Isaiah about the Temple: 'they who destroy this temple shall themselves build it.' Barnabas comments: 'This is happening now. For owing to the war, it was destroyed by the enemy; at present even the servants of the enemy will build it up again.' Such a statement would accord with someone who had seen the destruction of Jerusalem by the Romans in AD 70. But it might also apply to the year AD 132, when the Jews were entertaining fresh hopes that the Temple might be rebuilt, at a time when Bar-Cochba had roused all Palestine against the Romans.

But whenever Barnabas was written, the letter affords a fascinating glimpse into the mind of some of the very first Christian converts, anxious to escape the laws of Judaism while not overthrowing their Old Testament inheritance. It raises some of the same questions as the canonical scriptures, above all, what is the real relationship between Christianity and the Jewish context in which it was born.

Brooke Foss Westcott also found Hermas deeply rewarding. Although Codex Sinaiticus revealed a major part of the work, it is known also from a text assigned to the early second century found on the back of a local government register dug up in Egypt. It therefore must have been written very early in the Christian era. Westcott described it as a 'remarkable book — a threefold collection of Visions, Commandments and Parables'. He observed that it 'is commonly published among the writings of the Apostolic Fathers, and was for some time attributed to the Hermas saluted by St Paul' in his letter to the Romans.

In fact the Muratorian canon says Hermas wrote his *Shepherd* 'in the city of Rome, where Bishop Pius, his brother, occupied the chair of the Roman church'. The book itself claims that Hermas was a contemporary of Clement of Rome, who died around the year AD 96. Bishop Pius died in the middle of the second century AD, and most scholars have taken this second, later date as the true time when the *Shepherd* was composed. The book says Hermas was a Christian slave, bought in Rome by a woman called Rhoda who freed him. He then married, and became rich, sometimes by dubious practices. When the time of persecution came, Hermas lost all his property. His own children denounced him, but eventually he and his family were reconciled and together did penance.

So the book offers the possibility of pardon even to sinners after baptism. Tertullian came to deny this possibility, and thus changed his mind about the value of Hermas. He called Hermas's book, 'the Shepherd of the adulterers'. But penance in Hermas is not the only teaching (though in one vision the angel of penance appears as a shepherd, and thus gives the book its name). Hermas was writing at a time when many Christians were uncertain about the relationship between their faith and Judaism. 'Theologically the book is of the highest value,' wrote Westcott, 'as shewing in what way Christianity was endangered by the influence of Jewish principles as distinguished from Jewish forms.' Hermas himself proclaims Christianity as 'a rock higher than the mountains, able to hold the whole world, ancient and yet with a new gate'.

He proclaims the virtue of faith — 'the first of the seven virgins by which the church is supported' — and faith's daughter, abstinence. As a former greedy merchant, Hermas is very much concerned about the proper use of, and right abstinence from, earthly goods. And he has a social conscience connected with this. Christians, he urges, should fast on bread and water. But they must not thus save money for themselves by not eating finer foods. They should count the cost of the meals they have saved, and then give the same to a widow or some other poor person.

The five visions, twelve commandments, and ten parables of Hermas forcibly present in striking images not only abstruse theology but also deeply pondered principles of Christian behaviour by one who had known the vicissitudes of earthly success and failure. The desire of the church for a fixed authoritative canon of Holy Scripture, however, allowed this powerful Christian document and the letter of Barnabas, as much else, virtually to disappear from Christian history, until Tischendorf visited Mount Sinai. As he wrote, 'While so much had been lost in the course of centuries by the tooth of time and the carelessness of individual monks, an invisible eye had watched over this treasure'.

Yet in finding the treasure, Tischendorf gave to the scholarly world a document which raised many alarming questions about what he and other Christians had previously held sacrosanct.

We are forced to ask now what precisely is the force of describing Scripture as canonical. Is, for example, the story of the woman taken in adultery, which was not in the original manuscripts and represents one of many later additions to them, still to be regarded as 'canonical'? And does its value reside in its canonical status or in its own intrinsic authority and power? How is it superior to Barnabas and Hermas which *are* in Codex Sinaiticus?

Religion, Leo Tolstoy held, is not an external phenomenon, but 'something known to us by inward experience'. In 1866, at the age of thirty-seven, he had been asked to defend a soldier facing court-martial for striking his captain. The penalty for the offence was death. Tolstoy agreed to defend the man, but the defence failed. The soldier was found guilty and shot.

At the end of his long life Tolstoy passionately denounced his own action. He cried that he should have refused to argue about evidence; he should have set aside his earlier, inadequate defence of the soldier as mentally disturbed when he struck the captain; he was foolish to try to have his soldier tried under some lesser article of the penal code which did not carry the death penalty on conviction. In his innermost being he knew that he ought to have attacked capital punishment as a crime against God and against man. And at this point Tolstoy turned to the 'dubious' story of the woman taken in adultery:

Only one thing is possible and necessary and must be, to try to free those who judge people from the stupefaction that leads them towards such a wild and inhuman purpose . . . That it is repulsive and contrary to human nature was shown to men long ago in the story of the woman who was about to be stoned to death. Is it possible that since that time men have emerged . . . who are so righteous that they are no longer afraid to cast the first stone?

Clearly the force of Tolstoy's reference to the story of the woman does not depend on its canonical status. For Tolstoy himself, its force depended on the way the story tallied with his own inward experience.

Nevertheless, believers have frequently accepted difficult doctrines found in the received text of the Bible simply because they held it to be the inspired word of God. Codex Sinaiticus ought to have been a powerful indication that in the early church no-one was absolutely certain precisely what was part of the inspired word of God and what was not. Those who ordered the codex to be made must have wanted Barnabas and the *Shepherd of Hermas* included in their complete Bible, alongside the books now regarded as canonical. Those who wrote out the codex for them must have been perfectly willing to go along with this request, considering it neither heretical nor absurd. But in fact it took the discovery of Gnostic writings — and in particular of Gnostic gospels — in this century to open our eyes to the extraordinary diverse nature of early Christian writings, to their abundance, and to their widespread acceptance.

So the earliest complete New Testament we possess is not the same New Testament accepted by the churches today. By the mid-twentieth century scholars had ceased to find this either baffling or surprising.

CHAPTER IX

The Legacy

What is accessible to us in any book depends on our own expectations of it, as well as on what it contains. For centuries the conventional expectations of Christians had been conditioned by the church and by theologians in two directions, both of them making it difficult to approach Codex Sinaiticus with an open mind. One notion unquestioned over the centuries was that of 'canonical', 'authentic' Scriptures, penned by eye-witnesses of the life of Jesus or friends of these eye-witnesses. The other powerful convention, blinding readers to the proper impact of Codex Sinaiticus, was the traditional notion of the order of the four gospels. Neither convention was easily overthrown, and both survived well into the twentieth century.

In 1952 the respected theologian Vincent Taylor wrote in his commentary on Mark's Gospel: 'Significant of the stability of critical opinion is the fact that, in a modern commentary, it is no longer necessary to prove the priority of Mark'. Dr Taylor spoke too soon. Roman Catholic theologians lagged far behind Protestants in giving up their belief in the priority of Matthew's Gospel. Only a year before the appearance of Vincent Taylor's commentary on Mark, the Roman Catholic abbot of Downside, Dom B.C. Butler, published an extremely learned book defending the old view. And some Protestants also resisted the arguments for the priority of Mark. As late as 1964 W.R. Farmer's book on the question maintained that 'Mark wrote after Matthew and Luke and is dependent on both'.

Writings of this kind could not indefinitely postpone the general acceptance of the priority of Mark; but that came in the scholarly world only in the nineteen-sixties. Only now could the true importance of the ending of Mark's Gospel in Codex Sinaiticus begin to make its proper impact.

Scholars had long known that the Codex Vaticanus also omitted the spurious last twelve verses of Mark's gospel. But they had been able to discount that piece of evidence for the view that Mark recounted no stories of Jesus' physical resurrection, for the scribe who wrote that section of Codex Vaticanus had himself been anxious about the omission. Unlike the scribe of Sinaiticus, instead of immediately beginning the first words of the Gospel of Luke at the end of Mark, the scribe of Vaticanus left a space after the words 'for they were afraid', as it were in case the 'lost' ending did turn up somewhere and could then be written in. But his own sources contained no such resurrection story.

Meanwhile, however, other manuscripts of great importance were being discovered which supported Codex Sinaiticus in omitting any account of Jesus' bodily resurrection. Remarkably, the most important of these manuscripts, Codex Syriacus, also came from St Catherine's monastery on Mount Sinai. Scholars visiting the monastery were disturbed to find that this ancient translation of the gospels also lacked the last eleven verses of the traditional text of Mark.

Soon it was discovered that the manuscript known as
Codex Bobiensis (or, in scholarly shorthand, 'k') ends at
Mark 16, verse 8, as do around 100 early Armenian
manuscripts and our two oldest Georgian translations of
the Gospel (which date from AD 897 and 913). Scholars
perceived that Clement of Alexandria and Origen never
quoted any verses of Mark subsequent to the words 'for
they were afraid', and that the canons devised by Eusebius
do not provide for any Marcan account of the appearances
of the risen Lord. Manuscripts were found in which the
scribes themselves add a note that the last eleven verses of
Mark do not appear in older copies. In other manuscripts
the scribes included these verses, but marked them with
asterisks to show that they probably needed deleting.

Now so long as the Gospel of Mark could be judged as
essentially secondary to Matthew, Luke, and John, these
successive confirmations of the disturbing witness of
Codex Sinaiticus could still be set aside. But, as the British
scholar C.F. Evans wrote in 1969, once it was shown that
Mark was the earliest of the Gospels and that Matthew and
Luke, if not John, had certainly written their Gospels by
reference to Mark's, then the situation was radically
changed. 'At the heart of the resurrection tradition',
observed Professor Evans, 'appeared a vacuum, the nature
and meaning of which scholars continue to debate.' Laymen and women too ought to ask about and debate the
same disturbing phenomenon.

Fortified by the erroneous notion that Mark, written
after Matthew, *must* have known about the physical
resurrection appearances of Jesus, earlier Christian scholars had devoted much ingenuity to speculating why the
codex from Mount Sinai ended where it does. Some
suggested that the evangelist had, perhaps, suddenly died,
after writing chapter 16 as far as verse 8. Others proposed
the idea that Mark did manage to finish his Gospel with

resurrection appearances, but that the final page or so of his manuscript was torn away or somehow lost. Neither of these hypotheses explains why no-one else bothered to finish the text, for in the earliest days of the Christian community many must have had access to accounts of resurrection appearances. If Mark was either killed or had died, other Christians could have added final verses. If, on the other hypothesis, the original manuscript was torn, this must have happened before Matthew or Luke got hold of Mark, since they have their own (differing) accounts of the resurrection appearances, which do not rely on him. The supposed mutilation must somehow have affected every copy of the earliest gospel.

Moreover, as Dr Austin Farrer pointed out, such theories are based on no historical evidence whatsoever. Dr Farrer wrote, 'It is immoral to invoke accident, whether physical accident such as the damaging of the unique original before even St Matthew saw a copy, or personal accident, such as St Mark's death or arrest in the middle of a sentence, when he had a couple more paragraphs only to write. Such accidents could happen, but they are not at all likely; and history would become a field for uncontrolled fantasy, if historians allowed themselves the free use of such suppositions.'

Nevertheless the fancies, more or less uncontrolled, of many twentieth-century Christians went far beyond merely speculating how Mark's Gospel had been somehow 'accidentally' truncated. Just as earlier believers, as we have seen, felt obliged to provide spurious endings to Mark's Gospel, so twentieth-century Christians often refused to accept that the gospel could have ended where it does, and they set about providing reconstructions of what he ought to have written or intended to write.

Strongly at work here was the powerful presupposition, reinforced over many centuries by the church, that a gospel *must* end with appearances of the risen Jesus. Writing in 1907 Professor Kirsopp Lake, for example, insisted that 'few people will ever doubt that the original Mark ended with an account of the risen Lord with the disciples in Galilee'. Professor F.C. Burkitt similarly contended 'That the Gospel was originally intended to finish at verse 8 [of chapter 16] is quite inconceivable'.

This supposedly eternal truth about what constitutes a gospel is in fact contradicted by the very earliest of our canonical gospels as witnessed to in Codex Sinaiticus. Unwilling or unable to see this, twentieth-century Christian scholars repeatedly speculated about the 'true' ending of Mark. Inevitably their speculations differed.

In 1936, for instance, Professor E.J. Goodspeed wrote that in its complete form Mark's Gospel 'doubtless contained a brief account of . . . [Jesus'] appearances to the two Marys and Salome after his burial'. Kirsopp Lake was not so certain exactly to whom Jesus would have appeared in a 'completed' Mark, but he supposed 'that the end of Mark contained an appearance in Galilee of a Risen Lord in a form which was not that of flesh and blood'. A.E.J. Rawlinson, on the other hand, was 'virtually certain that Mark must have intended to chronicle an appearance of the Risen Lord to St Peter, and probably other appearances as well'. And Professor C.H. Turner reconstructed the ending of Mark to include appearances of the risen Jesus to the two Marys and Salome (to calm their fears), to the women and the disciples together, to Peter and perhaps the other ten faithful disciples, and then to the eleven and many others (perhaps even 500 persons at once) in Galilee!

In spite of his sternness against the uncontrolled fantasies of historians, Dr Austin Farrer was unwilling to accept that Mark's Gospel ended at chapter 16, verse 8. He added a further, somewhat lame sentence: 'But Jesus sent forth his disciples to preach the gospel among all nations'. By now the impetus to invent appearances of Jesus to end Mark was running into the sand. Even so, the notion that Mark must have known such appearances was given up with great reluctance. Even in 1972 R.H. Fuller, Baldwin professor of sacred literature at Union Theological Seminary, declared 'In its original form Mark — the earliest Gospel — contained no resurrection appearances,' and then added, 'though the writer seemed to know of such appearances, apparently to Peter and the others in Galilee'. Few were willing to follow such theologians as C.F. Evans through to the conclusion that 'in Mark the visit to the tomb is the means by which the resurrection itself is declared, and not a prelude to, or presupposition of, appearances of the risen Lord to follow'.

The traditional conventions, overthrown by Codex Sinaiticus, had taken over a century to be finally demolished — if demolished they are yet. But at last the question could be faced of the true teaching of the first canonical gospel and its implications for the Christian faith. If Mark's belief that Jesus was still alive did not depend on the notion that Jesus after his crucifixion somehow 'bodily' appeared to his disciples, how may that fact alter belief in the resurrection for Jesus' twentieth-century followers?

In the early nineteen-seventies two Cambridge theologians, Don Cupitt and C.F.D. Moule, came to different conclusions when debating this whole question. For both men, the ending of St Mark was a crucial element in the debate. Professor Moule read Mark in the context of the rest of the New Testament, and not as the earliest gospel which once stood alone. In consequence, he still held that in its original form the gospel must have contained appearances of the risen Lord. Belief in the resurrection amongst the first disciples must have been caused, according to Professor Moule, by 'sense-communications from

God through Jesus, interpreting the past experiences in a new way'. Professor Moule insisted that the Bible records 'a very specific sort of revelation' of an exceptional sort, 'in that it was received by a plurality of persons, and was not compatible with private "visions" '.

Don Cupitt, on the other hand, asserted his conviction that the experiences of the earliest believers, after the death of Jesus, included not *meetings* with a physically risen Lord but *visions* of him. The resurrection experiences described (outside the four gospels) by St Paul, are all visions. The apostles' faith that Jesus was still alive arose from deep reflection — theological and personal — on what he had done while he walked on earth. 'My faith is apostolic,' wrote Don Cupitt, 'because I believe in the same sort of way. I arrive at the faith by a like train of reasoning, I share the same sort of experiences as the first disciples. The only difference is that they saw Jesus in the days of his flesh, and came to faith in him on the basis of their own acquaintance with him, whereas I have to read their testimony to him in the gospels.'

The Easter stories — Christ meeting his disciples in the flesh, eating with them, giving them commands, and so on — are, according to Don Cupitt, 'not to be taken as *reasons for believing* the Easter faith, but rather as picturesque *expressions* of the Easter faith'. And for this reason Mark could do without them.

So the debate comes back to the evidence of Sinaiticus, confirmed by the later witnesses. 'On my view St Mark's Gospel is, artistically at least, satisfactory in its present form, because it leaves the reader to draw the conclusion from what he has read', wrote Cupitt. And here he is 'as well-equipped as the very first Christians, because the story, from the Baptist to the burial and the women's continuing love for their dead Master's body, supplies the evidence for the Resurrection'.

The great manuscript hidden away for so long in the monastery of St Catherine on Mount Sinai is thus strikingly modern in its witness to the Christian faith. It contains the traditions as set down by the later evangelists about the resurrection appearances of Jesus. But in Mark's Gospel it also preserves the witness of a Christian who believed that his Lord was alive, without needing to offer accounts of those who had seen him alive after death as proofs of this faith.

But Codex Sinaiticus is also a document of its own time, as well as being a remarkable witness to the controversies of the early church. We have seen how it contains two early Christian writings which were later rejected as canonical by Christianity. But in provoking the twentieth-century debate about the true nature of Jesus' resurrection, it strikingly ties together that debate and one on the same, crucial subject which took place in the early church. And for the most part, the writings of those who opposed the notion of a physical resurrection, of Jesus or of Christians in general, were — like Barnabas and the *Shepherd of Hermas* — declared uncanonical and ultimately suppressed.

Writing at the end of the second century AD Tertullian insisted that 'a person who denies that resurrection which Christians confess cannot be a Christian'. In fact, many found the faith most difficult precisely at this point, and their different interpretations of the resurrection caused bitter disputes. Writing about thirty years before Tertullian, a Syrian called Celsus observed that the various groups of Christians 'slander one another with dreadful and unspeakable words of abuse, and they would not make even the least concession to come to agreement; for they utterly detest one another'. The disagreement was over the physical resurrection.

Until recently our only evidence about those who

denied the physical resurrection came from their victorious orthodox opponents. Now the texts from Nag
Hammadi enable us to judge these 'heretical' Christians
from their own writings. Very many of them regarded
faith in a literal resurrection of the body as the 'faith of
fools'. Nor did Mark find it a necessary part of the gospel.

A whole treatise found at Nag Hammadi, the *Letter to
Rhenigos*, is entirely devoted to the question of the resurrection. It assumes that there is no resurrection of a
physical body. Rather, human reason, or *nous*, can escape
from the world and the body into primeval nakedness. In
this, Christians are following the way of Jesus. 'He gave us
the way of immortality', wrote the author of the letter,
and he quotes St Paul: 'we suffered with him, we arose
with him, and we went to heaven with him'. So, according to this remarkable letter, 'We are drawn to heaven by
him like the beams of the sun, not being restrained by
anything. This is the spiritual resurrection'. So Christians
are urged not to live 'in conformity with this flesh,
. . . but to flee from the divisions and the fetters'. In this
way, 'already you have the resurrection'.

The *Letter to Rhenigos* conceives the resurrection as 'a
transformation of all things, and a transition into newness.
For imperishability descends upon the perishable'. In the
end, however, the spiritual interpretation of the resurrection was decreed heretical. Irenaeus declared of the gnostics that 'what they have published is utterly unlike what
has been handed down to us by the apostles'.

As Professor Elaine Pagels has pointed out, the notion
that some men had actually seen the risen Christ in the
flesh could be used to legitimize their clerical authority.
Thus St Peter's special relationship to Jesus is continually
bolstered by special reference to the Lord's appearance to
him after the resurrection. And according to the Acts of
the Apostles, Peter is responsible for replacing among the

apostles Judas Iscariot, who had betrayed Jesus, insisting that

> one of the men who have accompanied us during all the time that the Lord Jesus went in and out among us, beginning from the baptism of John until the day he was taken up from us — *one of these men must become with us a witness to his resurrection.* (The emphasis is Professor Pagels'.)

So, Professor Pagels argues, in the second century Christian leaders used the account in the Acts of the Apostles to establish specific, restricted chains of command. Only the apostles who had seen Christ in the flesh held definitive religious authority, so the theory went, and their only legitimate heirs were those who could trace their ordination back to that same apostolic succession. 'Even today,' concludes Professor Pagels, 'the pope traces his — and the primacy he claims over the rest — to Peter himself, "first of the apostles", since he was "first witness of the resurrection".'

Leon Trotsky once cynically observed that 'Of Christ's twelve apostles, Judas alone proved to be a traitor. But if he had acquired power, he would have represented the other eleven apostles as traitors, and also all the lesser apostles, whom Luke numbered as seventy'. The victorious tend to write history to glorify themselves, suppressing the achievements of their rivals. So the writings of the gnostics disappeared almost entirely from Christian history until this century, just as spurious endings were concocted for that odd-man-out, the Gospel of St Mark.

These who believed in the physical resurrection triumphed not simply for reasons of clerical politics. The doctrine of Christ's physical body was used to insist on the identical nature of the risen Lord and the life of Jesus on earth. In Christian theology it had the additional merit of symbolizing the possibility that all creation might be redeemed, not just the souls or *nous* of men and women. It carried with it the implication — in Dr Harry Carpenter's words — that 'God the creator of this world will bring all its richness and variety to perfection in the life to come, and our own complete human nature to its fullness'.

But the suppression of the alternative side to the great debate seriously distorted the truth about Christian history. As Athenagoras said of the early Christians, 'With regard to the resurrection, we find some utterly disbelieving, others doubting, and . . . some who are at loss what to believe'. That is closer to the position of our own age. In our time the debate has become alive again. I quote two foreign scholars. On the one hand Gerhard Ebeling insisted that 'The faith of the days after Easter knows itself to be nothing else but the right understanding of the Jesus of the days before Easter'. Asked what has now happened to Jesus he replies that Jesus has been 'raised to the right hand of God'. On the other hand the Swiss theologian Karl Barth maintained that more than this was required. According to Barth the Scriptures make it clear that it is 'the fact that the risen Christ can be touched which puts beyond all doubt that He is the man Jesus and no-one else'.

This is not quite true. The Gospels of Matthew and Luke use the empty tomb as a prelude to physical, flesh-and-blood appearances of the risen Jesus. But their predecessor Mark did not. In order to diverge from Mark's presentation of the faith, they were obliged to suppress his information that the two Marys and Salome told no-one of their experiences at the empty tomb. Instead, with the Gospel of John, they repeat a series of resurrection appearances of which not a single one appears in two Gospels at once.

Mark, on the other hand, shorn of his spurious endings, leads us directly from the story of the empty tomb to ask precisely what experiences persuaded the followers of

Jesus that he was alive. In the second and third centuries of the Christian era it came to be heretical for anyone to consider that these might have been other than face to face meetings with a bodily-risen Saviour. In making this judgment, the orthodox appealed to the witness of the four canonical gospels. Tischendorf's discovery of the great codex on Mount Sinai enables us today to see that this appeal was by no means so securely founded as these orthodox early Christian theologians imagined. Mark shows that there was no need to touch the risen Lord to believe in the resurrection.

In spite of our human desire for security and certainty, the earliest canonical gospel ends on a note of terror. Later Christians were not willing, it seems, to remain silent before the mystery of the resurrection. They canonized a spurious happy ending to the gospel. In his quest for the authentic gospels, Tischendorf discovered the truth in the monastery of St Catherine on Mount Sinai. It was not a truth that he himself would have welcomed. But the authentic Mark accords more closely with our own feelings of terror and hope in facing the grave and the mystery of life after death.

This concept of life, death and life after death accords more with the spiritual discipline of a monk of Mount Sinai than cruder notions of the Christian hope as something once for all proven by a physical resurrection of the corpse of Jesus. Instinctively most of us feel that, as St Paul expressed it, we inhabit both a physical body and a spiritual one. Paul vividly contrasted the resurrection body with the earthly body, as the difference between what is imperishable and what perishes, between glory and dishonour, between power and weakness.

'The spiritual body', said St Paul, 'does not come first; the physical body comes first, and then the spiritual.' Flesh and blood, he wrote, 'can never possess the kingdom of

God'. The vision of Christ granted to him was Christ raised in glory, raised (in his words) 'a spiritual body'. And the Christian hope, as St Paul expressed it, is that 'as we have worn the likeness of the man made of dust, so we shall wear the likeness of the heavenly man'. The Gospel of Mark, ending as it does, accords with St Paul's notion of the mystery of Christ's transformation, and the possibility that we too may be transformed like him. Only the later gospels, by emphasizing the physical resurrection, diminish this notion of transformation — and even they do not lose the idea that the body of the risen Jesus remains mysteriously different from ours. In the words of the great textual critic and theologian, Brooke Foss Westcott, 'The continuity, the intimacy, the simple familiarity of former intercourse is gone. He is seen and recognized only as He wills, and when He wills. In the former sense of the phrase, He is no longer with the disciples. They have, it appears, no longer a natural power of recognizing Him. Feeling and thought require to be purified and enlightened in order that He may be known under the conditions of earthly life'.

This purification and enlightenment in order to be granted a vision of the risen Lord is the meaning of monastic discipline. It involves renunciation of the physical body in the hope of living the spiritual life even in this world. The monastic father St Gregory of Sinai saw this process not only as a kind of progression towards the future resurrection life but also as a return to our original created glory. 'When, "in the beginning", God created the body, he did not place in it anger and mindless desire', wrote Gregory of Sinai. 'Only later, through the transgression, did the body become . . . mortal, corruptible and bestial.'

St Gregory of Sinai believed this taint of mortality and bestiality had affected soul as well as body. 'The soul was given over to the passions — or rather, to the demons — and the body became captive to a mindless bestiality, with the energy of that condition and under the domination of corruption.' Men and women, in both soul and body, had become, in the teaching of Gregory of Sinai and many other desert and monastic father, 'a single, senseless animality, subject to anger and to lust', for the soul and body interact with one another.

Precisely because of this, in Gregory of Sinai's scheme of salvation, it is possible, by discipline and mortification of the body and the soul, to escape from this condition: 'for the body, say the theologians, although able to receive corruption, was created incorruptible, and so it will be resurrected, just as the soul was created without passions, and will be resurrected without passions'.

For the early monks in the Egyptian desert and on Mount Sinai, martyrdom was clearly the swiftest way to overcome the lusts of the flesh. When the church became recognized by the imperial powers, this possibility was not so frequently available (though the marauders who murdered desert fathers still offered hope of a swift passage to the life hereafter). But (to quote Professor W.H.C. Frend) 'the true aim of the monk still remained the spiritual imitation of martyrdom. This was never better expressed than in a seventh-century romance, the *Book of Barlaam and Joseph*, "Monasticism arose from men's desire to become martyrs in intention" .' Even today the monastic life is a kind of spiritual martyrdom.

Professor Frend instances Origen, who was born in Egypt around the year AD 185, as a Christian who all his life desired to die a martyr's death. He would have achieved his ambition during the persecution in the city of Alexandria in 202, when his father was killed, had his mother not hid his clothes, thus forcing him to stay indoors out of harm's way.

Eventually, however, Origen — whose influence on the monastic ideal was great — developed a fresh notion of self-mortification. The Christian, he taught, can subdue the body by matyring the spirit. The ascetic life disciplines both soul and body at once. Some later criticized Origen for too great a zeal even in this divine endeavour. (He took literally Matthew chapter 19, verse 12, 'there are eunuchs which made themselves eunuchs for the kingdom of heaven's sake', and mutilated himself.) But the power of his example — fasting, renouncing earthly goods, going about barefoot — remained profound.

To renounce wealth is to take literally an injunction of Jesus: 'If you will be perfect, go and sell what you have, and give to the poor, and you shall have treasure in heaven'. To this was added a sometimes savage discipline of the body, in order to overcome what Gregory of Sinai called 'senseless animality'. It was the influence of St Basil the Great, in the middle of the fourth century, which persuaded men and women that this discipline could best be practised in a monastic community rather than as a solitary. But the monastery needed to be far from the world, according to Basil, 'lest through our eyes and ears we receive incitements to sin and become accustomed to it'. Basil insisted that 'to overcome our accustomed mode of life, a life alienated from the commandments of God, entails no small struggle'. Only by toiling in prayer and assiduous meditation upon the will of God 'shall we be able to rub out the stains of sin'.

So, even though Basil's rule of life involved living in a community, that community needed to shut itself off from the world, 'for it is impossible to meditate and pray in a crowd, which distracts the soul and introduces worldly cares'.

The great walls of Justinian's monastery on Mount Sinai serve, therefore, not only as a protection from attack but also as a defence against the distractions of the world which keep the soul and body from the vision of God. Such walls became a striking feature of the later form of Greek monasticism on Mount Athos, where again the monasteries are fortified, to defend soul and body from the outsider. Justinian's code of laws regulating the monastic life in his empire asserts that the purity and prayers of monks serve the whole world. But the emperor perceived that this was not the principal aim of monasticism. In the preface to his laws Justinian wrote, 'The monastic life, with the contemplation that a monk practises, is a holy thing, for it leads the soul to God'.

But the soul can reach God through the death of the body. So, in a remarkable phrase, Justinian's court historian Procopius wrote of the new monastery built by his emperor, 'On this Mount Sinai live monks, whose life is a kind of careful rehearsal of death'. For centuries a permanent reminder of the reality of death has, for the monks of Mount Sinai, been the ossuary where are kept the bones of their dead predecessors. In part this is simply a convenience. There are few graves in the cemetery attached to St Catherine's monastery. When a monk dies, the oldest grave is opened up, and the bones it contains are transferred to the ossuary. Most of these bones are divided up and placed on various heaps. But a few mummified corpses remain intact. One, said to be that of a sixth-century monk named Stephen, sits in a chair, dressed in the robes of a deacon, guarding the entrance to the ossuary. Such grisly reminders of mortality are found, too, on Mount Athos.

In the monastic life of St Catherine's, the traditions of the desert fathers and theologians have lasted throughout the centuries, alongside this slightly off-putting treatment of corpses. St Basil's rules, gently as they are expressed, speak ultimately of the renunciation of the flesh in order to achieve in this world the vision of God, and in the next, life everlasting. The monk, he wrote, 'must first of all possess nothing. His lot must be physical solitude. He must be disciplined in dress, conversation and tone of voice. He must eat quietly and not be obsessed with food and drink'. The monk, says Basil, must cultivate silence. He should avoid carnal men, think much, and talk little. He has to be obedient and to learn to work with his hands. Basil's finest paradox is that a monk must be 'adorned with shame'.

The Archbishop of Sinai himself spoke to me about the present-day life of a monk in phrases which entirely coincide with those of St Basil. The monastic life, he said, expresses the spiritual life at its deepest. It makes no concessions to a worldly life. The monastic life calls for no luxury, though a monk must be skilled and self-sufficient, with the aid of his fellows. Monks need no property of their own and are against possessions. A monk has more time and should have a greater impulse towards prayer than one who lives in the everyday world. His life is a training for humility, leading to a greater love for others. And its ultimate goal is the union of the soul with God.

Another monk of Mount Sinai who joined me one evening as I was eating said, 'It's a hard life'. Yet this 'careful rehearsal of death' is also a preparation for the life of the resurrection, so that a monk, as St Basil says, 'lays up treasure in heaven by keeping the commandments', and 'remembering always his end, rejoices in hope'.

In St Catherine's monastery today the vision of God is symbolized supremely by the chapel of the burning bush, the spot where Moses is said to have come face to face with God. Each Saturday it is the custom of those monks who now live there to use this chapel to celebrate the eucharist, when in faith they receive the risen body and blood of Christ as their own.

Among the many icons adorning this chapel are images which intimately connect this earthly life with the resurrection life. Moses receives the commandments on Mount Sinai — those commandments which promise to the obedient treasure in heaven. St Catherine carries her wheel and a red cross, symbols of mortification through martyrdom. Moses removes his shoes before the burning bush, just as the monks assembled for the eucharist are shoeless. And a great icon of the glorified Christ, in high priestly garments, depicts him holding open a New Testament, the book of the new age of mankind. One page of the open book carries a text of the eucharist: 'This is my body, which was broken for the forgiveness of sins'.

The left-hand page of the open gospel carries the words Jesus spoke to the man who condemned him to death: 'My kingdom is not of this world'.

The theology of eastern orthodoxy over many centuries weaves all these images into a complex understanding of how men and women may rise from the death in this world to the eternal spiritual life of the next. In the eighth century AD the second Council of Nicaea declared that holy images, such as icons of the Saviour, should be kissed, venerated, and honoured, but not worshipped, for worship, it was decreed, 'is reserved for him who is the subject of our faith and is proper for the divine nature alone'. The church fathers at this Council added: 'The honour rendered to the image is, in effect, transmitted to the prototype; whoever venerates the image, venerates in it the reality for which it stands'. Venerating the image of Jesus, the monks of Mount Sinai worship their risen Lord and look towards his kingdom which is not of this world. So, as the present Archbishop of Sinai told me, 'The form of an icon is ascetic', that is to say, austere, disciplined and severe, 'pulling man from earth to God'.

The ultimate hope of the spiritual life on earth is to be

granted a vision of the invisible God. In the fourth century the younger brother of St Basil, St Gregory of Nyssa, and in the seventh century the great orthodox mystic, St Maximus the Confessor, both identified the divine vision granted to mystics with the vision granted to Moses on Mount Sinai. The Christian aim, as St John Klimakos, abbot of Mount Sinai, put it, is to strive to contain this spiritual vision in his earthly body. But ultimately, according to the mystical theology of St Maximus, the spiritual takes over. Human beings are, he says, even deified. 'Man becomes God, thereby completely abandoning all that belongs to him by nature . . . because the grace of the Holy Spirit triumphs in him and God alone manifestly acts in him.'

Fascinatingly enough, this notion of the resurrection is far more spiritual than the concept of a resurrected corpse with which many once erroneously supposed St Mark ended his Gospel.

CHAPTER X

A New Mystery

Today the precious manuscripts of Mount Sinai are properly stored and shelved in a well-built fireproof library. The first volume of a series cataloguing these manuscripts was published in Wiesbaden in 1970. Earlier a handlist of the monastery's Arabic manuscripts was published in Baltimore. The tools which scholars have come to see as indispensable are rapidly being provided for the monastery on Mount Sinai.

It would be a great gain to scholarship if more and more students were to find their way to the monastery. Sitting at work in the comfort of the library, I felt the need to stay for ever simply to tap a few of its riches. Apart from its store of manuscripts, the library possesses another 5000 printed books, some of them dating from the earliest years of printing. I saw an *Odyssey*, published in Florence in 1428 with spaces left for the insertion of ornamental capitals. I examined Christopher Plantin's edition of the works of St Gregory of Nazianzus, who in the fourth century had gone to university with St Basil. I looked at a copy of the works of St John Chrysostom, the fourth-century monk, hermit, and doctor of the church, printed at Verona in 1529. These were a tiny tip of a rich scholarly iceberg.

Now this rich store has been supplemented by the remarkable treasure-trove discovered by the monks on 26 May 1975. After they had finished cleaning and unfolding these manuscripts, the monks packed them away in forty-seven empty tinned-milk cartons, sorting them out as best they could into Greek, Arabic, Syrian, Armenian, Ethiopian, Georgian, and Latin documents. Many were uncial texts, that is manuscripts written entirely in capital letters between the fourth and the eighth centuries of the Christian era. Professors Linos Politis and M.N. Panagiotakis, two Greek scholars who were eventually allowed to examine the Greek texts for a short time, declared the find to include 'the most important and probably the most ancient uncial manuscripts so far known'. Now Professor Panayotis Nikolopoulos of the National Library of Greece is working on an historical and descriptive account of these new treasures of St Catherine's.

In spite of the great care taken of their manuscripts by the monks of Mount Sinai, it is easy to see why some could have been lost in the past, buried for two centuries as in the case of the most recent find. Over the centuries every corner inside Justinian's powerful walls has been utilized and then re-used in one way or another. Narrow staircases lead to covered walks. The ancient pulley, which was used to hoist visitors and goods until the narrow passage with its three fortified doors was built in 1861, still exists as if ready for use. Defensive slits in the walls, through which could be fired arrows at anyone attacking the monastery, testify to the dangers of the past — as do the various holes through which could be poured rubbish — perhaps onto the heads of unwelcome visitors outside the walls! In one wall is an ancient and now unused 'garderobe' or privy. Inexplicable bells hang from corners, sometimes cracked, no longer useful or even in some cases usable. In one broken-down cell a wood-burning stove and cooking range, which must once have fed the whole community, lies decaying and broken. Next to it a serving hatch pierces the metre-thick wall of the beautiful gothic and now little-used refectory. One of the doors to this refectory, with its finely carved lintel-stones, now opens out onto nothing. Anyone leaving today by that door would fall down twenty feet (about six metres) and kill himself. Shallow pointed arches in some cases now lead nowhere. The architecture of one century mingles haphazardly with that of another. A dome juxtaposes with an ancient arch, next to a plastered/ wall and a casement surrounded with machine-cut stones. Parts once inhabited are now empty and neglected.

And yet the monks continually rebuild, or rather employ others to do so. In 1798 a storm damaged the north wing. Napoleon Bonaparte paid for its reconstruction. On top of the ancient southern wall in 1951 was built a new fireproof library and an icon gallery. Until recently the monastery possessed its own iron foundry, for smelting iron brought by camel from Cairo. New drains are being installed, in preparation for reconstructing the interiors of the monks' cells (the exteriors are to be kept as they have been for many years) and to serve new guest rooms. Modern construction methods replace the old techniques — traditional from the Dordogne in France to the Egyptian desert — of using uncut stone, and earth for mortar, and then covering it all with plaster. Outside the monastery walls a concrete mixer rattles away. The monks no longer wash themselves in the stone double sink near the ancient well (said to be the well of Moses himself). The Greek inscription ΕΛΑΙΟΤΑΒΕΙΟΝ over an ancient door indicates that there the monks once made oil by grinding olives: but they no longer do so today.

In short, although the monastery of St Catherine on Mount Sinai is still very much alive, and still a place of pilgrimage after thirteen centuries of its existence, much has changed within the fortress of Justinian's builders and much — no longer needed — is neglected.

Archbishop Damianos, the present abbot of Mount Sinai, showed me the room in the great north wall where the 1975 find was made. The three windows still showed blackened traces of the fire that gutted the chapel of St George. The Archbishop explained why he thought the hidden manuscripts were there in the first place. This room was very close to the sacristy of the monastery. And until the eighteenth century, part of the monks' library was kept there too. When this library was moved, for three good reasons a number of manuscripts were left behind in their old place.

First, manuscripts in languages other than Greek — such as Slavic and Syrian texts — were no longer useful in an all-Greek community, and were put aside. Secondly, in the very early days of the monastery the whole Bible was used at worship for reading the set lessons. But because this proved cumbersome, the monks soon created or obtained lectionaries containing extracts from Holy Scripture, corresponding to the lessons of the day. The old unwieldy Bibles were no longer of practical daily use. Thirdly, Archbishop Damianos suggested, some manuscripts were left behind when the library moved, simply because they were in need of repair. Subsequently the whole collection was buried when the roof of the cell caved in.

Archbishop Damianos told me that he had personally suspected there might be manuscripts concealed in that part of the monastery. After the fire it was therefore natural to start clearing the whole area. When a monk found the first manuscript, the community started clearing out the cell far more methodically. For over a month they devoted as much time as possible to unearthing the

199

fragments of parchment and to restoring and stretching them. 'Some were like creased bundles', recalled the Archbishop.

The climate of Mount Sinai is virtually perfect for the preservation of ancient manuscripts and works of art. The church built by Justinian's architect inside the monastery walls preserves perfectly not only its great sixth-century doors, as we have seen, but also the original thirteen wooden roof-trusses, carved and painted in red and gold. The cedar wood from Lebanon out of which the doors were made is in almost the same condition as it was 1400 years ago.

The climate which so remarkably preserved these ancient timbers has also cared for the precious manuscript treasures of Mount Sinai. None of them is eaten by insects or rotted by damp. The dry atmosphere has crinkled some of them. For the same reason others have a tendency to crack. But all are beautifully preserved and are protected by the monks from excessive light.

But in 1975 the monks also decided to protect their find from the scholarly world. At that time their delicate political situation — living in Egyptian territory which the Israelis were occupying — made them even more anxious to lead an unobtrusive existence. But undoubtedly their resentment at the treachery of Constantin von Tischendorf decisively prompted their decision to keep the new discoveries secret. The monks made their own rough classification of the finds and stored them in the forty-seven tinned-milk cartons. They immediately spotted more leaves and fragments of the Codex Sinaiticus, and stored them separately. And they meticulously cleaned the broken pieces of icons, also found in the cell, which they (erroneously as it turned out) hoped might be as old as the sixth century AD.

Then, under terms of the utmost secrecy, the

Archbishop and monks of St Catherine's did inform the Greek ministry of culture and science of their remarkable new find. The then minister, Professor K. Trypanis, asked Professor Linos Politis, an expert palaeographer, to visit Mount Sinai and examine the findings.. He in turn asked for the help of Professor N.M. Panagiotakis, an expert in the literature of the Middle Ages. On 29 September 1975 these two men flew via Tel Aviv to Jerusalem, where they were met by Archbishop Damianos. On 2 October they were inside the monastery on Mount Sinai.

The Greek scholars were allowed to see and examine some of the newly found documents only under an oath of complete secrecy. In no way were they to speak of or publish what they had discovered in them. As Professor Politis observed, the whole affair was still covered by 'a veil of mystery'. And in spite of the oath of secrecy taken by the two professors, the monks seriously restricted their access to the precious new manuscripts. Their stay in the monastery was limited to three days. 'The few monks were so busy with their heavy duties,' wrote an understandably frustrated Professor Politis, 'that in these three days we managed to devote only eight hours to the study of the findings — and this under conditions not at all favourable (lighting was inadequate, the place inconvenient for work, and so on).'

What is odder is that the two scholars were not shown all forty-seven cartons of manuscripts. The monks let them see only twenty-five cartons, though Fr Sofronios, who was at that time sacristan of St Catherine's (and had in fact discovered the first of these new manuscripts), told them there were many more.

Professors Politis and Panagiotakis confined themselves to studying only the Greek manuscripts in the new find, which the monks had put into ten boxes. In spite of their difficulties, they did take photographs of some of these manuscripts. They separated parchments from paper sheets. They divided those (older) manuscripts written entirely in capital letters from the (later) ones with lower case letters. They classified the contents of the older parchments and some of the later documents. And they discovered some pieces of papyrus, written over in Greek or Arabic, but now stuck together to be used as an early kind of book-binder. Both scholars were well aware of the importance of the material they were handling.

The first priority, the two Greek professors believed, was to ensure the preservations of the findings. There was no question of removing them from St Catherine's — especially (as Professor Politis specifically observed) after the behaviour of Constantin von Tischendorf. 'The manuscripts were found in the Sinai monastery,' wrote Professor Panagiotakis, 'and of course they are its property.' The professor took care to labour this point! 'Nobody wants to claim the treasures from the monastery, and nobody disputes the ownership. Even if we consider logical the view that the monks in this case — as in other similar cases — are not arbitrary owners but merely keepers of the treasures handed down to them by history, it remains a fact that these treasures are historically linked with the place, and their removal from it should be considered unthinkable.' In short, the monks could trust the Greek scholars not to cheat them.

The new find therefore needed careful preservation *in situ*. 'It is fortunate that the find — in spite of being buried under the earth for more than two centuries — has been rather well preserved', reported Professor Politis. 'This is due to the great dryness of the Sinai heights. Under different conditions the parchments and papers would have rotted and been lost.' But, he pointed out, this self-same dryness was now the greatest problem for the future preservation of the find, for many parchments had shrunk and were now extremely rigid and inflexible. Preservation work would somehow have to deal with this.

In consequence, the Greek ministry of culture and science sent Professor Panayotis Nikolopoulos, keeper of manuscripts at the National Library of Athens, along with conservation experts, to Sinai on two visits in 1976 and 1977. Now a rather large number of people was privy to the monastery's secret, though all were sworn to silence. Soon the secret was bound to leak out — though not, as it happened, initially because of indiscretions either by the two Greek professors or Dr Nikolopoulos and his team.

Early in 1978 Professor S. Agouridis of the University of Athens visited the monastery and was shown the findings. He passed the news on to Professor Martin Hengel of the University of Tübingen in West Germany. Professor Hengel told a friend, and on 3 April 1978, a leading German newspaper, the *Frankfurter Allgemeine Zeitung*, carried an article signed by Carl Alfred Odin giving an accurate account of the new discoveries on Mount Sinai. 'Now the Aeolean bags have been opened,' wrote Professor Panagiotakis, 'and the secret has ceased to be a secret.'

Acrimonious controversy did not disappear from the scholarly world with the death of Constantin Tischendorf. European scholars now accused the Greeks of complete irresponsibility in keeping the new manuscripts to themselves. Others doubted the competence of Greek scholars to deal with the entire find. On 26 April the Greek newspapers published an Associated Press statement that Professor Kurt Aland had urged the Greeks to give up the work. 'Somebody should tell them that what is happening is a cultural scandal', were his alleged words.

Kurt Aland, who is director of the institute for New Testament research in Münster, later claimed he had been misquoted, but not before Professor Politis had declared his opinion to be 'unacceptable for its impudence'. The Greeks hastened to defend themselves. Greece, as Professor Politis pointed out, possesses the Academy of Athens, with its special research centres, four schools of philosophy and two of theology, as well as centres of Byzantine studies in Athens and Thessaloniki. Professor Panagiotakis said that initiatives from single institutions or people 'who have engineered ways of interfering' in the research ought to be discouraged. 'I do not mean people and institutions from Greece', he added! National pride was at stake, though this time the Germans in particular were dubbed interferers (whereas Tischendorf had most of all disliked the predatory ways of English scholars). 'I stress again,' wrote Professor Panagiotakis, 'that the initiative for the organization of the study should remain in Greek hands'. It would be marvellous, he declared, if the publication of the findings could be undertaken exclusively by Greek scholars.

Professor Panagiotakis conceded, however, that there were not enough scholars in Greece to deal with the new Greek manuscripts, let alone the non-Greek discoveries. 'I am sorry to say this,' he wrote, 'but it is to nobody's benefit if we loudly proclaim the worth and abilities of Greek scholars and are not in a position to support our claims.' He suggested that the Greek government should invite the co-operation of the centre for the research into textual history in Paris, the institute of papyrology in Vienna, and the centre for Byzantine Studies in Dumbarton Oaks. Perhaps, he added, some of these bodies could also be persuaded to help to finance the work. 'Megalomanic, sterile nationalism', he said, 'has never been part of our national character, and should have no place in a case such as this one.'

The article in the *Frankfurter Allgemeine Zeitung* not only produced the situation in which, as Professor Aland put it,

'Everyone is trying to reach the manuscripts'. It also persuaded Professors Politis and Panagiotakis that their irksome oaths of secrecy no longer applied. 'We promised not to proceed to any announcement,' Professor Politis wrote, 'until the holy fathers themselves judged the moment appropriate.' Both of them had kept that promise, he said, even though compulsory silence conflicted with the primary duty of a scholar as they saw it, namely to announce their findings to the scientific world. (The contrast with Tischendorf's behaviour over the provenance of Codex Sinaiticus could not be more complete.) 'However,' he continued, 'after the leakage of information on the matter from other sources . . . , we believe that we have become disengaged from our promise, since the reasons that made it necessary have been eclipsed.'

The announcement in the *Frankfurter Allgemeine Zeitung* appeared at the beginning of April. Before the end of May both Professor Politis and Professor Panagiotakis had written about their work on the new documents, in Greek daily newspapers. The monks of St Catherine's were less quick off the mark. Only in October 1981 did Archbishop Damianos announce to the International Byzantine Congress held in Vienna that the find would be made available to competent scholars — and even then, not until the monastery had published its own catalogue of the contents. The find was still not totally available to the outside world.

What then does it contain? No-one yet entirely knows, not even the monks themselves. A proper study of these documents, observes Professor Panagiotakis, 'requires lengthy, *in situ* work of many expert scholars, using the appropriate equipment'. The latest of the documents unearthed in 1975 dates from about the year AD 1750 (hence the conjecture that the roof of the cell caved in sometime in the late eighteenth century). The earliest documents are the pieces from the Codex Sinaiticus and others whose handwriting is in a near contemporary style to these.

Some of the manuscripts obviously came to St Catherine's monastery from elsewhere. But others are excitingly from the scribes of the monastery itself. A few of these (at least) are almost as old as Justinian's building itself. One such manuscript, dating from the seventh century AD, contains some of the writings of St John Klimakos. This manuscript is therefore virtually contemporary with the saint himself.

Without knowing the contents of anything like the whole of this new find, scholars are certain that it will shed entirely new light on the earliest history of our Christian civilization. The team assembled at Mount Sinai by Professor Nikolopoulos identified thirty-six pieces of papyrus being used as bindings on even earlier manuscripts. They found another nineteen early papyrus fragments, written in Greek. Altogether they discovered another 1148 manuscripts, either on parchment or paper, of which 305 were complete.

The majority (836) of these manuscripts were written in Greek. But the rest show the remarkably cosmopolitan character of the early centuries of St Catherine's monastery. The find contains manuscripts written in Arabic, Syrian, Slavic, Armenian, Ethiopian, Hebrew, and Latin. Until now it was thought that loss of contact between St Catherine's and Roman Catholic Christianity had led to the disappearance of all Latin manuscripts from the monastery. The fragments which contain music are a similarly unique find in St Catherine's. For two centuries the neglected cell in the monastery wall concealed these amazing riches.

Small wonder that Professor Panagiotakis describes the find as the greatest archaeological discovery of this century. These Gospel-books, Psalters, Calendars, Liturgies, and so on offer us hitherto undreamed of information about the way these early Christians worshipped. The find also contains speeches by early Christian fathers of the church, such as St John Chrysostom. And alongside these were found pagan works, such as eight pages of Homer's *Iliad* and four pages from a tenth-century edition of the works of Aristotle.

The concerns of the scholar and those of the man or woman in the street do not always coincide. Nevertheless, it is possible to sense the excitement of the scholarly world at these new finds. Nowhere else is there such a wealth of uncial books as have now been discovered on Mount Sinai. A question long pondered by historians of our early culture is who first switched from writing in these capital letters to the kind of script we still use today. Professor Linos Politis, on the evidence of the new find, now thinks it might have happened in the monastery of St Catherine itself.

Again, for a long time scholars have puzzled over a huge gap in our sources for Byzantine history, stretching from about AD 650 to 850. Now many of the documents discovered in St Catherine's monastery can be used to fill that gap.

But twentieth-century men and women will also want to know whether or not this new find alters our understanding of the Christian faith itself. Oddly enough, the monks of Mount Sinai, when I talked with them about this, seemed anxious to play down the importance of the find. Although the documents are of a fantastic richness, I was told not to expect any text the substance of which was hitherto unknown. Indeed, I was informed, there are fragments from the early centuries of the Christian era; but the find includes no new gospel comparable, say, to the *Gospel of Thomas*. It contains nothing comparable to the

Dead Sea Scrolls. In that sense at least the newly-revealed secrets of Mount Sinai are not revolutionary ones.

I personally disagree with the Holy Fathers. It took over a century for the full impact of the Codex Sinaiticus on our understanding of the development of Christianity to make itself felt. I agree with the judgment of Professor N.M. Panagiotakis that the new manuscripts discovered on Mount Sinai have great significance, not simply for the ancient culture of the Greek-speaking world, but also for the civilization of the first Christian centuries. There is, he has written, 'a significance locked up in these remains which perhaps has an enormous importance for the culture and history of all Christian folk'. But, as in the case of Codex Sinaiticus, to unlock that significance will take time.

One reason is that many of the newly-discovered parchments are palimpsests — that is, parchments re-used after the original text has been scraped away. Only when these palimpsests have been examined under ultra-violet light will be known what the earlier text contained. Another reason is that so far no-one has collated the newly-discovered Biblical texts with our present editions of Holy Scripture. It is perfectly possible that we shall find unknown writings of the early Christian centuries in the new manuscripts. We may also unlock fresh secrets about the original text of our present Bible.

The richness of the find on Mount Sinai will gradually be revealed as the oriental manuscripts (120 Arabic, 96 Syrian, 56 Armenian documents, and so on) as well as the more accessible Greek ones, are studied and deciphered. And although it will take many years for the new manuscripts to be translated, when they are made available the result will certainly further the contemporary revaluation of Christian belief.

Epilogue

Tischendorf was absolutely right to remove Codex Sinaiticus from Mount Sinai, declared Professor Philip Schaff in the 1870s, 'for these ignorant monks would never have made use of it, and Biblical scholars could not travel to Mount Sinai to examine it'. The slander on the monks was inexcusable in the eighteen-seventies. And today travel to Mount Sinai is relatively simple. The treasures of St Catherine's monastery can be made available to the scholarly world.

Yet should this increasingly happen, it would undoubtedly drastically change the life of that monastery. For the task of caring for ancient treasures and modern scholars savagely conflicts with the monastic vocation. Monasteries are ultimately about contemplating God and nothing else — a contemplation that promises peace passing human understanding.

In the nineteen-fifties a distinguished soldier and Philhellene, Patrick Leigh Fermor, visited and stayed in a Benedictine abbey in France. He then visited the priory of St Peter of Solesmes, before going on to what he described as 'a far stranger monastery: la Grande Trappe, the fountain head of the Cistercian order of Strict Obedience'.

Here he found peace, what he called 'the slow and cumulative spell of healing quietness'.

The monks of St Catherine's on Mount Sinai seek the peace which St Basil enjoined on his monastic followers. A hermit in the east is still known as a *hesychast*, from the word *hesychia*, which means 'quiet' or 'spiritual repose'. This ideal passed from the life of a hermit to the life of a monk. St John Klimakos observed that 'If the remembrance of Jesus is present with each breath, you will know the value of solitude'. Is the life of peace and solitude compatible with devotion to scholarship and with the charge of a great library visited by many secular scholars?

St Basil urged silence on a monk. Silence, he observed, makes a monk forget his old habits of speaking too much, even if his speech were good rather than bad. He counselled against too much laughter. I have, indeed, seen the monks of Mount Sinai laugh. Once when I was there a commotion at the metalled doorway provoked the guest-master to lean over the wall, only to perceive that a wandering Bulgarian had hitched his way to the monastery and was attempting to converse with some of the Dschebelijah. The guest-master let him in, and then introduced this wanderer to an aged monk from Romania (who, in spite of his age, still from time to time conducted visitors to the top of Mount Sinai). The comedy of the two eastern Europeans attempting and totally failing to converse in sign language, provoked enormous hilarity.

But by and large a monk cuts himself off from the world, and — according to the rules of St Basil — keeps a seemly spiritual distance even from his fellow-monks. This, I think, explains the difficulties present-day scholars have experienced in St Catherine's monastery. A monastery like St Catherine's, far from what we know as civilization, has existed over the centuries as a self-contained unit. The monks possessed their own ironworks. They baked their own bread. They grew their own food and made their own wine. Clothes were stored and mended; shoes were made; the sick were tended; buildings were repaired, or altered and put to new uses; and all this was done with the monastery's own resources. The intrusion of the outside world disturbed this self-sufficient pursuit of the godly life. And this pattern of life in St Catherine's today conflicts with the equally legitimate claims of the scholar who seeks to probe its cultural riches. As a result, the monastery, in spite of the hospitality it displays to the twentieth-century visitor, does not offer the scholar the facilities he would ask for in any other great centre of learning. The three paltry days, offering only eight meagre hours of working time, allowed to Professors Panagiotakis and Politis when they visited St Catherine's monastery to examine the newly discovered ancient documents are a striking example of the incompatibility of the demands made by the monastic life and the demands made by scholars.

Yet the monks of Mount Sinai are, whether or not they welcome it, the custodians of part of the spiritual and cultural heritage of the whole world. Legitimately, they cling to it. It seems to me that far more must be done to make this heritage available to scholars and through them to others. In St Catherine's monastery today there are not enough monks to see to the needs of those scholars who might wish to examine the treasures housed there.

One possible solution is for some such body as UNESCO to recruit and pay (and perhaps also train) persons who would work entirely in the library of the monastery and with its other treasures. These persons would have to be of a temper acceptable to the Archbishop and confraternity of St Catherine's. They would be the ones who exercised the day to day care of the monastery's cultural treasures. They alone would have the time and expertise to cater for the needs of international scholarship and visiting researchers. If therefore Codex Sinaiticus is ever returned to Mount Sinai, the monks of St Catherine's, notwithstanding their vocation to prayer, must in turn accept the demands which Christendom and the scholarly world have a right to make on them.

Those who, like myself and many before me, grew enchanted with staying in the monastery of St Catherine on Mount Sinai, have to avoid romanticizing it. Some scholars have come away from Mount Sinai frustrated at their lack of access to the monastery's treasures. Others, such as Kirsopp and Sylvia Lake, who in 1927 were able to spend five hours a day for six weeks working in the library of St Catherine's, found the atmosphere of the monastery entirely congenial. None exhausted its treasures or unlocked all its secrets.

Only three passengers were in the plane that flew me on a Thursday morning from St Catherine's airport. As no-one was in a hurry, we persuaded the pilot to take us over the monastery. We flew over the huge wide sandy gorge, as far as the tiny village where the road turns towards Mount Sinai. Trees grow first on the left and then on both sides of the road, as it snakes up the mountain side. Ahead the mountains appeared green. And then, far below, the monastery appeared, with its red tiles, and the church clearly visible, off-centre inside Justinian's great walls, its corrugated metal roof less offensive from such a height. I tried to make out the place of the burning bush, and then the plane turned away towards Cairo. My most distinct feeling was that I was leaving behind a great store-house of unexplored treasures.

Pierre Loti felt the same, as he left the chapel of the burning bush, with its icons and hanging lamps. He was conscious of a life of prayer and the preservation of countless treasures going back to the earliest ages of the church. 'People and empires have passed away,' he wrote, 'while these precious things slowly tarnished in this dim crypt. Even the monk who accompanies us resembles, with the pale beauty of his ascetic face, the mystics of the early ages; and his thoughts are infinitely removed from ours. And the vague reflection of the sunlight which arrives through a single little window in the thick wall, and falls in a circle of ghostly radiance on the icons and mosaics, seems to be some gleam from a far-off, ancient day, a gleam from an age wholly different from the sordid, impious century in which we live.'

Pierre Loti was perhaps too romantic. And there have been centuries quite as sordid as his or even ours. But from those far-off ancient days the monastery of St Catherine on Mount Sinai has preserved treasures of inestimable value for our century and for centuries to come. What else is to be found there?

Appendix

These extracts from *The Epistle of Barnabas* and *The Shepherd of Hermas* are reprinted by permission of the publishers and The Loeb Classical Library from *The Apostolic Fathers*, translated by Kirsopp Lake, London: William Heinemann 1912 and 1913 and Cambridge, Massachusetts: Harvard University Press, 1912 and 1913. The translator's original footnotes are also reproduced.

THE EPISTLE OF BARNABAS

I

1. HAIL, sons and daughters, in the name of the Lord who loved us, in peace. Greeting and introduction

2. Exceedingly and abundantly do I rejoice over your blessed and glorious spirit for the greatness and richness of God's ordinances towards you; so innate a grace of the gift of the spirit have you received. 3. Wherefore I congratulate myself the more in my hope of salvation, because I truly see in you that the Spirit has been poured out upon you from the Lord, who is rich in his bounty;[1] so that the sight of you, for which I longed, amazed me. 4. Being persuaded then of this, and being conscious that since I spoke among you I have much understand-

[1] Literally "spring."

ing because the Lord has travelled with me in the way of righteousness, I am above all constrained to this, to love you above my own life, because great faith and love dwell in you in the "hope of his life." 5. I have therefore reckoned that, if I make it my care in your behalf to communicate somewhat of that which I received, it shall bring me the reward of having ministered to such spirits, and I hasten to send you a short letter in order that your knowledge may be perfected along with your faith.

6. There are then three doctrines[1] of the Lord: "the *The three doctrines* hope of life" is the beginning and end of our faith; and righteousness is the beginning and end of judgment; love of joy and of gladness is the testimony of the works of righteousness. 7. For the Lord made known to us *Prophets* through the prophets things past and things present and has given us the firstfruits of the taste of things to come; and when we see these things coming to pass one by one, as he said, we ought to make a richer and deeper offering for fear of him. 8. But I will show you a few things, not as a teacher but as one of yourselves, in which you shall rejoice at this present time.

II

1. SEEING then that the days are evil, and that the *The n of vir.* worker of evil himself is in power, we ought to give heed to ourselves, and seek out the ordinances of the Lord. 2. Fear then, and patience are the helpers of our faith, and long-suffering and continence are our allies. 3. While then these things remain in holiness towards the Lord, wisdom, prudence, understanding, and knowledge rejoice with them. 4. For he has made plain *The abolition of* to us through all the Prophets that he needs neither *Jewish sacrifices* sacrifices nor burnt-offerings nor oblations, saying in one place, 5. "What is the multitude of your sacrifices unto me? saith the Lord. I am full of burnt offerings and desire not the fat of lambs and the blood of bulls and goats, not even when ye come to appear before me. For who has required these things at your hands? Hence-

[1]Or possibly "ordinances" or "decrees."

forth shall ye tread my court no more. If ye bring flour, it is vain. Incense is an abomination to me. I cannot away with your new moons and sabbaths." 6. These things then he abolished in order that the new law of our Lord Jesus Christ, which is without the yoke of necessity, might have its oblation not made by man. 7. And again he says to them, "Did I command your fathers when they came out of the land of Egypt to offer me burnt offerings and sacrifices? 8. Nay, but rather did I command them this: Let none of you cherish any evil in his heart against his neighbour, and love not a false oath." 9. We ought then to understand, if we are not foolish, the loving intention of our Father, for he speaks to us, wishing that we should not err like them, but seek how we may make our offering to him. 10. To us then he speaks thus: "Sacrifice for the Lord is a broken heart, a smell of sweet savour to the Lord is a heart that glorifieth him that made it."[1] We ought, therefore, brethren, carefully to enquire concerning our salvation, in order that the evil one may not achieve a deceitful entry into us and hurl us away from our life.

III

1. To them he says then again concerning these things, "Why do ye fast for me, saith the Lord, so that your voice is heard this day with a cry! This is not the fast which I chose, saith the Lord, not a man humbling his soul; 2. nor though ye bend your neck as a hoop, and put on sackcloth, and make your bed of ashes, not even so shall ye call it an acceptable fast." 3. But to us he says, "Behold this is the fast which I chose," saith the Lord, "loose every bond of wickedness, set loose the fastenings of harsh agreements, send away the bruised in forgiveness, and tear up every unjust contract, give to the hungry thy bread, and if thou seest a naked man clothe him, bring the homeless into thy house, and if thou seest a humble man, despise him not, neither thou

Concerning fasting

[1]The first part of this quotation is Ps. 51, 19; the second part according to a note in C is from the Apocalypse of Adam, which is no longer extant.

216

nor any of the household of thy seed. 4. Then shall thy
light break forth as the dawn, and thy robes shall rise
quickly, and thy righteousness shall go before thee, and
the glory of God shall surround thee." 5. "Then thou
shalt cry and God shall hear thee; while thou art still
speaking He shall say, 'Lo I am here'; if thou puttest
away from thee bondage, and violence, and the word of
murmuring, and dost give to the poor thy bread with a
cheerful heart, and dost pity the soul that is abased." 6.
So then, brethren, the long-suffering one foresaw that
the people whom He prepared in his Beloved should
believe in guilelessness, and made all things plain to us
beforehand that we should not be shipwrecked by
conversion to their law.

IV

1. WE ought then, to enquire earnestly into the things
which now are, and to seek out those which are able to
save us. Let us then utterly flee from all the works of
lawlessness, lest the works of lawlessness overcome us,
and let us hate the error of this present time, that we
may be loved in that which is to come. 2. Let us give no
freedom to our souls to have power to walk with
sinners and wicked men, lest we be made like to them.
3. The final stumbling block is at hand of which it was
written, as Enoch says, "For to this end the Lord has cut
short the times and the days, that his beloved should
make haste and come to his inheritance." 4. And the
Prophet also says thus: "Ten kingdoms shall reign upon
the earth and there shall rise up after them a little king,
who shall subdue three of the kings under one."
5. Daniel says likewise concerning the same: "And I
beheld the fourth Beast, wicked and powerful and
fiercer than all the beasts of the sea, and that ten horns
sprang from it, and out of them a little excrescent horn,
and that it subdued under one three of the great horns."
6. You ought then to understand. And this also I ask
you, as being one of yourselves, and especially as loving
you all above my own life; take heed to yourselves now,
and be not made like unto some, heaping up your sins

Warning that the final trial is at hand

217

and saying that the covenant is both theirs and ours. 7. It is ours: but in this way did they finally lose it when Moses had just received it, for the Scripture says: "And Moses was in the mount fasting forty days and forty nights, and he received the covenant from the Lord, tables of stone written with the finger of the hand of the Lord." 8. But they turned to idols and lost it. For thus saith the Lord: "Moses, Moses, go down quickly, for thy people, whom thou broughtest forth out of the land of Egypt, have broken the Law." And Moses understood and cast the two tables out of his hands, and their covenant was broken, in order that the covenant of Jesus the Beloved should be sealed in our hearts in hope of his faith. 9. (And though I wish to write much, I hasten to write in devotion to you, not as a teacher, but as it becomes one who loves to leave out nothing of that which we have.)[1] Wherefore let us pay heed in the last days, for the whole time of our life and faith will profit us nothing, unless we resist, as becomes the sons of God in this present evil time, against the offences which are to come, that the Black One may have no opportunity of entry. 10. Let us flee from all vanity, let us utterly hate the deeds of the path of wickedness. Do not by retiring apart live alone as if you were already made righteous, but come together and seek out the common good. 11. For the Scripture says: "Woe to them who are prudent for themselves and understanding in their own sight." Let us be spiritual, let us be a temple consecrated to God, so far as in us lies let us "exercise ourselves in the fear" of God, and let us strive to keep his commandments in order that we may rejoice in his ordinances. 12. The Lord will "judge" the world "without respect of persons." Each will receive according to his deeds. If he be good his righteousness will lead him, if he be evil the reward of iniquity is before him. 13. Let us never rest as though we were 'called'[2] and slumber in our sins, lest the wicked ruler gain power over us and thrust us out from the Kingdom of the Lord. 14. And consider this also, my brethren, when you see that after such great signs and wonders were wrought in Israel they

The covenant. Christian or Jewish?

Admonition to stedfastness

[1]It is possible that the odd change of construction is due to some reference to a well known maxim: but the source of such quotation or reference has not been found.

[2]Apparently a loose expression = "confiding in our call."

218

were even then finally abandoned;—let us take heed lest as it was written we be found "many called but few chosen."

V

1. FOR it was for this reason that the Lord endured to deliver up his flesh to corruption, that we should be sanctified by the remission of sin, that is, by his sprinkled blood. 2. For the scripture concerning him relates partly to Israel, partly to us, and it speaks thus: "He was wounded for our transgressions and bruised for our iniquities, by his stripes we were healed. He was brought as a sheep to the slaughter, and as a lamb dumb before its shearer." 3. Therefore we ought to give great thanks to the Lord that he has given us knowledge of the past, and wisdom for the present, and that we are not without understanding for the future. 4. And the Scripture says, "Not unjustly are the nets spread out for the birds." This means that a man deserves to perish who has a knowledge of the way of righteousness, but turns aside into the way of darkness. 5. Moreover, my brethren, if the Lord endured to suffer for our life, though he is the Lord of all the world, to whom God said before the foundation of the world, "Let us make man in our image and likeness," how, then, did he endure to suffer at the hand of man? 6. Learn:—The Prophets who received grace from him prophesied of him, and he, in order that he "might destroy death," and show forth the Resurrection from the dead, because he needs must be made "manifest in the flesh," endured 7. in order to fulfil the promise made to the fathers, and himself prepare for himself the new people and show while he was on earth that he himself will raise the dead and judge the risen. 8. Furthermore, while teaching Israel and doing such great signs and wonders he preached to them and loved them greatly; 9. but when he chose out his own Apostles who were to preach his Gospel, he chose those who were iniquitous above all sin to show that "he came not to call the righteous but sinners,"—then he manifested himself as God's Son. 10. For if he had not come in the flesh men could in no

The reason for the Passion of Christ

way have been saved by beholding him; seeing that they have not the power when they look at the sun to gaze straight at its rays, though it is destined to perish, and is the work of his hands. 11. So then the Son of God came in the flesh for this reason, that he might complete the total of the sins of those who persecuted his prophets to death. 12. For this cause he endured. For God says of the chastisement of his flesh that it is from them: "When they shall smite their shepherd, then the sheep of the flock shall be destroyed." 13. And he was willing to suffer thus, for it was necessary that he should suffer on a tree, for the Prophet says of him, "Spare my soul from the sword" and, "Nail my flesh, for the synagogues of the wicked have risen against me." 14. And again he says: "Lo, I have given my back to scourges, and my cheeks to strokes, and I have set my face as a solid rock."

VI

1. WHEN therefore he made the commandment what does he say? "Who is he that comes into court with me? Let him oppose me; or, who is he that seeks justice against me? Let him draw near to the Lord's servant. 2. Woe unto you, for ye shall all wax old as a garment and the moth shall eat you up." And again the Prophet says that he was placed as a strong stone for crushing, "Lo, I will place for the foundations of Sion a precious stone, chosen out, a chief corner stone, honourable." 3. Then what does he say? "And he that hopeth on it shall live for ever." Is then our hope on a stone? God forbid. But he means that the Lord placed his flesh in strength. For he says, "And he placed me as a solid rock." 4. And again the Prophet says, "The stone which the builders rejected, this is become the head of the corner," and again he says, "This is the great and wonderful day which the Lord made." 5. I write to you more simply that you may understand: I am devoted to your love. 6. What then does the Prophet say again? "The synagogue of the sinners compassed me around, they surrounded me as bees round the honeycomb" and, "They

Proofs from the Prophets

220

cast lots for my clothing." 7. Since therefore he was destined to be manifest and to suffer in the flesh his Passion was foretold. For the Prophet says concerning Israel, "Woe unto their soul, for they have plotted an evil plot against themselves, saying, 'Let us bind the Just one, for he is unprofitable to us.' " 8. What does the other Prophet, Moses, say to them? "Lo, thus saith the Lord God, enter into the good land which the Lord sware that he would give to Abraham, Isaac, and Jacob, and inherit it, a land flowing with milk and honey." 9. But learn what knowledge says. Hope, it says, on that Jesus[1] who will be manifested to you in the flesh. For man is earth which suffers, for the creation of Adam was from the face of the earth. 10. What then is the meaning of "into the good land, a land flowing with milk and honey"? Blessed be our Lord, brethren, who has placed in us wisdom and understanding of his secrets. For the prophet speaks a parable of the Lord: "Who shall understand save he who is wise, and learned, and a lover of his Lord?" 11. Since then he made us new by the remission of sins he made us another type, that we should have the soul of children as though he were creating afresh. 12. For it is concerning us that the scripture says that he says to the Son, "Let us make man after our image and likeness, and let them rule the beasts of the earth, and the birds of heaven, and the fishes of the sea." And the Lord said, when he saw our fair creation, "Increase and multiply and fill the earth"; these things were spoken to the Son. 13. Again I will show you how he speaks to us. In the last days he made a second creation; and the Lord says, "See, I make the last things the first." To this then the Prophet referred when he proclaimed, "Enter into a land flowing with milk and honey, and rule over it." 14. See then, we have been created afresh, as he says again in another Prophet, "See," saith the Lord, "I will take out from them" (that is those whom the Spirit of the Lord foresaw) "the hearts of stone and I will put in hearts of flesh." Because he himself was going to be manifest in the flesh and to dwell among us. 15. For, my brethren, the habitation of our hearts is a shrine holy to the Lord.

---

[1] A contrast is here no doubt implied between "that Jesus who will be manifested" and the Jesus, or Joshua (the two names are the same in Greek) who led the Israelites over the Jordan.

16. For the Lord says again, "And wherewith shall I appear before the Lord my God and be glorified?" He says, "I will confess to thee in the assembly of my brethren, and will sing to thee in the midst of the assembly of saints." We then are they whom he brought into the good land. 17. What then is the milk and the honey? Because a child is first nourished with honey, and afterwards with milk. Thus therefore we also, being nourished on the faith of the promise and by the word, shall live and possess the earth. 18. And we have said above, "And let them increase and multiply and rule over the fishes." Who then is it who is now able to rule over beasts or fishes or the birds of heaven? For we ought to understand that to rule implies authority, so that one may give commandments and have domination. 19. If then this does not happen at present he has told us the time when it will;—when we ourselves also have been made perfect as heirs of the covenant of the Lord.

VII

1. UNDERSTAND therefore, children of gladness, that the good Lord made all things plain beforehand to us, that we should know him to whom we ought to give thanks and praise for everything. 2. If then the Son of God, though he was the Lord and was "destined to judge the living and the dead" suffered in order that his wounding might make us alive, let us believe that the Son of God could not suffer except for our sakes. 3. But moreover when he was crucified "he was given to drink vinegar and gall." Listen how the priests of the Temple foretold this. The commandment was written, "Whosoever does not keep the fast shall die the death," and the Lord commanded this because he himself was going to offer the vessel of the spirit as a sacrifice for our sins, in order that the type established in Isaac, who was offered upon the altar, might be fulfilled. 4. What then does he say in the Prophet? "And let them eat of the goat which is offered in the fast for all their sins." Attend carefully,—"and let all the priests alone eat the entrails unwashed with vinegar." 5. Why? Because you

Fasting and the scapegoat

222

are going "to give to me gall and vinegar to drink" when I am on the point of offering my flesh for my new people, therefore you alone shall eat, while the people fast and mourn in sackcloth and ashes. To show that he must suffer for them. 6. Note what was commanded: "Take two goats, goodly and alike, and offer them, and let the priest take the one as a burnt offering for sins." 7. But what are they to do with the other? "The other," he says, "is accursed." Notice how the type of Jesus is manifested: 8. "And do ye all spit on it, and goad it, and bind the scarlet wool about its head, and so let it be cast into the desert." And when it is so done, he who takes the goat into the wilderness drives it forth, and takes away the wool, and puts it upon a shrub which is called Rachél,[1] of which we are accustomed to eat the shoots when we find them in the country: thus of Rachél alone is the fruit sweet. 9. What does this mean? Listen: "the first goat is for the altar, but the other is accursed," and note that the one that is accursed is crowned, because then "they will see him" on that day with the long scarlet robe "down to the feet" on his body, and they will say, "Is not this he whom we once crucified and rejected and pierced and spat upon? Of a truth it was he who then said that he was the Son of God." 10. But how is he like to the goat? For this reason: "the goats shall be alike, beautiful, and a pair," in order that when they see him come at that time they may be astonished at the likeness of the goat. See then the type of Jesus destined to suffer. 11. But why is it that they put the wool in the middle of the thorns? It is a type of Jesus placed in the Church, because whoever wishes to take away the scarlet wool must suffer much because the thorns are terrible and he can gain it only through pain. Thus he says, "those who will see me, and attain to my kingdom must lay hold of me through pain and suffering."

---

[1] It is probable that Barnabas has mistaken a word meaning a hill for the name of a herb with which he was familiar; but it is not clear whether the confusion was made in Hebrew or in Greek (ῥαχός = a brier, and sometimes a wild-olive, and ῥαχις = a mountain ridge, seems to suggest some such possibility). But the identity of the herb is unknown. There is an interesting article on it in the *Journal of Biblical Literature*, 1890, by Rendel Harris.

VIII

1. BUT what do you think that it typifies, that the commandment has been given to Israel that the men in whom sin is complete offer a heifer and slay it and burn it, and that boys then take the ashes and put them into vessels and bind scarlet wool on sticks (see again the type of the Cross and the scarlet wool) and hyssop, and that the boys all sprinkle the people thus one by one in order that they all be purified from their sins? 2. Observe how plainly he speaks to you. The calf is Jesus; the sinful men offering it are those who brought him to be slain. Then there are no longer men, no longer the glory[1] of sinners. 3. The boys who sprinkle are they who preached to us the forgiveness of sins, and the purification of the heart, to whom he gave the power of the Gospel to preach, and there are twelve as a testimony to the tribes, because there are twelve tribes of Israel. 4. But why are there three boys who sprinkle? As a testimony to Abraham, Isaac, and Jacob, for these are great before God. 5. And why was the wool put on the wood? Because the kingdom of Jesus is on the wood,[2] and because those who hope on him shall live for ever. 6. But why are the wool and the hyssop together? Because in his kingdom there shall be evil and foul days, in which we shall be saved, for he also who has pain in his flesh is cured by the foulness of the hyssop. 7. And for this reason the things which were thus done are plain to us, but obscure to them, because they did not hear the Lord's voice.

The sacrifice of a heifer

IX

1. FOR he speaks again concerning the ears, how he circumcised our hearts; for the Lord says in the Prophet: "In the hearing of the ear they obey me." And again he says, "They who are afar off shall hear clearly, they shall

The circumcision

[1] This seems to be the only possible translation, but the text must surely be corrupt.
[2] Or "on the tree."

know the things that I have done," and "Circumcise your hearts, saith the Lord." 2. And again he says, "Hear, O Israel, thus saith the Lord thy God," and again the Spirit of the Lord prophesies, "Who is he that will live for ever? Let him hear the voice of my servant." 3. And again he says, "Hear, O heaven, and give ear, O earth, for the Lord hath spoken these things for a testimony." And again he says, "Hear the word of the Lord, ye rulers of this people." And again he says, "Hear, O children, a voice of one crying in the wilderness." So then he circumcised our hearing in order that we should hear the word and believe. 4. But moreover the circumcision in which they trusted has been abolished. For he declared that circumcision was not of the flesh, but they erred because an evil angel was misleading them. 5. He says to them, "Thus saith the Lord your God" (here I find a commandment), "Sow not among thorns, be circumcised to your Lord." And what does he say? "Circumcise the hardness of your heart, and stiffen not your neck." Take it again: "Behold, saith the Lord, all the heathen are uncircumcised in the foreskin, but this people is uncircumcised in heart." 6. But you will say, surely the people has received circumcision as a seal? Yes, but every Syrian and Arab and all priests of the idols have been circumcised; are then these also within their[1] covenant?—indeed even the Egyptians belong to the circumcision. 7. Learn fully then, children of love, concerning all things, for Abraham, who first circumcised, did so looking forward in the spirit to Jesus, and had received the doctrines of three letters. 8. For it says, "And Abraham circumcised from his household eighteen men and three hundred."[2]. What then was the knowledge that was given to him? Notice that he first mentions the eighteen, and after a pause the three hundred. The eighteen is **I** (= ten) and **H** (= 8)— you have Jesus[3] —and because the cross was destined to have grace in the **T** he says "and three hundred."[4] So he indicates Jesus in the two letters and the cross in the other. 9. He knows this who placed the gift of his teaching in our hearts. No one has heard a more excellent lesson from me, but I know that you are worthy.

[1]*I.e.* of the Jews.

[2]In Greek, which expresses numerals by letters, this is **TIH**.

[3]Because **IH** are in Greek the first letters of the word Jesus.

[4]The Greek symbol for 300 is **T**.

225

X

1. Now, in that Moses said, "Ye shall not eat swine, nor an eagle, nor a hawk, nor a crow, nor any fish which has no scales on itself," he included three doctrines in his understanding. 2. Moreover he says to them in Deuteronomy, "And I will make a covenant of my ordinances with this people." So then the ordinance of God is not abstinence from eating, but Moses spoke in the spirit. 3. He mentioned the swine for this reason: you shall not consort, he means, with men who are like swine, that is to say, when they have plenty they forget the Lord, but when they are in want they recognise the Lord, just as the swine when it eats does not know its master, but when it it hungry it cries out, and after receiving food is again silent. 4. "Neither shalt thou eat the eagle nor the hawk nor the kite nor the crow." Thou shalt not, he means, join thyself or make thyself like to such men, as do not know how to gain their food by their labour and sweat, but plunder other people's property in their iniquity, and lay wait for it, though they seem to walk in innocence, and look round to see whom they may plunder in their covetousness, just as these birds alone provide no food for themselves, but sit idle, and seek how they may devour the flesh of others, and become pestilent in their iniquity. 5. "Thou shalt not eat," he says, "the lamprey nor the polypus nor the cuttlefish." Thou shalt not, he means, consort with or become like such men who are utterly ungodly and who are already condemned to death, just as these fish alone are accursed, and float in the deep water, not swimming like the others, but living on the ground at the bottom of the sea. 6. Sed[1] nec "leporem manducabis." Non eris, inquit, corruptor puerorum nec similabis talibus. Quia lepus singulis annis facit ad adsellandum singula foramina; et quotquot annis vivit, totidem foramina facit. 7. Sed "nec beluam, inquit, manducabis";[2] hoc est non eris moecus aut adulter, nec corruptor, nec similabis talibus. Quia haec bestia alternis annis mutat naturam et fit modo masculus, modo femina. 8. Sed et quod dicit mustelam odibis. Non eris, inquit, talis, qui audit

[1]The Latin here given is that of the Old Latin version, and does not in all places correspond quite accurately to the Greek.
[2]This prohibition is not in the O.T.

iniquitatem et loquitur immunditiam. Non inquit adhaerebis immundis qui iniquitatem faciunt ore suo. 9. Moses received three doctrines concerning food and thus spoke of them in the Spirit; but they received them as really referring to food, owing to the lust of their flesh. 10. But David received knowledge concerning the same three doctrines, and says: "Blessed is the man who has not gone in the counsel of the ungodly" as the fishes go in darkness in the deep waters, "and has not stood in the way of sinners" like those who seem to fear the Lord, but sin like the swine, "and has not sat in the seat of the scorners" like the birds who sit and wait for their prey. Grasp fully the doctrines concerning food. 11. Moses says again, "Eat of every animal that is cloven hoofed and ruminant." What does he mean? That he who receives food knows him who feeds him, and rests on him and seems to rejoice. Well did he speak with regard to the commandment. What then does he mean? Consort with those who fear the Lord, with those who meditate in their heart on the meaning of the word which they have received, with those who speak of and observe the ordinances of the Lord, with those who know that meditation is a work of gladness, and who ruminate on the word of the Lord. But what does "the cloven hoofed" mean? That the righteous both walks in this world and looks forward to the holy age. See how well Moses legislated. 12. But how was it possible for them to understand or comprehend these things? But we having a righteous understanding of them announce the commandments as the Lord wished. For this cause he circumcised our hearing and our hearts that we should comprehend these things.

The explanation in the Psalter

XI

1. BUT let us enquire if the Lord took pains to foretell the water of baptism and the cross. Concerning the water it has been written with regard to Israel that they will not receive the baptism that brings the remission of sins, but will build for themselves. 2. For the Prophet says, "Be astonished O heaven, and let the earth tremble

Baptism

the more at this, that this people hath committed two evils: they have deserted me, the spring of life, and they have dug for themselves a cistern of death. 3. Is my holy mountain Sinai a desert rock? For ye shall be as the fledgling birds, fluttering about when they are taken away from the nest." 4. And again the Prophet says, "I will go before you and I will make mountains level, and I will break gates of brass, and I will shatter bars of iron, and I will give thee treasures of darkness, secret, invisible, that they may know that I am the Lord God." 5. And, "Thou shalt dwell in a lofty cave of a strong rock." And, "His water is sure, ye shall see the King in his glory, and your soul shall meditate on the fear of the Lord." 6. And again he says in another Prophet, "And he who does these things shall be as the tree, which is planted at the partings of the waters, which shall give its fruit in its season, and its leaf shall not fade, and all things, whatsoever he doeth, shall prosper. 7. It is not so with the wicked, it is not so; but they are even as the chaff which the wind driveth away from the face of the earth. Therefore the wicked shall not rise up in judgment, nor sinners in the counsel of the righteous, for the Lord knoweth the way of righteousness, and the way of the ungodly shall perish." 8. Mark how he described the The Cross water and the cross together. For he means this: blessed are those who hoped on the cross, and descended into the water. For he speaks of their reward "in his season"; at that time, he says, I will repay. But now when he says, "Their leaves shall not fade," he means that every word which shall come forth from your mouth in faith and love, shall be for conversion and hope for many. 9. And again another Prophet says, "And the land of Jacob was praised above every land." He means to say that he is glorifying the vessel of his Spirit. 10. What does he say next? "And there was a river flowing on the right hand, and beautiful trees grew out of it, and whosoever shall eat of them shall live for ever." 11. He means to say that we go down into the water full of sins and foulness, and we come up bearing the fruit of fear in our hearts, and having hope on Jesus in the Spirit. "And whosoever shall eat of them shall live for ever." He means that whosoever hears and believes these things spoken shall live for ever.

XII

1. SIMILARLY, again, he describes the cross in another Prophet, who says "And when shall all these things be accomplished? saith the Lord. When the tree shall fall and rise, and when blood shall flow from the tree." Here again you have a reference to the cross, and to him who should be crucified. 2. And he says again to Moses, when Israel was warred upon by strangers, and in order to remind those who were warred upon that they were delivered unto death by reason of their sins—the Spirit speaks to the heart of Moses to make a representation of the cross, and of him who should suffer, because, he says, unless they put their trust in him, they shall suffer war for ever. Moses therefore placed one shield upon another in the midst of the fight, and standing there raised above them all kept stretching out his hands, and so Israel again began to be victorious: then, whenever he let them drop they began to perish. 3. Why? That they may know that they cannot be saved if they do not hope on him. 4. And again he says in another Prophet, "I stretched out my hands the whole day to a disobedient people and one that refuses my righteous way." 5. Again Moses makes a representation of Jesus, showing that he must suffer, and shall himself give life, though they will believe that he has been put to death, by the sign given when Israel was falling (for the Lord made every serpent bite them, and they were perishing, for the fall[1] took place in Eve through the serpent), in order to convince them that they will be delivered over to the affliction of death because of their transgression. 6. Moreover, though Moses commanded them:—"You shall have neither graven nor molten image for your God," yet he makes one himself to show a type of Jesus. Moses therefore makes a graven serpent, and places it in honour and calls the people by a proclamation. 7. So they came together and besought Moses that he would offer prayer on their behalf for their healing. But Moses said to them, "Whenever one of you," he said, "be bitten, let him come to the serpent that is placed upon the tree, and let him hope, in faith that it though dead is able to give life, and he shall straightway be saved." And they did so. In this also you have again the glory of

[1]Literally the "transgression."

Jesus, for all things are in him and for him. 8. Again, Joshua
why does Moses say to Jesus, the son of Naue,[1] when he
gives him, prophet as he is, this name, that the whole
people should listen to him alone? Because the Father
was revealing everything concerning his Son Jesus.
9. Moses therefore says to Jesus the son of Naue, after
giving him this name, when he sent him to spy out the
land, "Take a book in thy hands and write what the
Lord saith, that the Son of God shall in the last day tear
up by the roots the whole house of Amalek." 10. See
again Jesus, not as son of man, but as Son of God, but
manifested in a type in the flesh. Since therefore they are
going to say that the Christ is David's son, David
himself prophesies, fearing and understanding the error
of the sinners, "The Lord said to my Lord sit thou on
my right hand until I make thy enemies thy footstool."
11. And again Isaiah speaks thus, "The Lord said to
Christ my Lord, whose right hand I held, that the
nations should obey before him, and I will shatter the
strength of Kings." See how "David calls him Lord"
and does not say Son.

XIII

1. Now let us see whether this people or the former Jews and Christians
people is the heir, and whether the covenant is for us or as heirs of the
for them. 2. Hear then what the Scripture says concern- covenant
ing the people: "And Isaac prayed concerning Rebecca
his wife, because she was barren, and she conceived.
Then Rebecca went forth to enquire of the Lord and the
Lord said to her: two nations are in thy womb, and two
peoples in thy belly, and one people shall overcome a
people, and the greater shall serve the less." 3. You
ought to understand who is Isaac and who is Rebecca,
and of whom he has shown that this people is greater
than that people. 4. And in another prophecy Jacob
speaks more plainly to Joseph his son, saying, "Behold
the Lord hath not deprived me of thy presence; bring
me thy sons, that I may bless them." 5. And he brought
Ephraim and Manasses, and wished that Manasses

[1]*i.e.* Joshua the son of Nun, of which names Jesus and Naue are the
Greek forms.

should be blessed, because he was the elder; for Joseph brought him to the right hand of his father Jacob. But Jacob saw in the spirit a type of the people of the future. And what does he say? "And Jacob crossed his hands, and placed his right hand on the head of Ephraim, the second and younger son, and blessed him; and Joseph said to Jacob, Change thy right hand on to the head of Manasses, for he is my first-born son. And Jacob said to Joseph, I know it, my child, I know it; but the greater shall serve the less, and this one shall indeed be blessed." 6. See who it is of whom he ordained that this people is the first and heir of the covenant. 7. If then besides this he remembered it also in the case of Abraham, we reach the perfection of our knowledge. What then does he say to Abraham, when he alone was faithful, and it was counted him for righteousness? "Behold I have made thee, Abraham, the father of the Gentiles who believe in God in uncircumcision."

XIV

1. So it is. But let us see whether the covenant which he sware to the fathers to give to the people—whether he has given it. He has given it. But they were not worthy to receive it because of their sins. 2. For the Prophet says, "And Moses was fasting on Mount Sinai, to receive the covenant of the Lord for the people, forty days and forty nights. And Moses received from the Lord the two tables, written by the finger of the hand of the Lord in the Spirit"; and Moses took them, and carried them down to give them to the people. 3. And the Lord said to Moses, "Moses, Moses, go down quickly, for thy people whom thou didst bring out of the land of Egypt have broken the Law. And Moses perceived that they had made themselves again molten images, and he cast them out of his hands, and the tables of the covenant of the Lord were broken." 4. Moses received it, but they were not worthy. But learn how we received it. Moses received it when he was a servant, but the Lord himself gave it to us, as the people of the inheritance, by suffering for our sakes. 5. And it was

The fulfilment of the promise to the Jews

231

made manifest both that the tale of their sins should be completed in their sins, and that we through Jesus, the Lord who inherits the covenant, should receive it, for he was prepared for this purpose, that when he appeared he might redeem from darkness our hearts which were already paid over to death, and given over to the iniquity of error, and by his word might make a covenant with us. 6. For it is written that the Father enjoins on him that he should redeem us from darkness and prepare a holy people for himself. 7. The Prophet therefore says, "I the Lord thy God did call thee in righteousness, and I will hold thy hands, and I will give thee strength, and I have given thee for a covenant of the people, for a light to the Gentiles, to open the eyes of the blind, and to bring forth from their fetters those that are bound and those that sit in darkness out of the prison house." We know then whence we have been redeemed. 8. Again the Prophet says, "Lo, I have made thee a light for the Gentiles, to be for salvation unto the ends of the earth, thus saith the Lord the God who did redeem thee." 9. And again the Prophet saith, "The Spirit of the Lord is upon me, because he annointed me to preach the Gospel of grace to the humble, he sent me to heal the brokenhearted, to proclaim delivery to the captives, and sight to the blind, to announce a year acceptable to the Lord, and a day of recompense, to comfort all who mourn."

XV

1. FURTHERMORE it was written concerning the Sabbath in the ten words which he spake on Mount Sinai face to face to Moses. "Sanctify also the Sabbath of the Lord with pure hands and a pure heart." 2. And in another place he says, "If my sons keep the Sabbath, then will I bestow my mercy upon them." 3. He speaks of the Sabbath at the beginning of the Creation, "And God made in six days the works of his hands and on the seventh day he made an end, and rested in it and sanctified it." 4. Notice, children, what is the meaning of "He made an end in six days"? He means this: that

The Sabbath

232

the Lord will make an end of everything in six thousand years, for a day with him means a thousand years. And he himself is my witness when he says, "Lo, the day of the Lord shall be as a thousand years." So then, children, in six days that is in six thousand years, everything will be completed. 5. "And he rested on the seventh day." This means, when his Son comes he will destroy the time of the wicked one, and will judge the godless, and will change the sun and the moon and the stars, and then he will truly rest on the seventh day. 6. Furthermore he says, "Thou shalt sanctify it with clean hands and a pure heart." If, then, anyone has at present the power to keep holy the day which God made holy, by being pure in heart, we are altogether deceived. 7. See that we shall indeed keep it holy at that time, when we enjoy true rest, when we shall be able to do so because we have been made righteous ourselves and have received the promise, when there is no more sin, but all things have been made new by the Lord: then we shall be able to keep it holy because we ourselves have first been made holy. 8. Furthermore he says to them, "Your new moons and the sabbaths I cannot away with." Do you see what he means? The present sabbaths are not acceptable to me, but that which I have made, in which I will give rest to all things and make the beginning of an eighth day, that is the beginning of another world. 9. Wherefore we also celebrate with gladness the eighth day in which Jesus also rose from the dead, and was made manifest, and ascended into Heaven.

XVI

1. I WILL also speak with you concerning the Temple, The Temple and show how the wretched men erred by putting their hope on the building, and not on the God who made them, and is the true house of God. 2. For they consecrated him in the Temple almost like the heathen. But learn how the Lord speaks, in bringing it to naught, "Who has measured the heaven with a span, or the earth with his outstretched hand? Have not I? saith the Lord.

Heaven is my throne, and the earth is my footstool, what house will ye build for me, or what is the place of my rest?" You know that their hope was vain. 3. Furthermore he says again, "Lo, they who destroyed this temple shall themselves build it." 4. That is happening now. For owing to the war it was destroyed by the enemy; at present even the servants of the enemy will build it up again. 5. Again, it was made manifest that the city and the temple and the people of Israel were to be delivered up. For the Scripture says, "And it shall come to pass in the last days that the Lord shall deliver the sheep of his pasture, and the sheep-fold, and their tower to destruction." And it took place according to what the Lord said. 6. But let us inquire if a temple of God exists. Yes, it exists, where he himself said that he makes and perfects it. For it is written, "And it shall come to pass when the week is ended that a temple of God shall be built gloriously in the name of the Lord." 7. I find then that a temple exists. Learn then how it will be built in the name of the Lord. Before we believed in God the habitation of our heart was corrupt and weak, like a temple really built with hands, because it was full of idolatry, and was the house of demons through doing things which were contrary to God. 8. "But it shall be built in the name of the Lord." Now give heed, in order that the temple of the Lord may be built gloriously. Learn in what way. When we received the remission of sins, and put our hope on the Name, we became new, being created again from the beginning; wherefore God truly dwells in us, in the habitation which we are. 9. How? His word of faith, the calling of his promise, the wisdom of the ordinances, the commands of the teaching, himself prophesying in us, himself dwelling in us, by opening the door of the temple (that is the mouth) to us, giving repentance to us, and thus he leads us, who have been enslaved to death into the incorruptible temple. 10. For he who desires to be saved looks not at the man, but at him who dwells and speaks in him, and is amazed at him, for he has never either heard him speak such words with his mouth, nor has he himself ever desired to hear them. This is a spiritual temple being built for the Lord.

XVII

1. So far as possibility and simplicity allow an explanation to be given to you my soul hopes that none of the things which are necessary for salvation have been omitted, according to my desire. 2. For if I write to you concerning things present or things to come, you will not understand because they are hid in parables. This then suffices.

XVIII

1. Now[1] let us pass on to another lesson and teaching. There are two Ways of teaching and power, one of Light and one of Darkness. And there is a great difference between the two Ways. For over the one are set light-bringing angels of God, but over the other angels of Satan. 2. And the one is the Lord from eternity and to eternity, and the other is the ruler of the present time of iniquity.

XIX

1. The Way of Light is this: if any man desire to journey to the appointed place, let him be zealous in his works. Therefore the knowledge given to us of this kind that we may walk in it is as follows:— 2. Thou shalt love thy maker, thou shalt fear thy Creator, thou shalt glorify Him who redeemed thee from death, thou shalt be simple in heart, and rich in spirit; thou shalt not join thyself to those who walk in the way of death, thou shalt hate all that is not pleasing to God, thou shalt hate all hypocrisy; thou shalt not desert the commandments of the Lord. 3. Thou shalt not exalt thyself, but shall be humble-minded in all things; thou shalt not take glory to thyself. Thou shalt form no evil plan against thy neighbour, thou shalt not let thy soul be froward.

4. Thou shalt not commit fornification, thou shalt not commit adultery, thou shalt not commit sodomy. Thou shalt not let the word of God depart from thee among the impurity of any men. Thou shalt not respect persons in the reproving of transgression. Thou shalt be meek, thou shalt be quiet, thou shalt fear the words which thou hast heard. Thou shalt not bear malice against thy brother. 5. Thou shalt not be in two minds whether it shall be or not. "Thou shalt not take the name of the Lord in vain." Thou shalt love thy neighbour more than thy own life. Thou shalt not procure abortion, thou shalt not commit infanticide. Thou shalt not withhold thy hand from thy son or from thy daughter, but shalt teach them the fear of God from their youth up. 6. Thou shalt not covet thy neighbour's goods, thou shalt not be avaricious. Thou shalt not be joined in soul with the haughty but shalt converse with humble and righteous men. Thou shalt receive the trials that befall thee as good, knowing that nothing happens without God. 7. Thou shalt not be double-minded or talkative. Thou shalt obey thy masters as a type of God in modesty and fear; thou shalt not command in bitterness thy slave or handmaid who hope on the same God, lest they cease to fear the God who is over you both; for he came not to call men with respect of persons, but those whom the Spirit prepared. 8. Thou shalt share all things with thy neighbour and shall not say that they are thy own property; for if you are sharers in that which is incorruptible, how much more in that which is corruptible? Thou shalt not be forward to speak, for the mouth is a snare of death. So far as thou canst, thou shalt keep thy soul pure. 9. Be not one who stretches out the hands to take, and shuts them when it comes to giving. Thou shalt love "as the apple of thine eye" all who speak to thee the word of the Lord. 10. Thou shalt remember the day of judgment day and night, and thou shalt seek each day the society of the saints, either labouring by speech, and going out to exhort, and striving to save souls by the word, or working with thine hands for the ransom of thy sins. 11. Thou shalt not hesitate to give, and when thou givest thou shalt not grumble, but thou shalt know who is the good paymaster of the reward. "Thou shalt keep the precepts" which thou hast received, "adding nothing and taking nothing away." Thou shalt

236

utterly hate evil. "Thou shalt give righteous judgment." 12. Thou shalt not cause quarrels, but shalt bring together and reconcile those that strive. Thou shalt confess thy sins. Thou shalt not betake thyself to prayer with an evil conscience. This is the Way of Light.

XX

1. BUT the Way of the Black One is crooked and full of cursing, for it is the way of death eternal with punishment, and in it are the things that destroy their soul: idolatry, frowardness, arrogance of power, hypocrisy, double-heartedness, adultery, murder, robbery, pride, transgression, fraud, malice, self-sufficiency, enchantments, magic, covetousness, the lack of the fear of God; 2. persecutors of the good, haters of the truth, lovers of lies, knowing not the reward of righteousness, who "cleave not to the good," nor to righteous judgment, who attend not to the cause of the widow and orphan, spending wakeful nights not in the fear of God, but in the pursuit of vice, from whom meekness and patience are far and distant, "loving vanity, seeking rewards," without pity for the poor, working not for him who is oppressed with toil, prone to evil speaking, without knowledge of their Maker, murderers of children, corrupters of God's creation, turning away the needy, oppressing the afflicted, advocates of the rich, unjust judges of the poor, altogether sinful.

The Way of Darkness

XXI

1. IT is good therefore that he who has learned the ordinances of the Lord as many as have been written should walk in them. For he who does these things shall be glorified in the kingdom of God, and he who chooses the others shall perish with his works. For this reason there is a resurrection, for this reason there is a recompense. 2. I beseech those who are in high positions, if

Final exhortation

you will receive any counsel of my goodwill, have among yourselves those to whom you may do good; fail not. 3. The day is at hand when all things shall perish with the Evil one; "The Lord and his reward is at hand." 4. I beseech you again and again be good lawgivers to each other, remain faithful counsellors of each other, remove from yourselves all hypocrisy. 5. Now may God, who is the Lord over all the world, give you wisdom, understanding, prudence, knowledge of his ordinances, patience. 6. And be taught of God, seeking out what the Lord requires from you, and see that ye be found faithful in the day of Judgment. 7. If there is any memory of good, meditate on these things and remember me, that my desire and my watchfulness may find some good end. I beseech you asking it of your favour. 8. While the fair vessel[1] is with you fail not in any of, them but seek these things diligently, and fulfil every commandment; for these things are worthy. 9. Wherefore I was the more zealous to write to you of my ability, to give you gladness. May you gain salvation, children of love and peace. The Lord of glory and of all grace be with your spirit.

The Epistle of Barnabas.

THE SHEPHERD

Vision 1

I

1. He who brought me up sold me to a certain Rhoda at Rome. After many years I made her acquaintance again, and began to love her as a sister.[2] 2. After some time I saw her bathing in the river Tiber, and gave her my hand and helped her out of the river. When I saw her

Hermas and Rhoda

---

[1] *i.e.* while you are in the body.

[2] As it stands this is hardly intelligible: presumably the meaning is that Hermas was born a slave, and that his owner sold him to Rhoda. It is implied that he then passed out of her possession, and later made her acquaintance again. The alternative is that ἀνεγνωρισάμην merely means "came to know her properly."

beauty I reflected in my heart and said: "I should be happy if I had a wife of such beauty and character." This was my only thought, and no other, no, not one. 3. After some time, while I was going to Cumae, and glorifying the creation of God, for its greatness and splendour and might, as I walked along I became sleepy. And a spirit seized me and took me away through a certain pathless district, through which a man could not walk, but the ground was precipitous and broken up by the streams of water. So I crossed that river, and came to the level ground and knelt down and began to pray to the Lord and to confess my sins. 4. Now while I was praying the Heaven was opened, and I saw that woman whom I had desired greeting me out of the Heaven and saying: "Hail, Hermas." 5. And I looked at her, and said to her: "Lady, what are you doing here?" and she answered me: "I was taken up to accuse you of your sins before the Lord." 6. I said to her: "Are you now accusing me?" "No," she said, "but listen to the words which I am going to say to you. 'God who dwells in Heaven' and created that which is out of that which is not, and 'increased and multiplied it' for the sake of his Holy Church, is angry with you because you sinned against me." 7. I answered and said to her: "Did I sin against you? In what place, or when did I speak an evil word to you? Did I not always look on you as a goddess? Did I not always respect you as a sister? Why do you charge me falsely, Lady, with these wicked and impure things?" 8. She laughed and said to me: "The desire of wickedness came up in your heart. Or do you not think that it is an evil deed for a righteous man if an evil desire come up in his heart? Yes, it is a sin," said she, "and a great one. For the righteous man has righteous designs. So long then as his designs are righteous his repute stands fast in Heaven, and he finds the Lord ready to assist him in all his doings. But they who have evil designs in their hearts bring upon themselves death and captivity, especially those who obtain this world for themselves, and glory in their wealth, and do not lay hold of the good things which are to come. 9. Their hearts will repent; yet have they no hope, but they have abandoned themselves and their life. But do you pray to God, and 'He shall heal the sins of yourself' and of all your house and of all the saints."

Hermas goes to Cumae

The vision of Rhoda speaking from Heaven

239

II

1. AFTER she had spoken these words the Heavens were shut, and I was all shuddering and in grief. And I began to say in myself: "If this sin is recorded against me, how shall I be saved? Or how shall I propitiate God for my completed sins? Or with what words shall I beseech the Lord to be forgiving unto me?" 2. While I was considering and doubting these things in my heart I saw before me a white chair made of snow-white wool of great size; and there came a woman, old and clothed in shining garments with a book in her hand, and she sat down alone and greeted me: "Hail, Hermas!" And I, in my grief and weeping, said: "Hail, Lady!" 3. And she said to me: "Why are you gloomy, Hermas? You who are patient and good-tempered, who are always laughing, why are you so downcast in appearance and not merry?" And I said to her: "Because of a most excellent lady, who says that I sinned against her." 4. And she said: "By no means let this thing happen to the servant of God; but for all that the thought did enter your heart concerning her. It is such a design as this which brings sin on the servants of God. For it is an evil and mad purpose against a revered spirit and one already approved, if a man desire an evil deed, and especially if it be Hermas the temperate, who abstains from every evil desire and is full of all simplicity and great innocence.

The vision of the ancient lady

III

1. "BUT it is not for this that God is angry with you, but in order that you should convert your family, which has sinned against the Lord, and against you, their parents. But you are indulgent, and do not correct your family, but have allowed them to become corrupt. For this reason the Lord is angry with you, but he will heal all the past evils in your family, for because of their sins and wickednesses have you been corrupted by the things of daily life. 2. But the great mercy of the Lord has had pity on you and on your family, and will make you strong and will establish you in his glory; only do

Why God is angry

not be slothful, but have courage and strengthen your family. For as the smith, by hammering his work, overcomes the task which he desires, so also the daily righteous word overcomes all wickedness. Do not cease, then, correcting your children, for I know that if they repent with all their heart, they will be inscribed in the books of life with the saints." 3. After she had ceased these words she said to me: "Would you like to hear me read aloud?" and I said: "I should like it, Lady." She said to me: "Listen then, and hear the glory of God." I heard great and wonderful things which I cannot remember; for all the words were frightful, such as a man cannot bear. So I remembered the last words, for they were profitable for us and gentle: 4. "Lo, 'the God of the powers,' whom I love, by his mighty power, and by his great wisdom 'created the world,' and by his glorious counsel surrounded his creation with beauty, and by his mighty word 'fixed the Heaven and founded the earth upon the waters,' and by his own wisdom and forethought created his holy Church, which he also blessed—Lo, he changes the heavens, and the mountains and the hills and the seas, and all things are becoming smooth for his chosen ones, to give them the promise which he made with great glory and joy, if they keep the ordinances of God, which they received with great faith."

The lady reads to Hermas

IV

1. So, when she had finished reading, and rose from the chair, there came four young men, and took up the chair and went away towards the East. 2. And she called me and touched my breast and said to me; "Did my reading please you?" and I said to her: "Lady, this last part pleases me, but the first part was hard and difficult." And she said to me: "This last part is for the righteous, but the first part was for the heathen and the apostates." 3. While she was speaking with me two men appeared, and took her by the arm and they went away towards the East, whither the chair had gone. But she went away cheerfully, and as she went said to me, "Play the man, Hermas."

The close of the vision

241

Vision 2

I

1. WHILE I was going to Cumae, at about the same time as the year before, as I walked along I remembered the vision of the previous year, and the spirit again seized me and took me away to the same place, where I had been the previous year. 2. So when I came to the place, I knelt down and began to pray to the Lord and 'to glorify his name,' because he had thought me worthy, and had made known to me my former sins. 3. But after I rose from prayer I saw before me the ancient lady, whom I had seen the year before, walking and reading out from a little book. And she said to me: "Can you take this message to God's elect ones?" I said to her: "Lady, I cannot remember so much; but give me the little book to copy." "Take it," she said, "and give it me back." 4. I took it and went away to a certain place in the country, and copied it all, letter by letter, for I could not distinguish the syllables.[1] So when I had finished the letters of the little book it was suddenly taken out of my hand; but I did not see by whom.

The second vision at Cumae

The ancient lady returns

The little book

II

1. BUT after fifteen days, when I had fasted and prayed greatly to the Lord, the knowledge of the writing was revealed to me. And these things were written: 2. Your seed, Hermas, have set God at naught, and have blasphemed the Lord, and have betrayed their parents in great wickedness, and they are called the betrayers of parents, and their betrayal has not profited them, but they have added to their sins wanton deeds and piled up wickedness, and so their crimes have been made complete. 3. But make these words known to all your children and to your wife, who shall in future be to you as a sister. For she also does not refrain her tongue, with

The contents of the little book

[1] Hermas no doubt means that it was written, like most early MSS., in a continuous script with no divisions between the words.

242

which she sins; but when she has heard these words she will refrain it, and will obtain mercy. 4. After you have made known these words to them, which the Master commanded me to reveal to you, all the sins which they have formerly committed shall be forgiven them, and they shall be forgiven to all the saints who have sinned up to this day,[1] if they repent with their whole heart, and put aside double-mindedness from their heart. 5. For the Master has sworn to his elect by his glory that if there be still sin after this day has been fixed, they shall find no salvation; for repentance for the just has an end; the days of repentance have been fulfilled for all the saints, but for the heathen repentance is open until the last day. 6. You shall say, then, to the leaders of the Church, that they reform their ways in righteousness to receive in full the promises with great glory. 7. You, therefore, 'who work righteousness,' must remain steadfast and be not double-minded, that your passing may be with the holy angels.[2] Blessed are you, as many as endure the great persecution which is coming, and as many as shall not deny their life. 8. For the Lord has sworn by his Son that those who have denied their Christ have been rejected from their life, that is, those who shall now deny him in the days to come. But those who denied him formerly have obtained forgiveness through his great mercy.

III

1. "But, Hermas, no longer bear a grudge against your children, nor neglect your sister, that they may be cleansed from their former sins. For they will be

---

[1] This is the main point of the "Shepherd." The primitive teaching was that for sin after baptism no repentance is possible (cf. Heb. vi.). Hermas now states that it has been revealed to him that "up to this day," i.e. the time of his revelation, sin will be forgiven to the repentant. But this offer of forgiveness will not be made a second time.

[2] Cf. Herm. *Sim.* ix, 25. and Martyr. Polycarp. ii 3 with the note on the latter passage as to the doctrine of a transformation of the just into angels after their death.

corrected with righteous correction, if you bear no grudge against them. The bearing of grudges works death. But you, Hermas, had great troubles of your own because of the transgressions of your family, because you did not pay attention to them. But you neglected them and became entangled in their evil deeds. 2. But you are saved by not 'having broken away from the living God,' and by your simplicity and great temperance. These things have saved you, if you remain in them, and they save all whose deeds are such, and who walk in innocence and simplicity. These shall overcome all wickedness and remain steadfast to eternal life. 3. 'Blessed' are all they 'who do righteousness'; they shall not perish for ever. 4. But you shall say to Maximus: 'Behold, persecution is coming, if it seems good to you deny the faith again.' 'The Lord is near those that turn to him,' as it is written in the Book of Eldad and Modat,[1] who prophesied to the people in the wilderness."

IV

1. AND a revelation was made to me, brethren, while I slept, by a very beautiful young man who said to me, "Who do you think that the ancient lady was from whom you received the little book?" I said, "The Sybil." "You are wrong," he said, "she is not." "Who is she, then?" I said. "The Church," he said. I said to him, "Why then is she old?" "Because," he said, "she was created the first of all things. For this reason is she old; and for her sake was the world established." 2. And afterwards I saw a vision in my house. The ancient lady came and asked me if I had already given the book to the elders. I said that I had not given it. "You have done well," she said, "for I have words to add. When therefore, I have finished all the words they shall be made known by you to all the elect. 3. You shall therefore write two little books and send one to

The revelation as to the ancient lady

The ancient lady returns

[1]This book is mentioned among the Apocrypha of the N.T. in the Athanasian Synopsis and in the Stichometry of Nicephorus, but is not extant. It is thought to be quoted in II Clem. xi. 2. Eldad and Modat are mentioned in Numbers xi. 26.

Clement and one to Grapte. Clement then shall send it to the cities abroad, for that is his duty; and Grapte shall exhort the widows and orphans; but in this city you shall read it yourself with the elders who are in charge of the church."

Vision 3

I

1. THE third vision which I saw, brethren, was as follows: 2. I had fasted for a long time, and prayed the Lord to explain to me the revelation which he had promised to show me through that ancient lady; and in the same night the ancient lady appeared to me and said to me: "Since you are so importunate and zealous to know everything, come into the country, where you are farming, and at the fifth hour I will appear to you, and show you what you must see." 3. I asked her, saying, "Lady, to what part of the field?" "Where you like," she said. I chose a beautiful secluded spot; but before I spoke to her and mentioned the place she said to me, "I will be there, where you wish." 4. I went, therefore, brethren, to the country, and I counted the hours, and I came to the spot where I had arranged for her to come, and I saw a couch of ivory placed there, and on the couch there lay a linen pillow, and over it a covering of fine linen was spread out. 5. When I saw these things lying there, and no one in the place I was greatly amazed, and, as it were, trembling seized me and my hair stood on end. And, as it were, panic came to me because I was alone. When therefore I came to myself, and remembered the glory of God and took courage, I knelt down and confessed my sins again to the Lord, as I had also done before. 6. And she came with six young men, whom I had also seen on the former occasion, and stood by me, and listened to me praying and confessing my sins to the Lord. And she touched me and said: "Hermas! stop asking all these questions about your sins, ask also concerning righteousness, that you may take presently some part of it to your family." 7. And she raised me up by the hand and took me to the couch and said to the young men: "Go and build." 8. And after the young

The ancient lady comes again

The couch of ivory

The six young men

245

men had gone away and we were alone, she said to me: "Sit here." I said to her: "Lady, let the elders sit first.[1]" She said: "Do what I tell you, and sit down." 9. Yet when I wished to sit on the right hand she would not let me, but signed to me with her hand to sit on the left. When therefore I thought about this, and was grieved because she did not let me sit on the right hand, she said to me: "Are you sorry, Hermas? The seat on the right is for others, who have already been found well-pleasing to God and have suffered for the Name. But you fall far short of sitting with them. But remain in your simplicity as you are doing, and you shall sit with them, and so shall all who do their deeds and bear what they also bore."

Hermas and the couch

The place of the martyrs

II

1. "WHAT," I said, "did they bear?" "Listen," she said: "Stripes, imprisonments, great afflictions, crucifixions, wild beasts, for the sake of the Name. Therefore is it given to them to be on the right hand of the Holiness, and to everyone who shall suffer for the Name; but for the rest there is the left side. But both, whether they sit on the right or the left, have the same gifts, and the same promises, only the former sit on the right and have somewhat of glory. 2. And you are desirous of sitting on the the right hand with them, but your failings are many. But you shall be cleansed from your failings, and all who are not double-minded shall be cleansed from all sins, up to this day." 3. When she had said this she wished to go away, but I fell at her feet and besought her by the Lord, to show me the vision which she had promised. 4. And she again took me by the hand and lifted me up, and made me sit on the couch on the left and she herself sat on the right. And she lifted up a certain glittering rod, and she said to me: "Do you see a great thing?" I said to her: "Lady, I see nothing." She said to me: "Behold, do you not see before you a

The vision of the town

[1]The meaning is obscure: 'the elders' is often explained as 'the Elders of the Church,' but it is more probably a mere formula of politeness 'seniores priores.'

great tower being built on the water with shining square stones?" 5. Now the tower was being built four-square by the six young men who had come with her; but tens of thousands of other men were bringing stones, some from the deep sea, and some from the land, and were giving them to the six young men, and these kept taking them and building. 6. The stones which had been The stones dragged from the deep sea, they placed without exception as they were into the building, for they had all been shaped and fitted into the joins with other stones. And they so fastened one to the other that their joins could not be seen. But the building of the tower appeared as if it had been built of a single stone. 7. Of the other stones, which were being brought from the dry ground, they cast some away, and some they put into the building and others they broke up and cast far from the tower. 8. And many other stones were lying round the tower, and they did not use them for the building, for some of them were rotten, and others had cracks, and others were too short, and others were white and round and did not fit into the building. 9. And I saw other stones being cast far from the tower, and coming on to the road, and not staying on the road, but rolling from the road into the rough ground. And others were falling into the fire, and were being burnt, and others were falling near the water, and could not be rolled into the water, although men wished them to be rolled on and to come into the water.

III

1. WHEN she had showed me these things she wished The explanation of
the vision to hasten away. I said to her: "Lady, what does it benefit me to have seen these things, if I do not know what they mean?" She answered me and said: "You are a persistent man, wanting to know about the tower." "Yes," I said, "Lady, in order that I may report to my brethren, and that they may be made more joyful, and when they hear these things may know the Lord in great glory." 2. And she said: "Many indeed shall hear, but some of them shall rejoice when they hear, and some shall mourn. But

these also, if they hear and repent, even they shall rejoice. Hear then, the parables of the tower, for I will reveal everything to you. And no longer trouble me about revelation, for these revelations are finished, for they have been fulfilled. Yet you will not cease asking for revelations, for you are shameless. 3. The tower which you see being built is myself, the Church, who have appeared to you both now and formerly. Ask, The tower therefore, what you will about the tower, and I will reveal it to you, that you may rejoice with the saints." 4. I said to her: "Lady, since you have once thought me worthy to reveal everything to me, proceed with the revelation." And she said to me: "What is permitted to be revealed to you shall be revealed; only let your heart be turned towards God and do not be double-minded as to what you see." 5. I asked her: "Why has the tower been built on the water, Lady?" "As I told you before, you are seeking diligently," said she, "and so by seeking you are finding out the truth. Hear, then, why the tower has been built upon the water: because your life was saved and shall be saved through water, and the tower has been founded by the utterance of the almighty and glorious Name, and is maintained by the unseen power of the Master."

IV

1. I answered and said to her: "Lady, great and The six young men wonderful is this thing. But, Lady, who are the six young men who are building?" "These are the holy angels of God, who were first created, to whom the Lord delivered all his creation to make it increase, and to build it up, and to rule the whole creation. Through them, therefore, the building of the tower shall be completed." 2. "But who are the others, who are bringing the stones?" "They also are holy angels of God, but these six are greater than they. Therefore the building of the tower shall be completed, and all shall rejoice together around the tower, and shall glorify God because the building of the tower has been completed." 3. I asked her saying: "Lady, I would like to know the

end of the stones, and what kind of force[1] they have."
She answered me and said: "It is not because you are
more worthy than all others that a revelation should be
made to you, for there were others before you and
better than you, to whom these visions ought to have
been revealed. But in order that 'the name of God might
be glorified' they have been, and shall be, revealed to
you because of the double-minded who dispute in their
heart whether these things are so or not. Tell them, that
all these things are true, and that there is nothing
beyond the truth, but that all things are strong and
certain and well-founded.

V

1. "LISTEN then concerning the stones which go into The stones
the building. The stones which are square and white and
which fit into their joins are the Apostles and bishops
and teachers and deacons who walked according to the
majesty of God, and served the elect of God in holiness
and reverence as bishops and teachers and deacons;
some of them are fallen asleep and some are still alive.
And they always agreed among themselves, and had
peace among themselves, and listened to one another;
for which cause their joins fit in the building of the
tower." 2. "But who are they who have been brought
out of the deep sea, and added on to the building, and
agree in their joins with the other stones which have
already been built?" "These are they who have suffered
for the name of the Lord." 3. "But I should like to
know, Lady, who are the other stones which are being
brought from the dry land?" She said: "Those which go
into the building without being hewed are they whom
the Lord approved because they walked in the upright-
ness of the Lord and preserved his commandments."
4. "But who are they who are being brought and placed
in the building?" "They are young in the faith and
faithful; but they are being exhorted by the angels to
good deeds, because wickedness has been found in

[1] Here almost the equivalent of 'meaning.' — 'What is their meaning in
the vision?'

them." 5. "But who are they whom they were rejecting The rejected stones and throwing away?" "These are they who have sinned and wish to repent; for this reason they have not been cast far away from the tower, because they will be valuable for the building if they repent. Those, then, who are going to repent, if they do so, will be strong in the faith if they repent now, while the tower is being built; but if the building be finished, they no longer have a place, but will be cast away. But they have only this,—that they lie beside the tower."

VI

1. "Do you wish to know who are those which are The stones which being broken up and cast far from the tower? These are were broken up the sons of wickedness; and their faith was hypocrisy, and no wickedness departed from them. For this cause they had no salvation, for because of their wickedness they are not useful for the building. Therefore they were broken up and cast far away, because of the anger of the Lord, for they had provoked his anger. 2. But the others The stones put of whom you saw many left lying and not going into on one side the building, of these those which are rotten are they who have known the truth, but are not remaining in it." 3. "And who are they which have the cracks?" "These are they who bear malice in their hearts against one another, and are not 'at peace among themselves,' but maintain the appearance of peace, yet when they depart from one another their wickednesses remain in their hearts. These are the cracks which the stones have. 4. And those which are too short are they which have believed, and they live for the greater part in righteousness, but have some measure of wickedness. Therefore, they are short and not perfect." 5. "But who, Lady, are the white and round ones which do not fit into the The round stones building?" She answered and said to me, "How long will you be stupid and foolish, and ask everything and understand nothing? These are they which have faith, but have also the riches of this world. When persecution comes, because of their wealth and because of business they deny their Lord." 6. And I answered and said to

250

her, "Lady, but then when will they be useful for the building?" "When," she said, "their wealth, which leads their souls astray, shall be cut off from them, then they will be useful to God. For just as the round stone cannot become square, unless something be cut off and taken away from it, so too they who have riches in this world cannot be useful to the Lord unless their wealth be cut away from them. 7. Understand it first from your own case; when you were rich, you were useless, but now you are useful and helpful for the Life. Be useful to God, for you yourself are taken from the same stones.[1]

VII

1. "BUT as for the other stones which you saw being cast far from the tower, and falling on to the road, and rolling from the road on to the rough ground; these are they who have believed, but because of their double-mindedness leave their true road. They think that it is possible to find a better road, and err and wander miserably in the rough ground. 2. And they who are falling into the fire and are being burnt, these are they who finally 'apostatise from the living God' and it no longer enters into their hearts to repent because of their licentious lusts, and the crimes which they have committed. 3. But do you wish to know who are the others which are falling near the water and cannot be rolled into the water? 'These are they who have heard the Word' and wish to be baptised 'in the name of the Lord.' Then, when the purity of the Truth comes into their recollection they repent and go again 'after their evil lusts.' " 4. So she ended the explanation of the tower. 5. I was still unabashed and asked her whether really all these stones which have been cast away, and do not fit into the building of the tower,—whether repentance is open to them, and they have a place in this tower. "Repentance," she said, "they have, but they cannot fit

The stones thrown away from the tower

The end of the rejected stones

---

[1]This appears to be the meaning; but the Greek is obscure and the early translations all paraphrase it so freely that they cannot be used to suggest any emendation.

into this tower. 6. But they will fit into another place much less honourable, and even this only after they have been tormented and fulfilled the days of their sins, and for this reason they will be removed,[1] because they shared in the righteous Word. And then[2] it shall befall them to be removed from their torments, because of the wickedness of the deeds which they committed. But if it come not into their hearts they have no salvation, because of the hardness of their hearts."

VIII

1. WHEN, therefore, I ceased asking her all these things, she said to me: "Would you like to see something else?" I was anxious to see it, and rejoiced greatly at the prospect. 2. She looked at me and smiled and said to me: "Do you see seven women round the tower?" "Yes," I said; "I see them." "This tower is being supported by them according to the commandment of the Lord. 3. Hear now their qualities. The first of them who is clasping her hands is called Faith. Through her the chosen of God are saved. 4. The second, who is girded and looks like a man, is called Continence; she is the daughter of Faith. Whosoever then shall follow her becomes blessed in his life, because he will abstain from all evil deeds, believing that if he refrains from every evil lust he will inherit eternal life." 5. "But who are the others, Lady?" "They are the daughters one of the other, and their names are Simplicity, Knowledge, Innocence, Reverence, and Love. When therefore you perform all the deeds of their mother, you can live." 6. "I would like, Lady," said I, "to know what are their several powers."[3] "Listen," she said, "to the powers which they have. 7. Their powers are supported one by the other, and they follow one another according to their birth. From Faith is born Continence, from Conti-

The vision of the seven women

The explanation

The powers of the Virtues

[1]*I.e.* from their punishment.

[2]Apparently the meaning is 'Then, *i.e.* if they repent,' but the text is obscure, and probably some words have been lost.

[3]Here also (cf. Vision III. iv. 3) 'powers' probably is almost equivalent to 'meaning' or 'signification.'

nence Simplicity, from Simplicity Innocence, from Innocence Reverence, from Reverence Knowledge, from Knowledge Love. Their works therefore are pure and reverent and godly. 8. Whosoever then serves them, and has the strength to lay hold of their works, shall have his dwelling in the tower with the saints of God." 9. And I began to ask her about the times, if the The end end were yet. But she cried out with a loud voice saying, "Foolish man, do you not see the tower still being built? Whenever therefore the building of the tower has been finished, the end comes. But it will quickly be built up; ask me nothing more. This reminder and the renewal of your spirits is sufficient for you and for the saints. 10. But the revelation was not for you alone, but for you to explain it to them all, 11. after three days, for you must understand it first. But I charge you first, Hermas, with these words, which I am going to say to you, to speak them all into the ears of the saints, that they may hear them and do them and be cleansed from their wickedness, and you with them.

IX

1. "LISTEN to me, children; I brought you up in great The charge of simplicity and innocence and reverence by the mercy of the Church God, who instilled righteousness into you that you should be justified and sanctified from all wickedness and all crookedness. But you do not wish to cease from your wickedness. 2. Now, therefore, listen to me and 'be at peace among yourselves' and regard one another and 'help one another' and do not take a superabundant share of the creatures of God for yourselves, but give also a part to those who lack. 3. For some are contracting illness in the flesh by too much eating, and are injuring their flesh, and the flesh of the others who have nothing to eat is being injured by their not having sufficient food and their body is being destroyed. 4. So this lack of sharing is harmful to you who are rich, and do not share with the poor. 5. Consider the judgment which is coming. Let therefore they who have overabundance seek out those who are hungry, so long as

the tower is not yet finished; for when the tower has been finished you will wish to do good, and will have no opportunity. 6. See to it then, you who rejoice in your wealth, that the destitute may not groan, and their groans go up to the Lord, and you with your good, be shut outside the door of the tower. 7. Therefore I speak now to the leaders of the Church and to those 'who take the chief seats.' Be not like the sorcerers, for sorcerers carry their charms in boxes, but you carry your charms and poison in your hearts. 8. You are hardened, and will not cleanse your hearts, and mix your wisdom together in a pure heart that you may find mercy by 'the great King.' 9. See to it, therefore, children, that these disagreements do not rob you of your life. 10. How will you correct the chosen of the Lord if you yourselves suffer no correction? Correct therefore one another and 'be at peace among yourselves,' that I also may stand joyfully before the Father, and give an account of you all to the Lord."

X

1. WHEN therefore she ceased speaking with me, the six young men who were building came and took her away to the tower, and four others took up the couch and bore it away also to the tower. I did not see their faces because they were turned away. 2. But as she was going I asked her to give me a revelation concerning the three forms in which she had appeared to me. She answered me and said, "Concerning these things you must ask some one else to reveal them to you." 3. Now she had appeared to me, brethren, in the first vision in the former year as very old and sitting on a chair. 4. But in the second vision her face was younger, but her body and hair were old and she spoke with me standing; but she was more joyful than the first time. 5. But in the third vision she was quite young and exceeding beautiful and only her hair was old; and she was quite joyful, and sat on a couch. 6. I was very unhappy about this, and wished to understand this revelation, and in a vision of the night I saw the ancient lady saying to me, "Every

The departure of the ancient lady

254

request needs humility: fast therefore and you shall receive what you ask from the Lord." 7. So I fasted one day and in the same night a young man appeared to me and said to me, "Why do you ask constantly for revelations in your prayer? Take care lest by your many requests you injure your flesh. 8. These revelations are sufficient for you. Can you see mightier revelations than you have seen?" 9. I answered and said to him, "Sir, I only ask you that there may be a complete revelation concerning the three forms of the ancient lady." He answered and said to me, "How long are you foolish? You are made foolish by your double-mindedness and because your heart is not turned to the Lord." 10. I answered and said again to him, "But from you, sir, we shall know them more accurately." *The young man*

XI

1. "LISTEN," he said, "concerning the forms which you are asking about. 2. Why did she appear to you in the first vision as old and seated on a chair? Because your[1] spirit is old and already fading away, and has no power through your weakness and double-mindedness. 3. For just as old people, who have no longer any hope of becoming young again, look for nothing except their last sleep, so also you, who have been weakened by the occupations of this life, have given yourself up to worry, and have not 'cast your cares upon the Lord.' But your mind was broken, and you grew old in your sorrows." 4. "Why, then, I should like to know, did she sit in a chair, sir?" "Because every sick person sits in a chair because of his sickness, that the weakness of the body may find support. Here you have the type of the first vision. *The three forms of the ancient lady*

---

[1]This 'your' is plural, in contrast to the 'you' in the preceding sentence, which is singular.

XII

1. "But in the second vision you saw her standing, and with a more youthful and more cheerful countenance than the former time, but with the body and hair of old age. Listen," he said, "also to this parable. 2. When anyone is old, he already despairs of himself by reason of his weakness and poverty, and expects nothing except the last day of his life. Then an inheritance was suddenly left him, and he heard it, and rose up and was very glad and put on his strength; and he no longer lies down but stands up, and his spirit which was already destroyed by his former deeds is renewed, and he no longer sits still, but takes courage. So also did you, when you heard the revelation, which the Lord revealed to you, 3. that he had mercy upon you, and renewed your spirit; and you put aside your weakness, and strength came to you, and you were made mighty in faith, and the Lord saw that you had been made strong and he rejoiced. And for this reason he showed you the building of the tower, and he will show you other things if you 'remain at peace among yourselves' with all your heart.

XIII

1. "But in the third vision you saw her young and beautiful and joyful and her appearance was beautiful. 2. For just as if some good news come to one who is in grief, he straightway forgets his former sorrow, and thinks of nothing but the news which he has heard, and for the future is strengthened to do good, and his spirit is renewed because of the joy which he has received; so you also have received the renewal of your spirits by seeing these good things. 3. And in that you saw her sitting on a couch, the position is secure, for a couch has four feet and stands securely, for even the world is controlled by four elements. 4. They, therefore, who have repented shall completely recover their youth and be well founded, because they have repented with all their heart. You have the revelation completed; no

256

longer ask anything about the revelation, but if anything be needed it shall be revealed to you."

Vision 4

I

1. THE fourth vision which I saw, brethren, twenty
days after the former vision, was a type of the persecution which is to come. 2. I was going into the country
by the Via Campana. The place is about ten furlongs
from the public road, and is easily reached. 3. As I
walked by myself I besought the Lord to complete the
revelations and visions which he had shown me by his
holy Church, to make me strong and give repentance to
his servants who had been offended, 'to glorify his'
great and glorious 'name' because he had thought me
worthy to show me his wonders. 4. And while I was
glorifying him and giving him thanks an answer came
to me as an echo of my voice, "Do not be double-
minded, Hermas." I began to reason in myself, and to
say, "In what ways can I be double-minded after being
given such a foundation by the Lord, and having seen
his glorious deeds?" 5. And I approached a little further,
brethren, and behold, I saw dust reaching as it were up
to heaven, and I began to say to myself, Are cattle
coming and raising dust? and it was about a furlong
away from me. 6. When the dust grew greater and
greater I supposed that it was some portent. The sun
shone out a little, and lo! I saw a great beast like some
Leviathan, and fiery locusts were going out of his
mouth. The beast was in size about a hundred feet and
its head was like a piece of pottery. 7. And I began to
weep and to pray the Lord to rescue me from it, and I
remembered the word which I had heard, "Do not be
double-minded, Hermas." 8. Thus, brethren, being
clothed in the faith of the Lord and remembering the
great things which he had taught me, I took courage and
faced the beast. And as the beast came on with a rush it
was as though it could destroy a city. 9. I came near to
it, and the Leviathan for all its size stretched itself out on
the ground, and put forth nothing except its tongue,
and did not move at all until I had passed it by. 10. And

The vision of
the Leviathan

257

the beast had on its head four colours, black, then the colour of flame and blood, then golden, then white.

II

1. AFTER I had passed the beast by and had gone about thirty feet further, lo! a maiden met me, 'adorned as if coming forth from the bridal chamber,' all in white and with white sandals, veiled to the forehead, and a turban for a head-dress, but her hair was white. 2. I recognised from the former visions that it was the Church, and I rejoiced the more. She greeted me saying, "Hail, O man," and I greeted her in return, "Hail, Lady." 3. She answered me and said, "Did nothing meet you?" I said to her, "Yes, Lady, such a beast as could destroy nations, but by the power of the Lord, and by his great mercy, I escaped it." 4. "You did well to escape it," she said, "because you cast your care upon God, and opened your heart to the Lord, believing that salvation can be found through nothing save through the great and glorious name. Therefore the Lord sent his angel, who is over the beast, whose name is Thegri[1] 'and shut his mouth that he should not hurt you.' You have escaped great tribulation through your faith, and because you were not double-minded when you saw so great a beast. 5. Go then and tell the Lord's elect ones of his great deeds, and tell them that this beast is a type of the great persecution which is to come. If then you are prepared beforehand, and repent with all your hearts towards the Lord, you will be able to escape it, if your heart be made pure and blameless, and you serve the Lord blamelessly for the rest of the days of your life. 'Cast your cares upon the Lord' and he will put them straight. 6. Believe on the Lord, you who are double-minded, that he can do all things, and turns his wrath away from you, and sends scourges on you who are double-minded. Woe to those who hear the words and disobey; it were better for them not to have been born."

The ancient lady

The explanation of the Leviathan

[1] No other mention of this Angel is found in Jewish or Christian literature, and no suitable meaning has been suggested for Thegri. Dr. Rendel Harris suggests Segri as an emendation, connecting it with the Hebrew word meaning 'to shut' (sagar), found in Dan. 6, 22.

III

1. I ASKED her concerning the four colours which the beast had on its head. She answered and said to me, "Are you again curious about such matters?" "Yes," I said, "Lady, let me know what they are." 2. "Listen," she said, "the black is this world, in which you are living; 3. the colour of fire and blood means that this world must be destroyed by blood and fire. 4. The golden part is you, who have fled from this world, for even as gold is 'tried in the fire' and becomes valuable, so also you who live among them,[1] are being tried. Those then who remain and pass through the flames shall be purified by them. Even as the gold puts away its dross, so also you will put away all sorrow and tribulation, and will be made pure and become useful for the building of the tower. 5. But the white part is the world to come, in which the elect of God shall dwell, for those who have been chosen by God for eternal life will be without spot and pure. 6. Therefore do not cease to speak to the ears of the saints. You have also the type of the great persecution to come, but if you will it shall be nothing. Remember what was written before." 7. When she had said this she went away, and I did not see to what place she departed, for there was a cloud, and I turned backwards in fear, thinking that the beast was coming.

The four colours on the Leviathan

THE FIFTH REVELATION[2]

1. WHILE I was praying at home and sitting on my bed, there entered a man glorious to look on, in the dress of a shepherd, covered with a white goatskin, with a bag on his shoulders and a staff in his hand. And he greeted me, and I greeted him back. 2. And at once he sat down by me, and said to me, "I have been sent by the most reverend angel to dwell with you the rest of the days of your life." 3. I thought he was come tempting me, and said to him, "Yes, but who are you?

The coming of the shepherd

---

[1]The "them" means "fire and blood"; but the construction of the sentence is awkward.

[1]This section is clearly intended as an introduction to the Mandates, but it is always quoted as the Fifth Vision.

259

for," I said, "I know to whom I was handed over." He said to me, "Do you not recognise me?" "No," I said. "I," said he, "am the shepherd to whom you were handed over."[1] 4. While he was still speaking, his appearance changed, and I recognised him, that it was he to whom I was handed over; and at once I was confounded, and fear seized me, and I was quite overcome with sorrow that I had answered him so basely and foolishly. 5. But he answered me and said, "Be not confounded, but be strong in my commandments which I am going to command you. For I was sent," said he, "to show you again all the things which you saw before, for they are the main points which are helpful to you. First of all write my commandments and the parables; but the rest you shall write as I shall show you. This is the reason," said he, "that I command you to write first the commandments and parables, that you may read them out at once, and be able to keep them." 6. So I wrote the commandments and parables as he commanded me. 7. If then you hear and keep them, and walk in them, and do them with a pure heart, you shall receive from the Lord all that he promised you, but if you hear them and do not repent, but continue to add to your sins, you shall receive the contrary from the Lord. All these things the shepherd commanded me to write thus, for he was the angel of repentance.

MANDATE 1

1. FIRST of all believe that God is one, 'who made all things and perfected them, and made all things to be out of that which was not,' and contains all things, and is himself alone uncontained. 2. Believe then in him, and fear him, and in your fear be continent. Keep these things, and you shall cast away from yourself all wickedness, and shall put on every virtue of righteousness, and shall live to God, if you keep this commandment.

Belief in God

[1]There is no mention of this in the preceding Visions.

260

MANDATE 2

1. HE said to me: "Have simplicity and be innocent Simplicity
and you shall be as the children who do not know the
wickedness that destroys the life of men. 2. In the first
place, speak evil of no one, and do not listen gladly to
him who speaks evil. Otherwise you also by listening
share in the sin of him who speaks evil, if you believe in
the evil-speaking which you hear. For by believing you
yourself also will have somewhat against your brother;
thus therefore, you will share the sin of the speaker of
evil. 3. Evil-speaking is wicked; it is a restless devil, Evil-speaking
never making peace, but always living in strife. Refrain
from it then, and you shall have well-being at all times
with all men. 4. And put on reverence, in which is no
evil stumbling-block, but all is smooth and joyful. Do
good, and of all your toil which God gives you, give in
simplicity to all who need, not doubting to whom you
shall give and to whom not: give to all, for to all God
wishes gifts to be made of his own bounties. 5. Those
then who receive shall render an account to God why
they received it and for what. For those who accepted
through distress shall not be punished, but those who
accepted in hypocrisy shall pay the penalty.[1] 6. He
therefore who gives is innocent; for as he received from
the Lord the fulfilment of this ministry, he fulfilled it in
simplicity, not doubting to whom he should give or not
give. Therefore this ministry fulfilled in simplicity was
honourable before God. He therefore who serves in
simplicity shall live to God. 7. Keep therefore this
commandment as I have told you, that your repentance
and that of your family may be found to be in simplicity, and that your innocence may be "pure and without
stain."

---

[1]This series of precepts is also found in the Didache (i.5) and is there
quoted as being "according to the commandment" (ἐντολή —the
same word as Hermas uses for the commandments or Mandates of the
Shepherd).

MANDATE 3

1. AGAIN he said to me, "Love truth: and let all truth Truth proceed from your mouth, that the spirit which God has made to dwell in this flesh may be found true by all men, and the Lord who dwells in you shall thus be glorified, for the Lord is true in every word and with him there is no lie. 2. They therefore who lie set the Lord at nought, and become defrauders of the Lord, not restoring to him the deposit which they received. For they received from him a spirit free from lies. If they return this as a lying spirit, they have defiled the commandment of the Lord and have robbed him." 3. When therefore I heard this I wept much, and when he saw me weeping he said, "Why do you weep?" "Because, sir," said I, "I do not know if I can be saved." "Why?" said he. "Because, sir," said I, "I have never yet in my life spoken a true word, but have ever spoken deceitfully with all men, and gave out that my lie was true among all, and no one ever contradicted me but believed my word. How then, sir," said I, "can I live after having done this?" 4. "Your thought," said he, "is good and true; for you ought to have walked in truth as God's servant, and an evil conscience ought not to dwell with the spirit of truth, nor ought grief to come on a spirit which is holy and true." "Never, sir," said I, "have I accurately understood[1] such words." 5. "Now then," said he, "you do understand them. Keep them that your former lies in your business may themselves become trustworthy now that these have been found true. For it is possible for those also to become trustworthy.[2] If you keep these things and from henceforth keep the whole truth, you can obtain life for yourself; and whoever shall hear this commandment, and abstain from the sin of lying shall live to God."

---

[1] The literal meaning of the Greek is "heard," but the meaning is clearly much more nearly "understood."

[2] The meaning is obscure, but it appears to be that Hermas having made untrue statements in the course of business must try so to act that his statements will be justified in fact: for instance, if he had made extravagant promises he must fulfil them.

MANDATE 4

I

1. "I COMMAND you," he said, " to keep purity and let Purity not any thought come into your heart about another man's wife, or about fornication or any such wicked things; for by doing this you do great sin. But if you always remember your own wife you will never sin. 2. For if this desire enter your heart you will sin, and if you do other such-like wicked things you commit sin. For this desire is a great sin for the servant of God. And if any man commit this wicked deed he works death for himself. 3. See to it then, abstain from this desire, for where holiness lives, lawlessness ought not to enter the heart of a righteous man." 4. I said to him, "Sir, allow me to ask you a few questions." "Say on," said he. "Sir," said I, "if a man have a wife faithful in the Lord, Man and wife and he finds her out in some adultery, does the husband sin if he lives with her?" 5. "So long as he is ignorant," said he, "he does not sin, but if the husband knows her sin, and the wife does not repent, but remains in her fornication, and the husband go on living with her, he becomes a partaker of her sin, and shares in her adultery." 6. "What then," said I, "sir, shall the husband do if the wife remain in this disposition?" "Let him put her away," he said, "and let the husband remain by himself. But 'if he put his wife away and marry another he also commits adultery himself.' " 7. "If then," said I, "sir, after the wife be put away she repent, and wish to return to her own husband, shall she not be received?" 8. "Yes," said he; "if the husband do not receive her he sins and covers himself with great sin; but it is necessary to receive the sinner who repents, but not often, for the servants of God have but one repentance. Therefore, for the sake of repentance the husband ought not to marry.[1]

[1]This mandate is really explaining the practical problem which arose from the conflict between the Christian precept against divorce (Mt. 10, 11 f.) and the equally early precept against having intercourse with immoral purposes. As the inserted clause "except for the cause of fornication" in the Matthaean version of Mk. 10, 11 f. (Mt. 19, 9; cf. Mt. 5, 32 and Lc. 16, 18) shows, the latter precept was regarded as more important, and immoral wives were put away, but Hermas and other writers always maintained that this was not strictly divorce, as the innocent party was not free to remarry in order to give the other the opportunity of repenting and of returning.

This is the course of action for wife and husband. 9. Not only," said he, "is it adultery if a man defile his flesh, but whosoever acts as do the heathen is also guilty of adultery, so that if anyone continue in such practices, and repent not, depart from him and do not live with him, otherwise you are also a sharer in his sin. 10. For this reason it was enjoined on you to live by yourselves, whether husband or wife, for in such cases repentance is possible. I, therefore," said he, "am not giving an opportunity to laxity that this business be thus concluded, but in order that he who has sinned sin no more,[1] and for his former sin there is one who can give healing, for he it is who has the power over all."

II

1. AND I asked him again, saying: "If the Lord has thought me worthy for you always to live with me, suffer yet a few words of mine, since I have no understanding and my heart has been hardened by my former deeds; give me understanding, for I am very foolish and have absolutely no understanding." 2. He answered me and said, "I am set over repentance, and I give understanding to all those who repent. Or do you not think," said he, "that this very repentance is itself understanding? To repent," said he, "is great understanding. For the sinner understands that he 'has done wickedly before the Lord,' and the deed which he wrought comes into his heart, and he repents and no longer does wickedly, but does good abundantly, and humbles his soul and punishes it because he sinned. You see, therefore, that repentance is great understanding." 3. "For this reason then, sir," said I, "I enquire accurately from you as to all things. First, because I am a sinner, that I may know what I must do to live, because my sins are many and manifold." 4. "You shall live," he said, "if you keep my commandments and walk in them, and

---

[1] Hermas is guarding against the imputation that he is lowering the standard of morality. This accusation was actually brought against him later by Tertullian.

whosoever shall hear and keep these commandments shall live to God."

III

1. I will yet, sir," said I, "continue to ask." "Say on," said he. "I have heard, sir," said I, "from some teachers[1] that there is no second repentance beyond the one given when we went down into the water and received remission of our former sins." 2. He said to me, "You have heard correctly, for that is so. For he who has received remission of sin ought never to sin again, but to live in purity. 3. But since you ask accurately concerning all things, I will explain this also to you without giving an excuse to those who in the future shall believe or to those who have already believed on the Lord. For those who have already believed or shall believe in the future, have no repentance of sins, but have remission of their former sin. 4. For those, then, who were called before these days, did the Lord appoint repentance, for the Lord knows the heart, and knowing all things beforehand he knew the weakness of man and the subtlety of the devil, that he will do some evil to the servants of God, and will do them mischief. 5. The Lord, therefore, being merciful, had mercy on his creation, and established this repentance, and to me was the control of this repentance given. 6. But I tell you," said he, "after that great and holy calling, if a man be tempted by the devil and sin, he has one repentance, but if he sin and repent repeatedly it is unprofitable for such a man, for scarcely shall he live."

Repentance for sin after baptism

In Codex Sinaiticus, because the final pages are defective, *The Shepherd of Hermas* breaks off here.

[1]Possibly a reference to Heb. 6, 4 ff.

Selected Bibliography

Unpublished Sources
Letters from C. Tischendorf to S. Davidson, Hunterian Library, University of Glasgow

Articles
Anon., 'Die Neuen Sinai–Funde', in *Bericht der Hermann Kunst-Stiftung zur Förderung der Neutestamentlichen Textforschung für die Jahre 1979 bis 1981,* Münster/Westfalen 1982, pp. 46–58
Politis, L., 'Nouveaux manuscrits grecs découverts au Mont Sinai', in *Scriptorium,* vol. xxxiv, Brussels 1980, pp. 5–17
Ševčenko, I., 'New Documents on Constantine Tischendorf and the *Codex Sinaiticus*', in *Scriptorium*, vol. xviii, Brussels 1964, pp. 55–80

Books
Behrend, H., *Auf der Suche nach Schätzen*, 5th edition, Berlin 1956
Codex Sinaiticus Petropolitanus, facsimile ed H. and K. Lake, Oxford 1911
Champdor, A., *Le Mont Sinai et le monastère Sainte-Catherine*, Albert Guillot, Paris 1963
Eckenstein, L., *A History of the Sinai*, New York 1921
Evans, C.F., *Resurrection and the New Testament*, London 1970
Farmer, W.F. *The Last Twelve Verses of Mark*, Cambridge 1974
Pagels, E., *The Gnostic Gospels*, London 1980
Rothenberg, B., and Weyer, H., *Sinai*, tr. E. Osers and B. Charleston, Washington and New York 1980

Index

269

270

271